Learn To Read English With Directions In Haitian Creole
Assessment
Color Edition

ISBN 978-1-945738-62-3
© 2022 – Wendy A. Charles & Alexander J. Charles
All Rights Reserved
Baldwin, New York
www.intellastic.com

All rights reserved. No portion of this book may be reproduced, stored in a retrieval system, or transmitted in any form or by any means – electronic, mechanical, photocopy, recording, video presentation, private instruction, scanning or other – except for brief quotations in critical reviews or articles, without the prior written permission of the writers.

All Rights Reserved. Printed in the USA.

Table of Contents

Unit A

Lesson 1.1	Reading Words with the Letter A/a	1
Lesson 1.2	Reading Words with the Short Vowel "a" Sound	2
Lesson 1.2	Reading & Writing Words with the Short Vowel "a" Sound	3
Lesson 1.3	Reading Words with the Long Vowel "a" Sound	4
Lesson 1.3	Reading & Writing Words with the Long Vowel "a" Sound	5
Lessons 1.2 & 1.3	Reading Short Vowel and Long Vowel Words	6
Lesson 1.4	Reading Words with the "age" Letter Combination	7
Lesson 1.5	Reading Words with the "ai" Vowel Pair	8
Lesson 1.6	Reading Letter "a" Words with the Schwa Sound	9
Lesson 1.7	Reading Words with the "ar" Letter Combination	10
Lesson 1.7	Reading Words with the "ar" Letter Combination	11
Lesson 1.8	Reading Words with a Silent Letter "a"	12
Unit Review - A/a	Reading Words with Vowel "a" Sounds: /ă/, /ā/, /ə/ & Silent	13
Lesson 1.9	Reading Multisyllable Words	14
Lesson 1.9	Reading Multisyllable Words	15
Lesson 1.10	Proper and Common Nouns and Adjectives	16

Unit B

Lesson 2.1	Reading Words with the Letter B/b	17
Lesson 2.2	Reading Words with the "br" Letter Combination	18
Lesson 2.3	Reading Words with the "bl" Letter Combination	19
Lesson 2.3	Reading Words with the "ble" Letter Combination	20
Lesson 2.4	Reading Words with the "mb" Letter Combination	21
Lesson 2.4	Reading Words with the "bt" Letter Combination	22
Lesson 2.5	Reading Words with a Silent Letter "b"	23
Lesson 2.6	Reading Multisyllable Words	24
Lesson 2.6	Reading Multisyllable Words	25
Lesson 2.7	Proper and Common Nouns and Adjectives	26

Unit C

Lesson 3.1	Reading Words with the Letter C/c	27
Lesson 3.1	Reading Words with the Hard Letter "c"	28
Lesson 3.2	Reading Words with the Soft Letter "c"	29
Lessons 3.1 & 3.2	Reading Hard Letter "c" and Soft Letter "c" Words	30
Lesson 3.3	Reading Words with the "cr" Letter Combination	31
Lesson 3.4	Reading Words with the "cl" Letter Combination	32
Lesson 3.4	Reading Words with the "cle" Letter Combination	33
Lesson 3.5	Reading Words with the "ct" Letter Combination	34
Lesson 3.6	Reading Soft Letter "c" Words	35
Lesson 3.6	Reading Soft Letter "c" Words	36
Lesson 3.7	Reading Words with the "ch" Letter Combination	37
Lesson 3.8	Reading Words with the "cc" Letter Combination	38
Lesson 3.9	Reading Words with a Silent Letter "c"	39
Lesson 3.10	Reading Multisyllable Words	40
Lesson 3.10	Reading Multisyllable Words	41
Lesson 3.11	Proper and Common Nouns and Adjectives	42

Unit D

Lesson 4.1	Reading Words with the Letter D/d	43
Lesson 4.2	Reading Letter "d" Words with the /d/ Sound & /j/ Sound	44
Lesson 4.2	Reading Words with the "dr" Letter Combination	45
Lesson 4.3	Reading Words with the "ed" Suffix/ Past Tense Verbs	46
Lesson 4.4	Reading Words with a Silent Letter "d"	47
Lesson 4.5	Reading Multisyllable Words	48
Lesson 4.5	Reading Multisyllable Words	49
Lesson 4.6	Proper and Common Nouns and Adjectives	50

Unit E

Lesson 5.1	Reading Words with the Letter E/e	51
Lesson 5.2	Reading Words with the Short Vowel "e" Sound	52
Lesson 5.2	Reading & Writing Words with the Short Vowel "e" Sound	53

Lesson 5.3	Reading Words with the Long Vowel "e" Sound	54
Lesson 5.3	Reading & Writing Words with the Long Vowel "e" Sound	55
Lessons 5.2 & 5.3	Reading Short Vowel and Long Vowel Words	56
Lesson 5.4	Reading Words with Letter "e" Vowel Pairs	57
Lesson 5.5	Reading Words with the Final Letter "e"	58
Lesson 5.6	Reading Letter "e" Words with the Schwa Vowel Sound	59
Lesson 5.7	Reading Words with the "er" Letter Combination	60
Lesson 5.8	Reading Words with the "eu" and "ew" Letter Combinations	61
Lesson 5.9	Reading Words with the "ey" Letter Combination	62
Lesson 5.10	Reading Words with a Silent Letter "e"	63
Unit Review	Reading Words with Vowel "e" Sounds: /ĕ/, /ē/, /ə/ & Silent	64
Lesson 5.11	Reading Multisyllable Words	65
Lesson 5.11	Reading Multisyllable Words	66
Lesson 5.12	Proper and Common Nouns and Adjectives	67

Unit F

Lesson 6.1	Reading Words with the Letter F/f	68
Lesson 6.2	Reading Words with the "fr" Letter Combination	69
Lesson 6.3	Reading Words with the "fl" Letter Combination	70
Lesson 6.3	Reading Words with the "fle" Letter Combination	71
Lesson 6.4	Reading Words with the "ft," "lf" and "ff" Letter Combinations	72
Lesson 6.5	Reading Words with a Silent Letter "f"	73
Lesson 6.6	Reading Singular and Plural forms of Words Ending in "-f" & "-fe"	74
Lesson 6.7	Reading Multisyllable Words	75
Lesson 6.7	Reading Multisyllable Words	76
Lesson 6.8	Proper and Common Nouns and Adjectives	77

Unit G

Lesson 7.1	Reading Words with the Letter G/g	78
Lesson 7.1	Reading Words with the Hard Letter "g"	79
Lesson 7.2	Reading Words with the Soft Letter G/g	80
Lessons 7.1 & 7.2	Reading Hard Letter "g" and Soft Letter "g" Words	81

Lessons 7.1 & 7.2	Reading Hard Letter "g" and Soft Letter "g" Words	82
Lesson 7.3	Reading Words with the "gr" Letter Combination	83
Lesson 7.4	Reading Words with the "gl" Letter Combination	84
Lesson 7.4	Reading Words with the "gle" Letter Combination	85
Lesson 7.5	Reading Words with the "gh" Letter Combination	86
Lesson 7.6	Reading Words with the "gn" Letter Combination	87
Lesson 7.7	Reading Words with a Silent Letter "g"	88
Lesson 7.8	Reading Multisyllable Words	89
Lesson 7.8	Reading Multisyllable Words	90
Lesson 7.9	Proper and Common Nouns and Adjectives	91

Unit H

Lesson 8.1	Reading Words with the Letter H/h	92
Lesson 8.2	Reading Words with the Letter "h" Combinations: "sh," "wh," "ch," "th," "rh," "ph" and "gh"	93
Lesson 8.2	Reading Words with the Letter "h" Combinations: "sh," "wh," "ch," "th," "rh," "ph," "gh" and "sch"	94
Lesson 8.3	Reading Words with a Silent Letter "h"	95
Lesson 8.4	Reading Multisyllable Words	96
Lesson 8.4	Reading Multisyllable Words	97
Lesson 8.5	Proper and Common Nouns and Adjectives	98

Unit I

Lesson 9.1	Reading Words with the Letter I/i	99
Lesson 9.2	Reading Words with the Short Vowel "i" Sound	100
Lesson 9.2	Reading & Writing Words with the Short Vowel "i" Sound	101
Lesson 9.3	Reading Words with the Long Vowel "i" Sound	102
Lesson 9.3	Reading & Writing Words with the Long Vowel "i" Sound	103
Lessons 9.2 & 9.3	Reading Short Vowel and Long Vowel Words	104
Lesson 9.4	Reading Words with Letter "i" Vowel Pairs	105
Lesson 9.5	Reading Words with the Final Letter "i"	106
Lesson 9.6	Reading Letter "i" Words with the Schwa Vowel Sound	107

Lesson 9.7	Reading Words with the "ir" Letter Combination	108
Lesson 9.8	Reading Letter "i" Words with the Long Vowel "e" Sound	109
Lesson 9.9	Reading Words with a Silent Letter "i"	110
Unit Review	Reading Words with Vowel "i" Sounds: /ĭ/, /ī/, /ə/ & Silent	111
Lesson 9.10	Reading Multisyllable Words	112
Lesson 9.10	Reading Multisyllable Words	113
Lesson 9.11	Proper and Common Nouns and Adjectives	114

Unit J

Lesson 10.1	Reading Words with the Letter J/j	115
Lesson 10.2	Reading Multisyllable Words	116
Lesson 10.2	Reading Multisyllable Words	117
Lesson 10.3	Proper and Common Nouns and Adjectives	118

Unit K

Lesson 11.1	Reading Words with the Letter K/k	119
Lesson 11.2	Reading Words with the Letter "k" and "ck" Letter Combination	120
Lesson 11.3	Reading Words with the "kle" Letter Combination	121
Lesson 11.4	Reading Words with a Silent Letter "k"	122
Lesson 11.5	Reading Multisyllable Words	123
Lesson 11.5	Reading Multisyllable Words	124
Lesson 11.6	Proper and Common Nouns and Adjectives	125

Unit L

Lesson 12.1	Reading Words with the Letter L/l	126
Lesson 12.2	Reading Words with the Letter "l" Combinations: "bl," "pl" & "sl"	127
Lesson 12.3	Reading Words with a Silent Letter "l"	128
Lesson 12.4	Reading Multisyllable Words	129
Lesson 12.4	Reading Multisyllable Words	130
Lesson 12.5	Proper and Common Nouns and Adjectives	131

Unit M

Lesson 13.1	Reading Words with the Letter M/m	132
Lesson 13.2	Reading Words with a Silent Letter "m"	133
Lesson 13.3	Reading Multisyllable Words	134
Lesson 13.3	Reading Multisyllable Words	135
Lesson 13.4	Proper and Common Nouns and Adjectives	136

Unit N

Lesson 14.1	Reading Words with the Letter N/n	137
Lesson 14.2	Reading Words with the "ng" Letter Combination	138
Lesson 14.3	Reading Words with a Silent Letter "n"	139
Lesson 14.4	Reading Multisyllable Words	140
Lesson 14.4	Reading Multisyllable Words	141
Lesson 14.5	Proper and Common Nouns and Adjectives	142

Unit O

Lesson 15.1	Reading Words with the Letter O/o	143
Lesson 15.2	Reading Words with the Short Vowel "o" Sound	144
Lesson 15.2	Reading & Writing Words with the Short Vowel "o" Sound	145
Lesson 15.3	Reading Words with the Long Vowel "o" Sound	146
Lesson 15.3	Reading & Writing Words with the Long Vowel "o" Sound	147
Lessons 15.2 & 15.3	Reading Short Vowel and Long Vowel Words	148
Lesson 15.4	Reading Words with Letter "o" Vowel Pairs	149
Lesson 15.5	Reading Words with the Final Letter "o"	150
Lesson 15.6	Reading Letter "o" Words with the Schwa Vowel Sound	151
Lesson 15.7	Reading Words with Vowel "o" Sounds: /ŏ/, /ō/ & /o͞o/	152
Lesson 15.8	Reading Words with the "or" Letter Combination	153
Lesson 15.8	Reading Words with the "or" Letter Combination	154
Lesson 15.9	Reading Words with a Silent Letter "o"	155
Unit Review	Reading Words with Vowel "o" Sounds: /ŏ/, /ō/, /ə/ & Silent	156
Lesson 15.10	Reading Multisyllable Words	157
Lesson 15.10	Reading Multisyllable Words	158

Lesson 15.11	Proper and Common Nouns and Adjectives	159

Unit P

Lesson 16.1	Reading Words with the Letter P/p	160
Lesson 16.2	Reading Words with the "ph" Letter Combination	161
Lesson 16.3	Reading Words with the "pr" Letter Combination	162
Lesson 16.4	Reading Words with the "pl" Letter Combination	163
Lesson 16.4	Reading Words with the "ple" Letter Combination	164
Lesson 16.5	Reading Words with a Silent Letter "p"	165
Lesson 16.6	Reading Multisyllable Words	166
Lesson 16.6	Reading Multisyllable Words	167
Lesson 16.7	Proper and Common Nouns and Adjectives	168

Unit Q

Lesson 17.1	Reading Words with the Letter Q/q	169
Lesson 17.2	Reading Words with the Letter "q" and "qu" Letter Combination	170
Lesson 17.2	Reading Words with the "qu" Letter Combination	171
Lesson 17.3	Reading Multisyllable Words	172
Lesson 17.3	Reading Multisyllable Words	173
Lesson 17.4	Proper and Common Nouns and Adjectives	174

Unit R

Lesson 18.1	Reading Words with the Letter R/r	175
Lesson 18.2	Reading Words with the Letter "r" Combinations: "br," "cr," "dr," "fr," "gr," "pr" and "tr"	176
Lesson 18.3	Reading Multisyllable Words	177
Lesson 18.3	Reading Multisyllable Words	178
Lesson 18.4	Proper and Common Nouns and Adjectives	179

Unit S

Lesson 19.1	Reading Words with the Letter S/s	180
Lesson 19.1	Reading Words with the Letter S/s	181

Lesson 19.2	Reading Words with the "sion," "sial" & "scious" Suffixes	182
Lesson 19.3	Reading Words with the "sch" Letter Combination	183
Lesson 19.4	Reading Words with the "scr," "shr," "spr" & "str" Letter Combinations	184
Lesson 19.5	Reading Words with the "sl" & "sle" Letter Combinations	185
Lesson 19.5	Reading Words with the "sle" Letter Combination	186
Lesson 19.6	Reading Words with the "sm" Letter Combination	187
Lesson 19.7	Reading Words with the "ss" Letter Combination	188
Lesson 19.8	Reading Words with a Silent Letter "s"	189
Lesson 19.9	Reading Multisyllable Words	190
Lesson 19.9	Reading Multisyllable Words	191
Lesson 19.10	Proper and Common Nouns and Adjectives	192

Unit T

Lesson 20.1	Reading Words with the Letter T/t	193
Lesson 20.2	Reading Words with the "thm" Letter Combination	194
Lesson 20.3	Reading Words with the "tion," "tial" & "tious" Suffixes	195
Lesson 20.4	Reading Words with the "tr" Letter Combination	196
Lesson 20.5	Reading Words with the "tle" Letter Combination	197
Lesson 20.6	Reading Words with the Letter "t" Sounds	198
Lesson 20.7	Reading Words with a Silent Letter "t"	199
Lesson 20.8	Reading Multisyllable Words	200
Lesson 20.8	Reading Multisyllable Words	201
Lesson 20.9	Proper and Common Nouns and Adjectives	202

Unit U

Lesson 21.1	Reading Words with the Letter U/u	203
Lesson 21.2	Reading Words with the Short Vowel "u" Sound	204
Lesson 21.2	Reading & Writing Words with the Short Vowel "u" Sound	205
Lesson 21.3	Reading Words with the Long Vowel "u" Sound	206
Lesson 21.3	Reading & Writing Words with the Long Vowel "u" Sound	207
Lessons 21.2 & 21.3	Reading Short Vowel and Long Vowel Words	208
Lesson 21.4	Reading Words with Letter "u" Vowel Pairs	209

Lesson 21.5	Reading Words with the Final Letter "u"	210
Lesson 21.6	Reading Letter "u" Words with the Schwa Vowel Sound	211
Lesson 21.7	Reading Words with the "ur" Letter Combination	212
Lesson 21.8	Reading Words with a Silent Letter "u"	213
Unit Review	Reading Words with Vowel "u" Sounds: /ŭ/, /o͞o/, /ə/ & Silent	214
Lesson 21.9	Reading Multisyllable Words	215
Lesson 21.9	Reading Multisyllable Words	216
Lesson 21.10	Proper and Common Nouns and Adjectives	217

Unit V

Lesson 22.1	Reading Words with the Letter V/v	218
Lesson 22.2	Reading Multisyllable Words	219
Lesson 22.2	Reading Multisyllable Words	220
Lesson 22.3	Proper and Common Nouns and Adjectives	221

Unit W

Lesson 23.1	Reading Words with the Letter W/w	222
Lesson 23.2	Reading Words with a Vowel before the Letter "w"	223
Lesson 23.3	Reading Words with a Silent "w" and "wr" Letter Combination	224
Lesson 23.3	Reading Words with a Silent Letter "w"	225
Lesson 23.4	Reading Multisyllable Words	226
Lesson 23.4	Reading Multisyllable Words	227
Lesson 23.5	Proper and Common Nouns and Adjectives	228

Unit X

Lesson 24.1	Reading Words with the Letter X/x	229
Lesson 24.1	Reading Words with the Letter X/x	230
Lesson 24.2	Reading Multisyllable Words	231
Lesson 24.2	Reading Multisyllable Words	232
Lesson 24.3	Proper and Common Nouns and Adjectives	233

Unit Y

Lesson 25.1	Reading Words with the Letter Y/y	234
Lesson 25.1	Reading Words with the Letter Y/y	235
Lesson 25.2	Reading Words with a Vowel before the Letter "y"	236
Lesson 25.3	Reading Words with the "cy" Letter Combination	237
Lesson 25.4	Reading Words with the Final Letter "y"	238
Lesson 25.5	Reading Words with the "yr" Letter Combination	239
Lesson 25.6	Reading Letter "y" Words with the Schwa Sound	240
Lesson 25.7	Reading Words with a Silent Letter "y"	241
Lesson 25.8	Reading Multisyllable Words	242
Lesson 25.8	Reading Multisyllable Words	243
Lesson 25.9	Proper and Common Nouns and Adjectives	244

Unit Z

Lesson 26.1	Reading Words with the Letter Z/z	245
Lesson 26.1	Reading Words with the Letter Z/z	246
Lesson 26.2	Reading Words with a Silent Letter "z"	247
Lesson 26.3	Reading Multisyllable Words	248
Lesson 26.3	Reading Multisyllable Words	249
Lesson 26.4	Proper and Common Nouns and Adjectives	250

Appendix

Appendix 1.0	Introduction of the Letter A/a	251
Appendix 2.0	Introduction of the Letter B/b	252
Appendix 2.0	Letter Recognition B/b	253
Appendix 3.0	Introduction of the Letter C/c	254
Appendix 3.0	Letter Recognition C/c	255
Appendix 4.0	Introduction of the Letter D/d	256
Appendix 4.0	Letter Recognition D/d	257
Appendix 5.0	Introduction of the Letter E/e	258
Appendix 6.0	Introduction of the Letter F/f	259
Appendix 6.0	Letter Recognition F/f	260

Appendix 7.0	Introduction of the Letter G/g	261
Appendix 7.0	Letter Recognition G/g	262
Appendix 8.0	Introduction of the Letter H/h	263
Appendix 8.0	Letter Recognition H/h	264
Appendix 9.0	Introduction of the Letter I/i	265
Appendix 10.0	Introduction of the Letter J/j	266
Appendix 10.0	Letter Recognition J/j	267
Appendix 11.0	Introduction of the Letter K/k	268
Appendix 11.0	Letter Recognition K/k	269
Appendix 12.0	Introduction of the Letter L/l	270
Appendix 12.0	Letter Recognition L/l	271
Appendix 13.0	Introduction of the Letter M/m	272
Appendix 13.0	Letter Recognition M/m	273
Appendix 14.0	Introduction of the Letter N/n	274
Appendix 14.0	Letter Recognition N/n	275
Appendix 15.0	Introduction of the Letter O/o	276
Appendix 16.0	Introduction of the Letter P/p	277
Appendix 16.0	Letter Recognition P/p	278
Appendix 17.0	Introduction of the Letter Q/q	279
Appendix 17.0	Letter Recognition Q/q	280
Appendix 18.0	Introduction of the Letter R/r	281
Appendix 18.0	Letter Recognition R/r	282
Appendix 19.0	Introduction of the Letter S/s	283
Appendix 19.0	Letter Recognition S/s	284
Appendix 20.0	Introduction of the Letter T/t	285
Appendix 20.0	Letter Recognition T/t	286
Appendix 21.0	Introduction of the Letter U/u	287
Appendix 22.0	Introduction of the Letter V/v	288
Appendix 22.0	Letter Recognition V/v	289
Appendix 23.0	Introduction of the Letter W/w	290
Appendix 23.0	Letter Recognition W/w	291

Appendix 24.0	Introduction of the Letter X/x	292
Appendix 24.0	Letter Recognition X/x	293
Appendix 25.0	Introduction of the Letter Y/y	294
Appendix 25.0	Letter Recognition Y/y	295
Appendix 26.0	Introduction of the Letter Z/z	296
Appendix 26.0	Letter Recognition Z/z	297

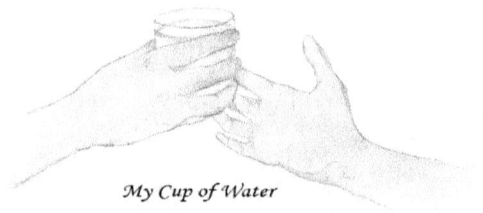

My Cup of Water

Name: _____ Date: ___/___/_____ Score: _____

Lesson 1.1

Reading Words with the Letter A/a

✓ Lesson Check Point

Directions: Read each target word. Find the letter "a" and put a check (✓) in the column that identifies its position: beginning, within or end.
Direksyons: Li chak mo objektif. Jwenn lèt "a" a epi mete yon tchèck (✓) nan kolòn ki idantifye pozisyon li an: nan kòmansman, ladan oubyen nan finisman.

Target Words	Beginning (First Letter)	Within	End (Last Letter)
1. baker			
2. sofa			
3. annex			
4. gorilla			
5. apples			

Directions: Read each target word. Read the words in the row and circle the word that has a different vowel "a" sound.
Direksyons: Li chak mo objektif. Li mo yo ki nan ranje a epi antoure mo a ki bay yon son vwayèl "a" ki diferan an.

Target Words				
6. flag	man	yam	cap	take
7. sad	clam	bag	save	brag
8. plan	rag	tag	pan	made
9. snap	cake	drag	add	has
10. trap	van	jazz	jam	wave

Learn to Read English With Directions In Haitian Creole

Name: _____ Date:___/___/_____ Score:_____

Lesson 1.2

Reading Words with the Short Vowel "a" Sound

✓ Lesson Check Point

 **Directions:** Read the words in the four boxes. Circle two words with the short vowel /ă/ sound. The anchor word for the short vowel /ă/ sound is apple.

Direksyons: Li mo yo ki nan kat ti bwat yo. Antoure de mo ki genyen son vwayèl kout /ă/ a. Mo referans pou son vwayèl kout /ă/ a se mo, apple.

flat	tail	safe	dad	Asia	pail
made	fast	spa	sat	ran	had

plate	sand	wage	label	slab	grab
ask	basic	cap	tab	away	game

 Directions: Read the words in the four boxes. Circle two words that rhyme. Rhyming words have the same ending sound, such as tap and map.

Direksyons: Li mo yo ki nan kat ti bwat yo. Antoure de mo ki rime. De mo oubyen plizyè mo ki rime genyen menm son nan finisman yo, tankou tap ak map.

ago	tan	barn	rat	mad	all
ran	aunt	cake	bat	fad	grape

pass	ball	past	last	fake	fall
jar	class	car	lake	glad	bad

Name: _____ Date: ___/___/_____ Score: _____

Lesson 1.2

Reading & Writing Words with the Short Vowel "a" Sound

✓ **Lesson Check Point**

Directions: Read each sentence and underline three words with the short vowel /ă/ sound. Then, write the underlined words on the lines below. The anchor word for the short vowel /ă/ sound is <u>apple</u>.

Direksyons: Li chak fraz epi soulinye twa mo ki genyen son vwayèl kout /ă/ a. Answit, ekri mo soulinye yo sou trè sa yo ki anba. Mo referans pou son vwayèl kout /ă/ a se mo, <u>apple</u>.

Model

<u>Ann</u> raised her <u>hand</u> in <u>class</u>.

      Ann   hand   class
    —————   —————   —————

1. Today, Dan sat on Pam's sofa.

   —————   —————   —————

2. Kate and Dave have two cats.

   —————   —————   —————

3. Dora cannot stand with the band.

   —————   —————   —————

4. My dad did not put gas in Nora's cab.

   —————   —————   —————

5. The campers ran in the rain with the flags.

   —————   —————   —————

 Name: _____ Date: ___/___/_____ Score: _____

Lesson 1.3

Reading Words with the Long Vowel "a" Sound

✓ **Lesson Check Point**

 Directions: Read the words in the four boxes. Circle two words with the long vowel /ā/ sound. The anchor word for the long vowel /ā/ sound is <u>ape</u>.

Direksyons: Li mo yo ki nan kat ti bwat yo. Antoure de mo ki genyen son vwayèl long /ā/ a. Mo referans pou son vwayèl long /ā/ a se mo, <u>ape</u>.

fail	clan	van	flat	sap	train
rat	day	rate	bait	tale	jam

gap	swam	tray	tail	lap	sale
way	fade	jam	ham	nag	mail

 Directions: Read the words in the four boxes. Circle two words that rhyme. Rhyming words have the same ending sound, such as <u>wait</u> and <u>date</u>.

Direksyons: Li mo ki nan kat ti bwat yo. Antoure de mo ki rime. De mo oubyen plizyè mo ki rime genyen menm son nan finisman yo, tankou <u>wait</u> ak <u>date</u>.

cab	race	strain	rain	bran	lay
lace	rag	jazz	grab	fat	way

late	brag	fade	Sam	tab	tan
gaps	mate	made	man	wait	rate

Name: _____ Date: ___/___/_____ Score: _____

Lesson 1.3

Reading & Writing Words with the Long Vowel "a" Sound

✓ **Lesson Check Point**

Directions: Read each sentence and underline three words with the long vowel /ā/ sound. Then, write the underlined words on the lines below. The anchor word for the long vowel /ā/ sound is <u>ape</u>.

Direksyons: Li chak fraz epi soulinye twa mo ki genyen son vwayèl long /ā/ a. Answit, ekri mo soulinye yo sou trè sa yo ki anba. Mo referans pou son vwayèl long /ā/ a se mo, <u>ape</u>.

Model

Ann has <u>grapes</u> and <u>cake</u> on her <u>plate</u>.

    grapes   cake   plate
   _____   _____   _____

1. Al saw the snake's tail in the cave.

2. Ann said, "It is not safe to skate in the rain."

3. We ate the glazed cake in the afternoon.

4. Kate said, "Papa, the square plates are on sale."

5. Last night, David and I were on the same plane.

Name: _____ Date: ___/___/_____ Score: _____

Review Lessons 1.2 & 1.3

Reading Short Vowel and Long Vowel Words

✓ **Lesson Check Point**

Directions: Read the target words in the word box. In the first column, write the words that have the short vowel /ă/ sound, as in the word apple. In the second column, write the words that have the long vowel /ā/ sound, as in the word ape.

Direksyons: Li mo yo objektif yo ki nan bwat mo a. Nan premye kolòn nan, ekri mo ki bay son vwayèl kout /ă/ yo, tankou li ye nan mo apple la. Nan dezyèm kolòn nan, ekri mo ki bay son vwayèl long /ā/ yo, tankou li ye nan mo ape la.

Target Word Box				
shack	made	rack	stay	camp
bag	plan	day	jazz	glass
tape	cave	stand	gate	pain
slam	plate	rain	lake	grab

Letter "a" has the /ă/ sound as in the word **apple**

Letter "a" has the /ā/ sound as in the word **ape**

 Name: _____ Date: ___/___/_____ Score: _____

Lesson 1.4

Reading Words with the "age" Letter Combination

✓ **Lesson Check Point**

 Directions: Read each target word. Find the "age" letter combination and put a check (✓) in the column that correctly identifies its sounds.
Direksyons: Li chak mo objektif. Jwenn konbinezon lèt "age" la epi mete yon tchèk (✓) nan kolòn nan ki idantifye son li yo kòrèkteman.

Target Words	"age" has the /ā/ + /j/ sounds as in the word stage	"age" has the /ĭ/ + /j/ sounds as in the word package	"age" has the /ä/ + /j/ or /ä/ + /zh/ sounds as in the word massage
1. fuselage			
2. discouraged			
3. sabotage			
4. backstage			
5. engaged			

 **Directions:** Read each sentence and underline the word that has an "age" letter combination that has the /ĭ/ + /j/ sounds, as in the word package.
Direksyons: Li chak fraz epi soulinye mo a ki genyen konbinezon lèt "age" la ki bay son /ĭ/ + /j/ a, tankou li ye nan mo package la.

6. Yesterday, they salvaged the plane's fuselage.

7. The backstage managers asked the teenagers to sing loudly.

8. The lizards by the cottage are camouflaged on the green leaves.

9. She encouraged the teenagers to look at the animals in the cage.

10. My agent's text message said the entourage is not allowed backstage.

Name: _____ Date:___/___/_____ Score: _____

Lesson 1.5

Reading Words with the "ai" Vowel Pair

✓ Lesson Check Point

Directions: Read each target word. Circle the word in the column that has the same "ai" sound as the target word.

Direksyons: Li chak mo objektif. Antoure mo a ki nan kolòn nan ki bay menm son "ai" la tankou mo objektif la.

claim	a. and
	b. race

paint	a. said
	b. cage

waist	a. wave
	b. read

await	a. adopt
	b. face

Directions: Read each target word. Put a check (✓) under the correct column heading.

Direksyons: Li chak mo objektif. Mete yon tchèk (✓) anba antèt kolòn ki kòrèk la.

Target Words	Words have the long "a" sound as in the word <u>sail</u>	Words do not have the long "a" sound
1. rain		
2. plaid		
3. said		
4. wait		

 Name: _____ Date: ___/___/_____ Score: _____

Lesson 1.6

Reading Letter "a" Words with the Schwa Vowel Sound

✓ **Lesson Check Point**

 Directions: Read each target word. Circle the word in the column that has the same "a" sound as the target word.
Direksyons: Li chak mo objektif. Antoure mo a ki nan kolòn nan ki bay menm son "a" a tankou mo ojektif la.

about	a. Bermuda
	b. hotcake

alone	a. performance
	b. having

normal	a. factors
	b. machine

cobra	a. obtain
	b. vitamin

 Directions: Read each sentence and underline the letter "a" word that has the schwa vowel /ə/ sound. The anchor word for the letter "a" schwa vowel sound is <u>sofa</u>.
Direksyons: Li chak fraz epi soulinye mo ki genyen lèt "a" a ki bay son schwa /ə/. Mo referans pou son schwa lèt "a" a se mo, <u>sofa</u>.

1. On Sunday, Dale will take a train to Canada.

2. The scholars in my class are obviously smart.

3. Annie saw beautiful, black snakes in Jamaica.

4. The awesome artist, Alexander, is very popular.

5. We were late for Mr. Anderson's grammar class.

6. The reggae performances in the park were awesome.

 Name: _____ Date: ___/___/_____ Score: _____

Lesson 1.7

Reading Words with the "ar" Letter Combination

✓ Lesson Check Point

Directions: Read each target word. Circle the word in the column that has the same "a" + "r" sounds as the target word.
Direksyons: Li chak mo objektif. Antoure mo a ki nan kolòn nan ki bay menm son "a" + "r" yo tankou mo ojektif la.

part	a. Arab
	b. farm

carry	a. baron
	b. dark

bark	a. care
	b. start

parole	a. artist
	b. cheddar

Directions: Read each target word. Put a check (✓) under the correct column heading.
Direksyons: Li chak mo objektif. Mete yon tchèk (✓) anba antèt kolòn ki kòrèk la.

Target Words	"ar" has the /ă/ + /r/ sounds as in the word <u>baron</u>	"ar" has the /ə/ + /r/ sounds as in the word <u>dollar</u>	"ar" has the /ä/ + /r/ sounds as in the word <u>car</u>	"ar" has the /ô/ + /r/ sounds as in the word <u>war</u>
1. part				
2. carry				
3. bark				
4. parole				

 Name: _____ Date:___/___/_____ Score:_____

Lesson 1.7

Reading Words with the "ar" Letter Combination

Dictionary Skills/ Vocabulary

✓ Lesson Check Point

 Directions: Read each target word and its definition. Write the target word on the line in front of its meaning. Use a dictionary or the Internet to check your answers.

Direksyons: Li chak mo objektif ak definisyon yo chak. Ekri mo objektif la sou trè ki devan definisyon li an. Itilize yon diksyonè oubyen entènèt pou tcheke repons ou yo.

Target Word Box				
guards	year	cheddar	triangular	hangar

1. _____ a structure used for housing aircrafts
2. _____ people who protect, oversee and defend
3. _____ a period of time that consists of 365 or 366 days
4. _____ shape with three sides, three corners and three angles
5. _____ a flavor of cheese that ranges from mild to extra sharp

 Directions: Read each sentence and write the target word that correctly completes the sentence.

Direksyons: Li chak fraz epi ekri mo objektif ki konplete fraz la kòrèkteman.

6. We measured the angles of three _____ figures.

7. The armed _____ are stationed throughout the airport.

8. Arnold received a four_____ scholarship to the university.

9. At the park, I will have _____ cheese sandwiches for lunch.

10. The airplane in the _____ is being repaired by the engineers.

Name: _____ Date:___/___/_____ Score:_____

Lesson 1.8

Reading Words with a Silent Letter "a"

✓ **Lesson Check Point**

Directions: Read the target words in the word box. Write the words that have a silent letter "a" in the first column. Write the words that do not have a silent letter "a" in the second column.

Direksyons: Li mo objektif yo ki nan ti bwat mo a. Ekri mo yo ki genyen lèt "a" ki pa pwononse a nan premye kolòn nan. Ekri mo yo ki pa genyen lèt "a" ki pa pwononse a nan dezyèm kolòn nan.

Target Word Box				
answer	beating	zealous	reaping	heater
faces	ago	alarms	sweat	back
Eastern	heads	bands	boats	always
have	stand	oats	cars	eating

Letter "a" is silent

_____
_____
_____
_____
_____
_____
_____
_____
_____

Letter "a" has a letter "a" sound

_____
_____
_____
_____
_____
_____
_____
_____
_____

Name: _____ Date: ___/___/_____ Score: _____

Unit Review - A/a

Reading Words with Vowel "a" Sounds: /ă/, /ā/, /ə/ & Silent

✓ **Lesson Check Point**

Directions: Read each target word. Circle the word in the column that has the same "a" sound as the target word.

Direksyons: Li chak mo objektif. Antoure mo a ki nan kolòn nan ki bay menm son "a" a tankou mo ojektif la.

China	a. camp
	b. larva

sand	a. ask
	b. plays

rain	a. class
	b. trade

oats	a. eaten
	b. snake

Directions: Read each target word. Put a check (✓) under the correct column heading.

Direksyons: Li chak mo objektif. Mete yon tchèk (✓) anba antèt kolòn ki kòrèk la.

Target Words	"a" has the /ă/ sound as in the word <u>apple</u>	"a" has the /ā/ sound as in the word <u>ate</u>	"a" has the /ə/ sound as in the word <u>sofa</u>	"a" is silent as in the word <u>boat</u>
1. China				
2. sand				
3. rain				
4. oats				

Name: _____ Date: ___/___/_____ Score: _____

The Reading Challenge

Lesson 1.9

Reading Multisyllable Words

✓ **Lesson Check Point**

Directions: Read and divide each target word into syllables. Write each word and place a hyphen (-) between the syllables in the second column. Write the number of syllables in the third column. Use a dictionary or the Internet to check your answers.

Direksyons: Li epi divize chak mo objektif an silab. Ekri chak mo epi mete yon tirè (-) ant silab yo nan dezyèm kolòn nan. Ekri kantite silab ke yo genyen an nan twazyèm kolòn nan. Itilize yon diksyonè oubyen entènèt pou tcheke repons ou yo.

Target Words	Words Divided into Syllables	Number of Syllables
1. distant	_____	_____
2. jubilant	_____	_____
3. mishap	_____	_____
4. burlap	_____	_____
5. doormat	_____	_____
6. transplant	_____	_____
7. brainwash	_____	_____
8. demanding	_____	_____
9. vibrantly	_____	_____
10. landing	_____	_____

Unit A Lesson 1.9

 Name: _____ Date: ___/___/_____ Score: _____

The Reading Challenge

Lesson 1.9

Reading Multisyllable Words

✓ **Lesson Check Point**

 **Directions:** Read each target word. Circle the word in the row that is divided correctly into syllables. Use a dictionary or the Internet to check your answers.

Direksyons: Li chak mo objektif. Antoure mo a ki nan ranje a ki divize an silab korèkteman yo. Itilize yon diksyonè oubyen entènèt pou tcheke repons ou yo.

Model

| important | a. im-por-tant (circled) | b. im-port-ant | c. im-porta-nt |

1. bureaucrat	a. bu-reau-crat	b. bur-eau-crat	c. bur-eauc-rat
2. thermostat	a. therm-os-tat	b. ther-mos-tat	c. ther-mo-stat
3. atmosphere	a. at-mos-phere	b. atm-o-sphere	c. at-mosp-here
4. handicap	a. han-dic-ap	b. hand-ic-ap	c. hand-i-cap
5. tolerant	a. to-ler-ant	b. tol-e-rant	c. tol-er-ant
6. pelican	a. pel-ic-an	b. pel-i-can	c. pe-li-can
7. radiant	a. rad-i-ant	b. ra-di-ant	c. ra-dia-nt
8. hesitant	a. hes-it-ant	b. he-sit-ant	c. hes-i-tant

Name: _____ Date: ___/___/_____ Score: _____

Lesson 1.10

Reading and Writing

Proper and Common Nouns and Adjectives

Directions: Read the words in the word box. Put an (X) on the line next to each word that is written incorrectly. Remember that all proper nouns and proper adjectives are capitalized. Use a dictionary or the Internet to check your answers.

Direksyons: Li chak mo yo ki nan bwat mo a. Met yon (X) sou ti trè a ki bò kote mo ki pa kri byen yo. Sonje ke tout non pwòp ak adjektif pwop ekri avèk yon lèt majiskil nan kòmansman yo. Itilize yon diksyonè oubyen entènèt pou tcheke repons ou yo.

Word Box		
__ Arabian	__ albania	__ Australia
__ announcer	__ atlantic Ocean	__ article
__ Algebra	__ anchor	__ Anthill
__ april	__ Angola	__ After

Directions: Read each unedited sentence and underline the word that is written incorrectly. Write each sentence correctly on the line.

Direksyons: Li chak fraz ki pa edite yo epi soulinye mo ki pa ekri byen an. Ekri chak fraz korèkteman sou liy lan.

Model

Andrew has a view of the <u>atlantic</u> Ocean from his apartment.
<u>Andrew has a view of the Atlantic Ocean from his apartment.</u>

1. alex's cats are Angora cats.

   _____

2. Anna ate an apple and an Avocado.

   _____

3. Mr. Aspen is an Assistant at Apple, Inc.

   _____

4. I read an Article about Africa and Asia.

   _____

Name: _____ Date: ___/___/_____ Score: _____

Lesson 2.1

Reading Words with the Letter B/b

✓ Lesson Check Point

Directions: Read each target word. Find the letter "b" and put a check (✓) in the column that identifies its position: beginning, within or end.
Direksyons: Li chak mo objektif. Jwenn lèt "b" a epi mete yon tchèck (✓) nan kolòn ki idantifye pozisyon li an: nan kòmansman, ladan oubyen nan finisman.

Target Words	Beginning (First Letter)	Within	End (Last Letter)
1. lab			
2. habit			
3. biker			
4. lubricate			
5. honeycomb			

Directions: Read each sentence and underline the words that begin with the letter "b." Write all the underlined words in alphabetical order on the lines below.
Direksyons: Li chak fraz epi soulinye mo ki kòmanse avèk lèt "b" yo. Ekri tout mo ki soulinye yo nan lòd alfabetik sou trè sa yo ki anba.

6. Beef is not good bait for fish.

7. The baseballs are on the bench.

8. Ann has a blog about baskets.

9. The baker baked a good cake.

10. My book is about birds and cats.

_____   _____   _____
_____   _____   _____
_____   _____   _____
                _____

Name: _____ Date: ___/___/_____ Score: _____

Lesson 2.2

Reading Words with the "br" Letter Combination

Dictionary Skills/ Vocabulary

✓ **Lesson Check Point**

Directions: Read each target word and its definition. Write the letter of the definition on the line of each target word. Use a dictionary or the Internet to check your answers.

Direksyons: Li chak mo objektif ak definisyon yo chak. Ekri lèt la ki koresponn ak definisyon an sou trè chak mo objektif yo. Itilize yon diksyonè oubyen entènèt pou tcheke repons ou yo.

Target Words	Definitions
1. __ braids	a. a gentle wind
2. __ brave	b. to weave strands together
3. __ breeze	c. the color of dirt and a tree bark
4. __ brother	d. description of a courageous person
5. __ brown	e. a male person who has the same parent(s) as another person

Directions: Read each sentence. Underline the word in the parentheses that correctly completes each sentence. Then, write the underlined word on the line.

Direksyons: Li chak fraz. Soulinye mo a ki nan parantèz yo ki konplete chak fraz kòrèkteman. Answit, ekri mo soulinye a sou trè a.

6. My _____ name is Brian. (braids, brother's)

7. Brad's favorite color is _____. (brags, brown)

8. Bridgette _____ her hair every day. (braids, brave)

9. Bret is the _____ boy who saved the baby. (brave, breeze)

10. When I opened the window, I felt a cool _____. (brags, breeze)

Name: _____ Date: ___/___/_____ Score: _____

Lesson 2.3

Reading Words with the "bl" Letter Combination

Dictionary Skills/ Vocabulary

✓ **Lesson Check Point**

Directions: Read each target word and its definition. Write the target word on the line in front of its meaning. Use a dictionary or the Internet to check your answers.

Direksyons: Li chak mo objektif ak definisyon yo chak. Ekri mo objektif la sou trè ki devan definisyon li an. Itilize yon diksyonè oubyen entènèt pou tcheke repons ou yo.

Target Word Box				
black	blank	blend	bloom	blue

1. _____ the opening of a flower bud
2. _____ the color of tar and the night sky
3. _____ the process of mixing things together
4. _____ the color of the sky on a clear sunny day
5. _____ a surface that does not have any words, images or marks

Directions: Read each sentence. Underline the word in the parentheses that correctly completes each sentence. Then, write the underlined word on the line.

Direksyons: Li chak fraz. Soulinye mo a ki nan parantèz yo ki konplete chak fraz kòrèkteman yo. Answit, ekri mo soulinye a sou trè a.

6. Bill's bike is_____. (blend, blue)

7. My boots are _____. (black, bloom)

8. My art book has _____ pages. (blank, bloom)

9. The flowers _____ by the brook. (bloom, blue)

10. I will _____ the berries in the blender. (blank, blend)

Name: _____ Date: ___/___/_____ Score: _____

Lesson 2.3

Reading Words with the "ble" Letter Combination

✓ Lesson Check Point

Directions: Read each target word. Find the "ble" letter combination and put a check (✓) in the column that identifies its position: beginning, within or end.

Direksyons: Li chak mo objektif. Jwenn konbinezon lèt "ble" a epi mete yon tchèk (✓) nan kolòn nan ki idantifye pozisyon li an: nan kòmansman, ladan oubyen nan finisman.

Target Words	Beginning (First 3 Letters)	Within	End (Last 3 Letters)
1. seasonable			
2. bleep			
3. nibbler			
4. bleaker			
5. assembler			

Directions: Read each target word. Put a check (✓) in the "yes" column if the "ble" letter combination has the /b/ + /ə/ + /l/ sounds. Put a check (✓) in the "no" column if the "ble" letter combination does not have the /b/ + /ə/ + /l/ sounds.

Direksyons: Li chak mo objektif. Mete yon tchèk (✓) nan kolòn "yes" an si konbinezon let "ble" a bay sons /b/ + /ə/ + /l/. Mete yon tchèk (✓) nan kolòn "no" an si konbinezon let "ble" a pa bay sons /b/ + /ə/ + /l/.

Target Words	Yes	No
6. syllable		
7. ramble		
8. bleak		
9. tumble		
10. blending		

Name: _____   Date: ___/___/_____   Score: _____

Lesson 2.4

Reading Words with the "mb" Letter Combination

✓ Lesson Check Point

Directions: Read each target word. Circle the word in the column that has the same "mb" sound(s) as the target word.

Direksyons: Li chak mo objektif. Antoure mo a ki nan kolòn nan ki bay menm son "mb" la (yo) tankou mo ojektif la.

amber	a. climb
	b. grumble

comb	a. numb
	b. jumbo

lamb	a. crumb
	b. humble

limbo	a. thumb
	b. thimble

Directions: Read each target word. In the second column, write the number of letters in the word. In the third column, write the number of letters heard in the word.

Direksyons: Li chak mo objektif. Nan dezyèm kolòn nan, ekri kantite lèt ki nan mo a. Nan twazyèm kolòn nan, ekri kantite lèt ou tande nan mo a.

Target Words	Number of letters in the word	Number of letters heard
1. amber		
2. comb		
3. lamb		
4. limbo		

Name: _____ Date: ___/___/_____ Score: _____

Lesson 2.4

Reading Words with the "bt" Letter Combination

✓ **Lesson Check Point**

Directions: Read each target word. Circle the word in the column that has the same "bt" sound(s) as the target word.

Direksyons: Li chak mo objektif. Antoure mo a ki nan kolòn nan ki bay menm son "bt" la (yo) tankou mo ojektif la.

debtor	a. doubting
	b. obtaining

debt	a. subtitle
	b. subtlety

subtropics	a. subtext
	b. indebted

subtract	a. subtle
	b. obtuse

Directions: Read each target word. In the second column, write the number of letters in the word. In the third column, write the number of letters heard in the word.

Direksyons: Li chak mo objektif. Nan dezyèm kolòn nan, ekri kantite lèt ki nan mo a. Nan twazyèm kolòn na, ekri kantite lèt ou tande nan mo a.

Target Words	Number of letters in the word	Number of letters heard
1. debtor		
2. debt		
3. subtropics		
4. subtract		

Name: _____ Date: ___/___/_____ Score: _____

Lesson 2.5

Reading Words with a Silent "b"

✓ Lesson Check Point

Directions: Read the target words in the word box. Write the words that have a silent letter "b" in the first column. Write the words that do not have a silent letter "b" in the second column.

Direksyons: Li mo objektif yo ki nan ti bwat mo a. Ekri mo yo ki genyen lèt "b" ki pa pwononse a nan premye kolòn nan. Ekri mo yo ki pa genyen lèt "b" ki pa pwononse a nan dezyèm kolòn nan.

Target Word Box				
comb	Arabic	subpoena	debtors	basketball
herb	lamb	obtain	doubting	subtleness
cobweb	debt	thumb	plumber	curb
bubbles	cab	bathtub	disturb	superb

Letter "b" is silent   Letter "b" has the /b/ sound

_____   _____
_____   _____
_____   _____
_____   _____
_____   _____
_____   _____
_____   _____
_____   _____

Learn to Read English With Directions In Haitian Creole

Name: _____ Date:___/___/_____ Score:_____

The Reading Challenge

Lesson 2.6

Reading Multisyllable Words

✓ **Lesson Check Point**

Directions: Read and divide each target word into syllables. Write each word and place a hyphen (-) between the syllables in the second column. Write the number of syllables in the third column. Use a dictionary or the Internet to check your answers.

Direksyons: Li epi divize chak mo objektif an silab. Ekri chak mo epi mete yon tirè (-) ant silab yo nan dezyèm kolòn nan. Ekri kantite silab ke yo genyen an nan twazyèm kolòn nan. Itilize yon diksyonè oubyen entènèt pou tcheke repons ou yo.

Target Words	Words Divided into Syllables	Number of Syllables
1. anybody	_____	_____
2. tugboat	_____	_____
3. subtracting	_____	_____
4. sandbox	_____	_____
5. banana	_____	_____
6. bankroll	_____	_____
7. suburb	_____	_____
8. barbecue	_____	_____
9. becoming	_____	_____
10. centerboard	_____	_____

Name: _____ Date:___/___/_____ Score:_____

The Reading Challenge

Lesson 2.6

Reading Multisyllable Words

✓ **Lesson Check Point**

Directions: Read each target word. Circle the word in the row that is divided correctly into syllables. Use a dictionary or the Internet to check your answers.

Direksyons: Li chak mo objektif. Antoure mo a ki nan ranje a ki divize an silab korèkteman yo. Itilize yon diksyonè oubyen entènèt pou tcheke repons ou yo.

Model

| because | a. be-cause (circled) | b. beca-use | c. b-ecause |

1. backyard	a. ba-ckyard	b. backy-ard	c. back-yard
2. Bahamas	a. Ba-ha-mas	b. Baha-mas	c. Bah-amas
3. bagel	a. bag-el	b. b-agel	c. ba-gel
4. bedtime	a. be-dtime	b. bed-time	c. bedt-ime
5. belonging	a. belong-ing	b. be-lo-nging	c. be-long-ing
6. between	a. be-tween	b. bet-ween	c. betw-een
7. byproduct	a. by-pro-duct	b. by-prod-uct	c. by-produ-ct
8. bifocal	a. bif-o-cal	b. bi-fo-cal	c. bi-foc-al

Learn to Read English With Directions In Haitian Creole

Name: _____ Date: ___/___/_____ Score: _____

Lesson 2.7

Reading and Writing

Proper and Common Nouns and Adjectives

Directions: Read the words in the word box. Put an (X) on the line next to each word that is written incorrectly. Remember that all proper nouns and proper adjectives are capitalized. Use a dictionary or the Internet to check your answers.

Direksyons: Li chak mo yo ki nan bwat mo a. Met yon (X) sou ti trè a ki bò kote mo ki pa kri byen yo. Sonje ke tout non pwòp ak adjektif pwop ekri avèk yon lèt majiskil nan kòmansman yo. Itilize yon diksyonè oubyen entènèt pou tcheke repons ou yo.

Word Box		
__ brother	__ Dr. brown	__ Boston
__ bolivia	__ bubbles	__ british
__ Baby	__ Burma	__ Brussels
__ baking	__ bahamas	__ Bridge

Directions: Read each unedited sentence and underline the word that is written incorrectly. Write each sentence correctly on the line.

Direksyons: Li chak fraz ki pa edite yo epi soulinye mo ki pa ekri byen an. Ekri chak fraz korèkteman sou liy lan.

Model
brandon's books are about big boats.
<u>Brandon's books are about big boats.</u>

1. bobby will borrow Ben's banjo.
   _____

2. The brown brick Building is a bank.
   _____

3. The breadbasket has Big buns and bread.
   _____

4. You can buy belts and brushes from benny.
   _____

Name: _____ Date: ___/___/_____ Score: _____

Lesson 3.1

Reading Words with the Letter C/c

✓ Lesson Check Point

Directions: Read each target word. Find the letter "c" and put a check (✓) in the column that identifies its position: beginning, within or end.

Direksyons: Li chak mo objektif. Jwenn lèt "c" a epi mete yon tchèck (✓) nan kolòn ki idantifye pozisyon li an: nan kòmansman, ladan oubyen nan finisman.

Target Words	Beginning (First Letter)	Within	End (Last Letter)
1. picture			
2. music			
3. economy			
4. control			
5. microbe			

Directions: Read each sentence and underline the words that begin with the letter "c." Write all the underlined words in alphabetical order on the lines below.

Direksyons: Li chak fraz epi soulinye mo ki kòmanse avèk lèt "c" yo. Ekri tout mo ki soulinye yo nan lòd alfabetik sou trè sa yo ki anba.

6. Cats do not like cheese.

7. The cheesecake is very cold.

8. Annie has cocoa on her chin.

9. Bob said, "The cab is parked by the cabin."

10. The coconut tart was baked with cranberries.

_____   _____   _____

_____   _____   _____

_____   _____   _____

               _____

Name: _____ Date:___/___/_____ Score:_____

Lesson 3.1

Reading Words with the Hard Letter "c"

✓ Lesson Check Point

Directions: Read each target word. Put a check (✓) under the correct column heading.

Direksyons: Li chak mo objektif. Mete yon tchèk (✓) anba antèt kolòn ki kòrèk la.

Target Words	Hard "c" has the /k/ sound as in the word <u>cat</u>	Soft "c" has the /s/ sound as in the word <u>cell</u>
1. comic		
2. created		
3. balance		
4. camels		
5. civilian		

Directions: Read each sentence and underline the words that have the hard "c" sound, as in the word <u>cat</u>. Write all the underlined words in alphabetical order on the lines below.

Direksyons: Li chak fraz epi souliye mo ki gen son "c" difisil, tankou nan mo <u>cat</u> la. Ekri tout mo ki soulinye yo nan lòd alfabetik sou trè sa yo ki anba.

6. Craig ate my cinnamon cherry cake.

7. I ate cheese at the Canadian cafeteria.

8. The carrots in the ceramic bowl are crunchy.

9. All the cheerful campers are in the big cabin.

10. The characters in my book like to eat cheap candy.

_____   _____   _____

_____   _____   _____

_____   _____   _____

_____

Name: _____ Date: ___/___/_____ Score: _____

Lesson 3.2

Reading Words with the Soft Letter "c"

✓ Lesson Check Point

Directions: Read each target word. Put a check (✓) under the correct column heading.

Direksyons: Li chak mo objektif. Mete yon tchèk (✓) anba antèt kolòn ki kòrèk la.

Target Words	Hard "c" has the /k/ sound as in the word cat	Soft "c" has the /s/ sound as in the word cell
1. pencil		
2. ice		
3. cage		
4. brace		
5. cute		

Directions: Read each sentence and underline the words that have the soft "c" sound, as in the word cell. Write all the underlined words in alphabetical order on the lines below.

Direksyons: Li chak fraz epi soulinye mo ki bay son dous "c" yo, tankou li ye nan mo cell la. Ekri tout mo ki soulinye yo nan lòd alfabetik sou trè sa yo ki anba.

6. The cooks have fancy ceramic pots.

7. I took a cab to the cinema in the city.

8. The country performer danced in a circle.

9. The cyclist has a cranberry-colored bicycle.

10. Mom placed vanilla icing on the coconut crumb cake.

_____ _____ _____

_____ _____ _____

_____ _____ _____

_____

Name: _____ Date: ___/___/_____ Score: _____

Review Lessons 3.1 & 3.2

Reading Hard Letter "c" and Soft Letter "c" Words

✓ **Lesson Check Point**

Directions: Read the target words in the word box. In the first column, write the words with the letter "c" that have the /k/ sound, as in the word cat. In the second column, write the words with the letter "c" that have the /s/ sound, as in the word cell.

Direksyons: Li mo objektif yo ki nan bwat mo a. Nan premye kolòn nan, ekri mo yo ki genyen lèt "c" ki bay son /k/ yo, tankou li ye nan mo cat la. Nan dezyèm kolòn nan, ekri mo yo ki genyen lèt "c" ki bay son /s/ yo, tankou li ye nan mo cell la.

Target Word Box				
faces	celery	coil	cider	cool
candy	cellar	fancy	code	come
ace	cute	cook	cent	place
curly	civil	cap	cure	bouncy

Hard letter "c" has the /k/ sound as in the word cat

Soft letter "c" has the /s/ sound as in the word cell

Name: _____ Date: ___/___/_____ Score: _____

Lesson 3.3

Reading Words with the "cr" Letter Combination

Dictionary Skills/ Vocabulary

✓ Lesson Check Point

Directions: Read each target word and its definition. Write the letter of the definition on the line of each target word. Use a dictionary or the Internet to check your answers.

Direksyons: Li chak mo objektif ak definisyon yo chak. Ekri lèt la ki koresponn ak definisyon an sou trè chak mo objektif yo. Itilize yon diksyonè oubyen entènèt pou tcheke repons ou yo.

Target Words	Definitions
1. __ cream	a. an insect that makes noises by rubbing its wings
2. __ crib	b. the firm, outer part of a loaf of bread or a pie
3. __ cricket	c. something made from milk; a dairy product
4. __ crop	d. harvested fruits, grains and/or vegetables
5. __ crust	e. a baby's bed with high sides

Directions: Read each sentence. Underline the word in the parentheses that correctly completes each sentence. Then, write the underlined word on the line.

Direksyons: Li chak fraz. Soulinye mo a ki nan parantèz yo ki konplete chak fraz kòrèkteman. Answit, ekri mo soulinye a sou trè a.

6. The _____ of my pie crumbles. (crust, cream)

7. The baby's _____ is very clean. (crib, crop)

8. The farmer has a large _____ of corn. (crust, crop)

9. I can hear the _____ by the cabin. (crust, crickets)

10. I like to put _____ on my cranberries. (cream, crop)

Name: _____ Date:___/___/_____ Score:_____

Lesson 3.4

Reading Words with the "cl" Letter Combination

Dictionary Skills/ Vocabulary

✓ Lesson Check Point

Directions: Read each target word and its definition. Write the target word on the line in front of its meaning. Use a dictionary or the Internet to check your answers.

Direksyons: Li chak mo objektif ak definisyon yo chak. Ekri mo objektif la sou trè ki devan definisyon li an. Itilize yon diksyonè oubyen entènèt pou tcheke repons ou yo.

Target Word Box				
class	classmates	climbed	clinic	closed

1. _____ the position of something that is not open
2. _____ students who are in the same class
3. _____ to have moved upward
4. _____ a group of students instructed by a teacher
5. _____ a place where patients receive medical treatment

Directions: Read each sentence. Underline the word in the parentheses that correctly completes each sentence. Then, write the underlined word on the line.

Direksyons: Li chak fraz. Soulinye mo a ki nan parantèz yo ki konplete chak fraz kòrèkteman. Answit, ekri mo soulinye a sou trè a.

6. Chad _____ the cab door. (class, closed)

7. The campers _____ up the cliff. (climbed, classmates)

8. I enrolled in a chemistry _____ at Cleveland College. (class, clinic)

9. My doctor works at the children's _____. (climbed, clinic)

10. Chad and Cindy are _____ at school. (classmates, closed)

Name: _____ Date: ___/___/_____ Score: _____

Lesson 3.4

Reading Words with the "cle" Letter Combination

✓ Lesson Check Point

Directions: Read each target word. Find the "cle" letter combination and put a check (✓) in the column that identifies its position: beginning, within or end.

Direksyons: Li chak mo objektif. Jwenn konbinezon lèt "cle" a epi mete yon tchèk (✓) nan kolòn nan ki idantifye pozisyon li an: nan kòmansman, ladan oubyen nan finisman.

Target Words	Beginning (First 3 Letters)	Within	End (Last 3 Letters)
1. clean			
2. clerk			
3. clerical			
4. uncle			
5. encirclement			

Directions: Read each target word. Put a check (✓) in the "yes" column if the "cle" letter combination has the /k/ + /ə/ + /l/ sounds. Put a check (✓) in the "no" column if the "cle" letter combination does not have the /k/ + /ə/ + /l/ sounds.

Direksyons: Li chak mo objektif. Mete yon tchèk (✓) nan kolòn "yes" an si konbinezon let "cle" a bay sons /k/ + /ə/ + /l/. Mete yon tchèk (✓) nan kolòn "no" an si konbinezon let "cle" a pa bay sons /k/ + /ə/ + /l/.

Target Words	Yes	No
6. clean		
7. clerk		
8. clerical		
9. uncle		
10. encirclement		

Name: _____ Date:___/___/_____ Score:_____

Lesson 3.5

Reading Words with the "ct" Letter Combination

✓ Lesson Check Point

Directions: Read each target word. Circle the word in the column that has the same "ct" sound(s) as the target word.

Direksyons: Li chak mo objektif. Antoure mo a ki nan kolòn nan ki bay menm son "ct" la (yo) tankou mo objektif la.

actor	a. impact
	b. indict

direct	a. victual
	b. effects

convict	a. connection
	b. inspect

Connecticut	a. indict
	b. factor

Directions: Read each target word. Put a check (✓) under the correct column heading.

Direksyons: Li chak mo objektif. Mete yon tchèk (✓) anba antèt kolòn ki kòrèk la.

Target Words	"ct" has the /k/ + /t/ sounds as in the word <u>fact</u>	"ct" has the silent "c" + /t/ sound as in the word <u>indict</u>
1. actor		
2. direct		
3. convict		
4. Connecticut		

Learn to Read English With Directions In Haitian Creole

Name: _____ Date: ___/___/_____ Score: _____

Lesson 3.6

Reading Soft Letter "c" Words

✓ Lesson Check Point

 Directions: Read each target word. Circle the word in the column that has the same "cean," "cian," "cial," "cious" or "cient" sound as the target word.

Direksyons: Li chak mo objektif. Antoure mo a ki nan kolòn nan ki bay menm son "cean," "cian," "cial," "cious" oubyen "cient" yo tankou mo objektif la.

official	a. physician
	b. commercial

beautician	a. crustacean
	b. American

conscious	a. cousins
	b. ferocious

deficient	a. decent
	b. efficient

 Directions: Read each target word. Put a check (✓) in the column that identifies the same "cean," "cian," "cial," "cious" or "cient" sound within the target word.

Direksyons: Li chak mo objektif. Mete yon tchèk (✓) nan kolòn nan ki idantifye menm son "cean," "cian," "cial," "cious" oubyen "cient" yo nan mo objektif la.

Target Words	"cean" has the /sh/+/ə/+/n/ sounds as in the word <u>ocean</u>	"cial" has the /sh/+/ə/+/l/ sounds as in the word <u>special</u>	"cious" has the /sh/+/ə/+/s/ sounds as in the word <u>delicious</u>	"cient" has the /sh/+/ə/+/n/+/t/ sounds as in the word <u>ancient</u>
1. official				
2. beautician				
3. conscious				
4. deficient				

Name: _____ Date: ___/___/_____ Score: _____

Lesson 3.6

Reading Soft Letter "c" Words

✓ Lesson Check Point

Directions: Read the target words in the word box. In the first column, write the words with the letter "c" that have the /s/ sound, as in the word cell. In the second column, write the words with the letter "c" that have the /sh/ sound, as in the word ocean.

Direksyons: Li mo objektif yo ki nan bwat la. Nan premye kolòn nan, ekri mo yo ki avèk lèt "c" ki bay son /s/ yo, tankou li ye nan mo cell. Nan dezyèm kolòn nan, ekri mo ki avèk lèt "c" ki bay son /sh/ yo, tankou li ye nan mo ocean.

Target Word Box				
proficient	voice	electrician	medicine	place
princess	official	pencil	capricious	judicious
artificial	lacy	dance	recipe	mercy
physician	sentence	clinician	pediatrician	commercial

Soft letter "c" has the /s/ sound as in the word cell

Soft letter "c" has the /sh/ sound as in the word ocean

Learn to Read English With Directions In Haitian Creole

 Name: _____ Date: ___/___/_____ Score: _____

Lesson 3.7

Reading Words with the "ch" Letter Combination

✓ **Lesson Check Point**

 Directions: Read each target word. Circle the word in the column that has the same "ch" sound as the target word.

Direksyons: Li chak mo objektif. Antoure mo a ki nan kolòn nan ki bay menm son "ch" a tankou mo objektif la.

echo	a. bunch
	b. scholar

chip	a. chalk
	b. character

chair	a. chaos
	b. chat

Chicago	a. chin
	b. chef

 Directions: Read each target word. Put a check (✓) under the correct column heading.

Direksyons: Li chak mo objektif. Mete yon tchèk (✓) anba antèt kolòn ki kòrèk la.

Target Words	"ch" has the /ch/ sound as in the word <u>chain</u>	"ch" has the /sh/ sound as in the word <u>chef</u>	"ch" has the /k/ sound as in the word <u>chaos</u>	"ch" is silent as in the word <u>yacht</u>
1. echo				
2. chip				
3. chair				
4. Chicago				

Name: _____ Date: ___/___/_____ Score: _____

Lesson 3.8

Reading Words with the "cc" Letter Combination

✓ Lesson Check Point

Directions: Read each target word. Circle the word in the column that has the same "cc" sound(s) as the target word.

Direksyons: Li chak mo objektif. Antoure mo a ki nan kolòn nan ki bay menm son "cc" la (yo) tankou mo objektif la.

| raccoon | a. soccer |
| | b. accept |

| succumb | a. hiccup |
| | b. accessory |

| accent | a. occur |
| | b. success |

| accessible | a. accelerate |
| | b. broccoli |

Directions: Read each target word. Put a check (✓) under the correct column heading.

Direksyons: Li chak mo objektif. Mete yon tchèk (✓) anba antèt kolòn ki kòrèk la.

Target Words	"cc" has the /k/ sound as in the word <u>soccer</u>	"cc" has the /k/ + /s/ sounds as in the word <u>accept</u>
1. raccoon		
2. succumb		
3. accent		
4. accessible		

Name: _____ Date: ___/___/_____ Score: _____

Lesson 3.9

Reading Words with a Silent Letter "c"

✓ **Lesson Check Point**

Directions: Read the target words in the word box. Write the words that have a silent letter "c" in the first column. Write the words that do not have a silent letter "c" in the second column.

Direksyons: Li mo objektif yo ki nan ti bwat mo a. Ekri mo yo ki genyen lèt "c" ki pa pwononse a nan premye kolòn nan. Ekri mo yo ki pa genyen lèt "c" ki pa pwononse a nan dezyèm kolòn nan.

Target Word Box				
recycle	science	exclude	campers	scene
corpuscle	kneecap	scuff	adolescent	yacht
local	increase	conscience	wildcats	scenery
comment	muscle	distance	scissors	scenario

Letter "c" is silent

Letter "c" has the /k/, /s/ or /sh/ sound

Name: _____ Date:___/___/_____ Score:_____

The Reading Challenge

Lesson 3.10

Reading Multisyllable Words

✓ **Lesson Check Point**

Directions: Read and divide each target word into syllables. Write each word and place a hyphen (-) between the syllables in the second column. Write the number of syllables in the third column. Use a dictionary or the Internet to check your answers.

Direksyons: Li epi divize chak mo objektif an silab. Ekri chak mo epi mete yon tirè (-) ant silab yo nan dezyèm kolòn nan. Ekri kantite silab ke yo genyen an nan twazyèm kolòn nan. Itilize yon diksyonè oubyen entènèt pou tcheke repons ou yo.

Target Words	Words Divided into Syllables	Number of Syllables
1. cavity	_____	_____
2. cabinet	_____	_____
3. chlorine	_____	_____
4. category	_____	_____
5. conception	_____	_____
6. ceremony	_____	_____
7. cardinal	_____	_____
8. continue	_____	_____
9. chandelier	_____	_____
10. cauliflower	_____	_____

Unit C Lesson 3.10

Learn to Read English With Directions In Haitian Creole

Name: _____ Date: ___/___/_____ Score: _____

The Reading Challenge

Lesson 3.10

Reading Multisyllable Words

✓ Lesson Check Point

Directions: Read each target word. Circle the word in the row that is divided correctly into syllables. Use a dictionary or the Internet to check your answers.

Direksyons: Li chak mo objektif. Antoure mo a ki nan ranje a ki divize an silab korèkteman yo. Itilize yon diksyonè oubyen entènèt pou tcheke repons ou yo.

Model

| calculus | a. calcu-lus | b. cal-cu-lus | c. cal-culus |

1. clerical	a. cler-i-cal	b. cle-ri-cal	c. cle-ric-al
2. circulate	a. cir-cul-ate	b. ci-rcul-ate	c. cir-cu-late
3. character	a. cha-ra-cter	b. char-ac-ter	c. char-act-er
4. Chicago	a. Chic-a-go	b. Chi-ca-go	c. Chi-cag-o
5. circular	a. cir-cu-lar	b. ci-rcu-lar	c. circu-lar
6. conclude	a. con-clude	b. con-clu-de	c. co-nclu-de
7. chestnut	a. che-st-nut	b. chest-n-ut	c. chest-nut
8. centipede	a. cen-ti-pede	b. cent-i-pede	c. ce-nti-pede

Name: _____ Date:___/___/_____ Score:_____

Lesson 3.11

Reading and Writing

Proper and Common Nouns and Adjectives

Directions: Read the words in the word box. Put an (X) on the line next to each word that is written incorrectly. Remember that all proper nouns and proper adjectives are capitalized. Use a dictionary or the Internet to check your answers.

Direksyons: Li chak mo yo ki nan bwat mo a. Met yon (X) sou ti trè a ki bò kote mo ki pa kri byen yo. Sonje ke tout non pwòp ak adjektif pwop ekri avèk yon lèt majiskil nan kòmansman yo. Itilize yon diksyonè oubyen entènèt pou tcheke repons ou yo.

Word Box					
__	Center	__	classical	__	Chapter
__	Connecticut	__	Canada	__	chain
__	carpet	__	Coffee	__	chinese
__	canada	__	celtic	__	classroom

Directions: Read each unedited sentence and underline the word that is written incorrectly. Write each sentence correctly on the line.

Direksyons: Li chak fraz ki pa edite yo epi soulinye mo ki pa ekri byen an. Ekri chak fraz korèkteman sou liy lan.

Model
The <u>Camp</u> in Cleveland is closed.
The camp in Cleveland is closed.

1. Carson City is not close to chicago.
_____

2. champion breakfast cereal is chewy.
_____

3. Chloe said, "Columbus is a Capital city."
_____

4. Mrs. Charles' Class is studying storybook characters.
_____

Name: _____ Date:___/___/_____ Score:_____

Lesson 4.1

Reading Words with the Letter D/d

✓ Lesson Check Point

Directions: Read each target word. Find the letter "d" and put a check (✓) in the column that identifies its position: beginning, within or end.
Direksyons: Li chak mo objektif. Jwenn lèt "d" a epi mete yon tchèck (✓) nan kolòn ki idantifye pozisyon li an: nan kòmansman, ladan oubyen nan finisman.

Target Words	Beginning (First Letter)	Within	End (Last Letter)
1. mud			
2. dream			
3. landing			
4. period			
5. medal			

Directions: Read each sentence and underline the words that begin with the letter "d." Write all the underlined words in alphabetical order on the lines below.
Direksyons: Li chak fraz epi soulinye mo ki kòmanse avèk lèt "d" yo. Ekri tout mo ki soulinye yo nan lòd alfabetik sou trè sa yo ki anba.

6. Andy drew a dog and a cat.

7. Dan always reads about dinosaurs.

8. Dr. Brown delivered Betty's baby boy.

9. The chicken drumstick costs one dollar.

10. Annie and Charles went to the desert for a day.

_____ _____ _____
_____ _____ _____
_____ _____ _____
              _____

Name: _____ Date: ___/___/_____ Score: _____

Lesson 4.2

Reading Letter "d" Words with the /d/ Sound & /j/ Sound

✓ **Lesson Check Point**

Directions: Read each target word. Circle the word in the column that has the same "d" sound as the target word.

Direksyons: Li chak mo objektif. Antoure mo a ki nan kolòn nan ki bay menm son "d" a tankou mo objektif la.

induct	a. sedulous
	b. extend

glandular	a. decide
	b. educable

schedule	a. completed
	b. modulate

ladder	a. cordial
	b. middle

Directions: Read each target word. Put a check (✓) under the correct column heading.

Direksyons: Li chak mo objektif. Mete yon tchèk (✓) anba antèt kolòn ki kòrèk la.

Target Words	"d" has the /d/ sound as in the word <u>doctor</u>	"d" has the /j/ sound as in the word <u>educate</u>
1. induct		
2. glandular		
3. schedule		
4. ladder		

 Name: _____ Date:___/___/_____ Score: _____

Lesson 4.2

Reading Words with the "dr" Letter Combination

Dictionary Skills/ Vocabulary

✓ **Lesson Check Point**

 Directions: Read each target word and its definition. Write the letter of the definition on the line of each target word. Use a dictionary or the Internet to check your answers.

Direksyons: Li chak mo objektif ak definisyon yo chak. Ekri lèt la ki koresponn ak definisyon an sou trè chak mo objektif yo. Itilize yon diksyonè oubyen entènèt pou tcheke repons ou yo.

Target Words	Definitions
1. __ drain	a. to have made a picture with a pencil or crayon
2. __ drawer	b. to allow liquid to gradually flow away
3. __ drew	c. the process of making a hole with a tool
4. __ drill	d. feeling sleepy or tired
5. __ drowsy	e. a boxlike pull-out section in furniture

 Directions: Read each sentence. Underline the word in the parentheses that correctly completes each sentence. Then, write the underlined word on the line.

Direksyons: Li chak fraz. Soulinye mo a ki nan parantèz yo ki konplete chak fraz kòrèkteman. Answit, ekri mo soulinye a sou trè a.

6. I will _____ the water into the sink. (drain, drill)

7. Daisy puts her dresses in the _____. (drawer, drain)

8. Dot and Dan will _____ a hole in the door. (drill, drowsy)

9. Dan went to bed because he was _____. (drawer, drowsy)

10. The boys _____ pictures of ducks and dogs. (drain, drew)

Name: _____ Date: ___/__/_____ Score: _____

Lesson 4.3

Reading Words with the "ed" Suffix/ Past Tense Verbs

✓ Lesson Check Point

Directions: Read each target word. Circle the word in the column that has the same "ed" sound(s) as the target word.
Direksyons: Li chak mo objektif. Antoure mo a ki nan kolòn nan ki bay menm son "ed" a tankou mo objektif la.

allowed	a. slapped
	b. returned

shaped	a. linked
	b. rained

waited	a. washed
	b. admitted

entered	a. framed
	b. walked

Directions: Read each target word.   Put a check (✓) under the correct column heading.
Direksyons: Li chak mo objektif. Mete yon tchèk (✓) anba antèt kolòn ki kòrèk la.

Target Words	"ed" has the /ĭ/ + /d/ sounds as in the word <u>rested</u>	"ed" has the /d/ sound as in the word <u>hugged</u>	"ed" has the /t/ sound as in the word <u>tipped</u>
1. allowed			
2. shaped			
3. waited			
4. entered			

Name: _____ Date: ___/___/_____ Score: _____

Lesson 4.4

Reading Words with a Silent Letter "d"

✓ Lesson Check Point

Directions: Read the target words in the word box. Write the words that have a silent letter "d" in the first column. Write the words that do not have a silent letter "d" in the second column.

Direksyons: Li mo objektif yo ki nan ti bwat mo a. Ekri mo yo ki genyen yon lèt "d" ki pa pwononse a nan premye kolòn nan. Ekri mo yo ki pa genyen yon lèt "d" ki pa pwononse a nan dezyèm kolòn nan.

Target Word Box				
shed	dislodge	third	adjust	landscape
adjunct	handsome	duck	date	grudge
side	dress	hedge	handrail	ready
bridge	handkerchief	doctors	Wednesday	judge

Letter "d" is silent	Letter "d" has the /d/ sound
_____	_____
_____	_____
_____	_____
_____	_____
_____	_____
_____	_____
_____	_____
_____	_____

Name: _____ Date: ___/___/_____ Score: _____

The Reading Challenge

Lesson 4.5

Reading Multisyllable Words

✓ Lesson Check Point

Directions: Read and divide each target word into syllables. Write each word and place a hyphen (-) between the syllables in the second column. Write the number of syllables in the third column. Use a dictionary or the Internet to check your answers.

Direksyons: Li epi divize chak mo objektif an silab. Ekri chak mo epi mete yon tirè (-) ant silab yo nan dezyèm kolòn nan. Ekri kantite silab ke yo genyen an nan twazyèm kolòn nan. Itilize yon diksyonè oubyen entènèt pou tcheke repons ou yo.

Target Words	Words Divided into Syllables	Number of Syllables
1. development		
2. demonstrator		
3. despondent		
4. digital		
5. duplication		
6. digestion		
7. derivation		
8. durable		
9. delinquency		
10. doctoral		

Name: _____ Date: ___/___/_____ Score: _____

The Reading Challenge

Lesson 4.5

Reading Multisyllable Words

✓ Lesson Check Point

 Directions: Read each target word. Circle the word in the row that is divided correctly into syllables. Use a dictionary or the Internet to check your answers.

Direksyons: Li chak mo objektif. Antoure mo a ki nan ranje a ki divize an silab korèkteman yo. Itilize yon diksyonè oubyen entènèt pou tcheke repons ou yo.

Model

| dictionary | a. di-ction-ary | b. dic-tion-ar-y (circled) | c. dic-tiona-ry |

| 1. decision | a. de-ci-sion | b. dec-i-sion | c. de-cis-ion |

| 2. disciple | a. di-sci-ple | b. disc-i-ple | c. dis-ci-ple |

| 3. decagram | a. de-ca-gram | b. dec-a-gram | c. de-cag-ram |

| 4. dynamite | a. dyn-a-mite | b. dy-nam-ite | c. dy-na-mite |

| 5. democrat | a. dem-o-crat | b. de-mo-crat | c. de-mocr-at |

| 6. dynasty | a. dyn-as-ty | b. dy-nast-y | c. dy-nas-ty |

| 7. decimal | a. de-cim-al | b. dec-i-mal | c. de-ci-mal |

| 8. document | a. doc-u-ment | b. do-cum-ent | c. do-cume-nt |

Name: _____ Date: ___/___/_____ Score: _____

Lesson 4.6

Reading and Writing

Proper and Common Nouns and Adjectives

Directions: Read the words in the word box. Put an (X) on the line next to each word that is written incorrectly. Remember that all proper nouns and proper adjectives are capitalized. Use a dictionary or the Internet to check your answers.

Direksyons: Li chak mo yo ki nan bwat mo a. Met yon (X) sou ti trè a ki bò kote mo ki pa kri byen yo. Sonje ke tout non pwòp ak adjektif pwop ekri avèk yon lèt majiskil nan kòmansman yo. Itilize yon diksyonè oubyen entènèt pou tcheke repons ou yo.

Word Box		
__ Delaware	__ danish	__ dresses
__ Dependent	__ Dishes	__ Diner
__ dense	__ doormat	__ Dominican
__ december	__ Denver	__ dr.

Directions: Read each unedited sentence and underline the word that is written incorrectly. Write each sentence correctly on the line.

Direksyons: Li chak fraz ki pa edite yo epi soulinye mo ki pa ekri byen an. Ekri chak fraz korèkteman sou liy lan.

Model
Dan said, "My daughter's name is <u>donna</u>."
Dan said, "My daughter's name is Donna."

1. The dictionary belongs to dean Douglas.
   _____

2. Dakota dreams about ducks in the Desert.
   _____

3. Bobby said, "diana's desk is by the front door."
   _____

4. denver Diner sells one dozen donuts for one dollar.
   _____

Name: _____ Date:___/___/_____ Score: _____

Lesson 5.1

Reading Words with the Letter E/e

✓ **Lesson Check Point**

Directions: Read each target word. Find the letter "e" and put a check (✓) in the column that identifies its position: beginning, within or end.

Direksyons: Li chak mo objektif. Jwenn lèt "e" a epi mete yon tchèck (✓) nan kolòn ki idantifye pozisyon li an: nan kòmansman, ladan oubyen nan finisman.

Target Words	Beginning (First Letter)	Within	End (Last Letter)
1. multiple			
2. after			
3. evict			
4. enchant			
5. indicate			

Directions: Read each target word. Read the words in the row and circle the word that has a different vowel "e" sound.

Direksyons: Li chak mo objektif. Li mo yo ki nan ranje a epi antoure mo a ki bay yon son vwayèl "e" ki diferan an.

Target Words				
6. neck	bend	tell	be	pest
7. flesh	me	vest	yell	felt
8. blend	went	she	fresh	tent
9. press	fell	then	cell	he
10. spend	nest	we	mend	bled

Name: _____ Date:___/___/_____ Score: _____

Lesson 5.2

Reading Words with the Short Vowel "e" Sound

✓ Lesson Check Point

Directions: Read the words in the four boxes. Circle two words with the short vowel /ĕ/ sound. The anchor word for the short vowel /ĕ/ sound is <u>egg</u>.

Direksyons: Li mo yo ki nan kat ti bwat yo. Antoure de mo ki genyen son vwayèl kout /ĕ/ a. Mo referans pou son vwayel kout /ĕ/a se mo, <u>egg</u>.

trend	leak
zero	bent

tent	reap
flesh	east

mend	beck
scene	lease

lean	bled
seek	end

heap	peace
dent	mesh

theme	knelt
wedge	peas

Directions: Read the words in the four boxes. Circle two words that rhyme. Rhyming words have the same ending sound, such as <u>set</u> and <u>wet</u>.

Direksyons: Li mo yo ki nan kat ti bwat yo. Antoure de mo ki rime. De mo oubyen plizyè mo ki rime genyen menm son nan finisman yo, tankou <u>set</u> ak <u>wet</u>.

leg	grease
me	beg

rent	sent
fleas	east

eat	fled
see	sled

spent	tea
cent	help

scene	wed
led	steak

real	beam
cell	fell

Name: _____ Date: ___/___/_____ Score: _____

Lesson 5.2

Reading & Writing Words with the Short Vowel "e" Sound

✓ **Lesson Check Point**

Directions: Read each sentence and underline three words with the short vowel /ĕ/ sound. Then, write the underlined words on the lines below. The anchor word for the short vowel /ĕ/ sound is <u>egg</u>.

Direksyons: Li chak fraz epi soulinye twa mo ki genyen son vwayèl kout /ĕ/ a. Answit, ekri mo soulinye yo sou trè sa yo ki anba. Mo referans pou son vwayèl kout /ĕ/ a se mo, <u>egg</u>.

Model

She placed her <u>legs</u> on the <u>wet</u> <u>deck</u>.

    legs   wet   deck
 ‾‾‾‾‾‾‾‾   ‾‾‾‾‾‾‾‾   ‾‾‾‾‾‾‾‾

1. On Tuesday, we met Ted at the shed.

   ‾‾‾‾‾‾‾‾   ‾‾‾‾‾‾‾‾   ‾‾‾‾‾‾‾‾

2. My pet is next to the neatly made bed.

   ‾‾‾‾‾‾‾‾   ‾‾‾‾‾‾‾‾   ‾‾‾‾‾‾‾‾

3. On Tuesday, Ken's jet did not set off.

   ‾‾‾‾‾‾‾‾   ‾‾‾‾‾‾‾‾   ‾‾‾‾‾‾‾‾

4. At camp, the men made the best eggs.

   ‾‾‾‾‾‾‾‾   ‾‾‾‾‾‾‾‾   ‾‾‾‾‾‾‾‾

5. Ed's little, red sled is on the car seat.

   ‾‾‾‾‾‾‾‾   ‾‾‾‾‾‾‾‾   ‾‾‾‾‾‾‾‾

 Name: _____ Date: ___/___/_____ Score: _____

Lesson 5.3

Reading Words with the Long Vowel "e" Sound

✓ **Lesson Check Point**

 Directions: Read the words in the four boxes. Circle two words with the long vowel /ē/ sound. The anchor word for the long vowel /ē/ sound is <u>me</u>.

Direksyons: Li mo yo ki nan kat ti bwat yo. Antoure de mo ki genyen son vwayèl long /ē/ a. Mo referans pou son vwayèl long /ē/ a se mo, <u>me</u>.

dell	zeal		peak	melt		seize	cress
wear	reap		head	bee		meet	sell

their	see		wheat	free		neat	met
each	swell		pear	pelt		steel	fled

 Directions: Read the words in the four boxes. Circle two words that rhyme. Rhyming words have the same ending sound, such as <u>beep</u> and <u>reap</u>.

Direksyons: Li mo yo ki nan kat ti bwat yo. Antoure de mo ki rime. De mo oubyen plizyè mo ki rime genyen menm son nan finisman yo, tankou <u>beep</u> ak <u>reap</u>.

led	mean		smelt	eight		learn	beat
hear	dean		heal	peel		feet	jets

glean	clean		heap	drench		real	gem
trench	vein		dear	leap		seal	tear

Name: _____ Date: ___/___/_____ Score: _____

Lesson 5.3

Reading & Writing Words with the Long Vowel "e" Sound

✓ **Lesson Check Point**

Directions: Read each sentence and underline three words with the long vowel /ē/ sound. Then, write the underlined words on the lines below. The anchor word for the long vowel /ē/ sound is <u>me</u>.

Direksyons: Li chak fraz epi soulinye twa mo ki genyen son vwayèl long /ē/ a. Answit, ekri mo soulinye yo sou trè sa yo ki anba. Mo referans pou son vwayèl long /ē/ a se mo, <u>me</u>.

Model

<u>We</u> are <u>reading</u> an article entitled, "<u>Eagles</u> Bird of Prey."

    We   reading   Eagles
  _____   _____   _____

1. Ed's hockey team reigns supreme.

  _____   _____   _____

2. The lead teacher wrote interesting themes on the board.

  _____   _____   _____

3. The athletes on the Swedish team are in good health.

  _____   _____   _____

4. For good health, people should eat and sleep well.

  _____   _____   _____

5. I noticed that the green leaves are falling off the trees.

  _____   _____   _____

Name: _____ Date: ___/___/_____ Score: _____

Review Lessons 5.2 & 5.3

Reading Short Vowel and Long Vowel Words

Directions: Read the target words in the word box. In the first column, write the words that have the short vowel /ĕ/ sound, as in the word <u>egg</u>. In the second column, write the words that have the long vowel /ē/ sound, as in the word <u>me</u>.

Direksyons: Li mo objektif yo ki nan bwat mo a. Nan premye kolòn nan, ekri mo ki bay son vwayèl kout /ĕ/ yo, tankou li ye nan mo <u>egg</u> la. Nan dezyèm kolòn nan, ekri mo ki bay son vwayèl long /ē/ yo, tankou li ye nan mo <u>me</u> la.

Target Word Box				
receive	sketch	clever	legacy	deceive
edit	eagle	eating	scheme	them
when	scream	Haitian Creole	eggshell	compete
people	vest	sending	concrete	medal

Letter "e" has the /ĕ/ sound as in the word <u>egg</u>

Letter "e" has the /ē/ sound as in the word <u>me</u>

Name: _____ Date: ___/___/_____ Score: _____

Lesson 5.4

Reading Words with Letter "e" Vowel Pairs

✓ **Lesson Check Point**

Directions: Read each target word. Circle the word in the column that has the same vowel "ea," "ee," "ei," "eo" or "eu" sound as the target word.

Direksyons: Li chak mo objektif. Antoure mo a ki nan kolòn nan ki bay menm son vwayèl "ea," "ee," "ei," "eo" oubyen "eu" a tankou mo objektif la.

keep	a. dear
	b. stream

eight	a. peer
	b. veil

people	a. Europe
	b. reader

cheese	a. peanut
	b. hear

Directions: Read each target word. Put a check (✓) under the correct column heading.

Direksyons: Li chak mo objektif. Mete yon tchèk (✓) anba antèt kolòn ki kòrèk la.

Target Words	Words have the long "e" sound as in the word <u>tea</u>	Words do not have the long "e" sound
1. keep		
2. eight		
3. people		
4. cheese		

Name: _____ Date: ___/___/_____ Score: _____

Lesson 5.5

Reading Words with the Final Letter "e"

✓ Lesson Check Point

Directions: Read each target word. Find the letter "e" and put a check (✓) in the column that identifies its position within the syllable.

Direksyons: Li chak mo objektif. Jwenn lèt "e" a epi mete yon tchèck (✓) nan kolòn ki idantifye pozisyon li an nan silab la.

Target Words	"e" is at the end of a one syllable word	"e" is at the end of the first syllable	"e" is at the end of a multi-syllable word
1. dispute			
2. she			
3. hero			
4. we			
5. began			

Directions: Read each target word. Put a check (✓) under the correct column heading.

Direksyons: Li chak mo objektif. Mete yon tchèk (✓) anba antèt kolòn ki kòrèk la.

Target Words	"e" has the /ĕ/ sound as in the word <u>egg</u>	"e" has the /ē/ sound as in the word <u>me</u>	"e" has the /ə/ sound as in the word <u>item</u>	"e" is silent as in the word <u>great</u>
6. label				
7. medical				
8. seedling				
9. cake				
10. tenant				

 Name: _____ Date:___/___/_____ Score:_____

Lesson 5.6

Reading Letter "e" Words with the Schwa Vowel Sound

✓ **Lesson Check Point**

Directions: Read each target word. Circle the word in the column that has the same "e" sound as the target word.

Direksyons: Li chak mo objektif. Antoure mo a ki nan kolòn nan ki bay menm son "e" a tankou mo objektif la.

father	a. else
	b. problem

pres<u>e</u>nt	a. liver
	b. lend

the	a. penny
	b. camel

en<u>e</u>my	a. wider
	b. meal

Directions: Read each sentence and underline the letter "e" word that has the schwa vowel /ə/ sound. The anchor word for the letter "e" schwa vowel sound is <u>item</u>.

Direksyons: Li chak fraz epi soulinye mo ki genyen lèt "e" ki bay son schwa /ə/ a. Mo referans pou son schwa lèt "e" a se mo, <u>item</u>.

1. We lived in Belize for five years.

2. My toy elephants are stuffed with cotton fibers.

3. Our education system focuses on teaching students.

4. My instructor said, "This year, I have a marvelous class!"

5. Mr. Eastman made nine food deliveries along our coastline.

6. We read an interesting short story entitled "Two Kinds" by Amy Tan.

Name: _____ Date:___/___/_____ Score:_____

Lesson 5.7

Reading Words with the "er" Letter Combination

Dictionary Skills/ Vocabulary

✓ Lesson Check Point

Directions: Read each target word and its definition. Write the letter of the definition on the line of each target word. Use a dictionary or the Internet to check your answers.

Direksyons: Li chak mo objektif ak definisyon yo chak. Ekri lèt la ki koresponn ak definisyon an sou trè chak mo objektif yo. Itilize yon diksyonè oubyen entènèt pou tcheke repons ou yo.

Target Words	Definitions
1. __ cherry	a. a written form of communication
2. __ terrible	b. a verbal or written response to a question
3. __ periscope	c. a sweet fruit that is small, round and red
4. __ letter	d. something very bad or unacceptable
5. __ answer	e. a viewing instrument that has a system of lenses

Directions: Read each sentence and write the target word that correctly completes the sentence.
Direksyons: Li chak fraz epi ekri mo objektif ki konplete fraz la kòrèkteman.

6. Jerry's milkshake has whipped cream and a _____ on top.

7. Sherry received a business _____ in the mail.

8. The clerk used his new _____ for entertainment.

9. My sister said the correct _____ to the difficult question.

10. The shaky ladder against the house is in a _____ place.

 Name: _____   Date: ___/___/_____   Score: _____

Lesson 5.8

Reading Words with the "eu" and "ew" Letter Combinations

✓ **Lesson Check Point**

 Directions: Read each sentence and underline the word that has a silent letter "e."

Direksyons: Li chak fraz epi soulinye mo a ki genyen lèt "e" ki pa pwononse a.

Model
My father said, "The apricot streusel is very tasty."

1. Ben read the eulogy at Mr. Edward's funeral.

2. The domestic cat was neutered by the veterinarian.

3. The driver skillfully maneuvers his red car in the parking lot.

4. Helen Evans, the author of the award-winning book, has a pseudonym.

 Directions: Read each sentence and underline the word with an "eu" or "ew" letter combination that has the long vowel /yōō/ or /ōō/ sound, as in the words feud and flew.

Direksyons: Li chak fraz epi soulinye mo a ki genyen yon konbinezon lèt "eu" oubyen "ew" ki bay son vwayèl long /yōō/ oubyen /ōō/ a, tankou li ye nan mo feud ak flew.

5. Last summer, Edward grew rather quickly.

6. Emily accidentally lost her gold and silver jewelry.

7. My mother is sewing a red dress for Mrs. Andrews.

8. The major family dispute was over a pot of beef stew.

9. It was difficult for the judge to maintain a neutral position.

10. The successful battle was directed by Lieutenant Edmonds.

Name: _____ Date: ___/___/_____ Score: _____

Lesson 5.9

Reading Words with the "ey" Letter Combination

✓ **Lesson Check Point**

Directions: Read each target word. Put a check (✓) under the correct column heading.

Direksyons: Li chak mo objektif. Mete yon tchèk (✓) anba antèt kolòn ki kòrèk la.

Target Words	"ey" has the long /ē/ sound as in the word <u>honey</u>	"ey" has the long /ā/ sound as in the word <u>hey</u>
1. kidney		
2. grey		
3. they		
4. volley		

Directions: Read each sentence and underline the word with the "ey" letter combination. Put a check (✓) under the correct column heading.

Direksyons: Li chak fraz epi soulinye mo a ki genyen konbinezon lèt "ey" la. Mete yon tchèk (✓) anba antèt kolòn ki kòrèk la.

	"ey" has the long /ē/ sound as in the word <u>honey</u>	"ey" has the long /ā/ sound as in the word <u>hey</u>
5. The students must obey the rules.	_____	_____
6. The eagle is looking for its prey.	_____	_____
7. Bradley is eating cheese for lunch.	_____	_____
8. They are eager to go to Europe.	_____	_____
9. Jeffery has a hockey game this evening.	_____	_____
10. Shama saw four fat monkeys at the zoo.	_____	_____

Unit E Lesson 5.9

Name: _____ Date: ___/___/_____ Score: _____

Lesson 5.10

Reading Words with a Silent Letter "e"

✓ **Lesson Check Point**

Directions: Read the target words in the word box. Write the words that have a silent letter "e" in the first column. Write the words that do not have a silent letter "e" in the second column.

Direksyons: Li mo objektif yo ki nan ti bwat mo a. Ekri mo yo ki genyen yon lèt "e" ki pa pwononse a nan premye kolòn nan. Ekri mo yo ki pa genyen yon lèt "e" ki pa pwononse a nan dezyèm kolòn nan.

Target Word Box				
issues	dependent	partake	clues	computer
restore	screen	effect	sideways	element
eating	elephants	made	seagulls	beneath
space	teapot	rake	pine	ending

Letter "e" is silent

_____
_____
_____
_____
_____
_____
_____
_____

Letter "e" has a letter "e" sound

_____
_____
_____
_____
_____
_____
_____
_____

Unit E
Lesson 5.10

Learn to Read English With Directions In Haitian Creole

Name: _____ Date:___/___/_____ Score:_____

Unit Review - E/e

Reading Words with Vowel "e" Sounds: /ĕ/, /ē/, /ə/ & Silent

✓ **Lesson Check Point**

Directions: Read each target word. Circle the word in the column that has the same "e" sound as the target word.

Direksyons: Li chak mo objektif. Antoure mo a ki nan kolòn nan ki bay menm son "e" a tankou mo objektif la.

| marvel | a. legged |
| | b. item |

| trade | a. blue |
| | b. smell |

| elephant | a. legacy |
| | b. east |

| navel | a. Belize |
| | b. paycheck |

Directions: Read each target word. Put a check (✓) under the correct column heading.

Direksyons: Li chak mo objektif. Mete yon tchèk (✓) anba antèt kolòn ki kòrèk la.

Target Words	"e" has the /ĕ/ sound as in the word <u>egg</u>	"e" has the /ē/ sound as in the word <u>me</u>	"e" has the /ə/ sound as in the word <u>item</u>	"e" is silent as in the word <u>great</u>
1. marvel				
2. trade				
3. elephant				
4. navel				

Name: _____ Date: ___/___/_____ Score: _____

The Reading Challenge

Lesson 5.11

Reading Multisyllable Words

✓ **Lesson Check Point**

Directions: Read and divide each target word into syllables. Write each word and place a hyphen (-) between the syllables in the second column. Write the number of syllables in the third column. Use a dictionary or the Internet to check your answers.

Direksyons: Li epi divize chak mo objektif an silab. Ekri chak mo epi mete yon tirè (-) ant silab yo nan dezyèm kolòn nan. Ekri kantite silab ke yo genyen an nan twazyèm kolòn nan. Itilize yon diksyonè oubyen entènèt pou tcheke repons ou yo.

Target Words	Words Divided into Syllables	Number of Syllables
1. problem	_____	_____
2. systemic	_____	_____
3. retelling	_____	_____
4. featuring	_____	_____
5. heartfelt	_____	_____
6. peacock	_____	_____
7. leaflet	_____	_____
8. kitchen	_____	_____
9. fifteen	_____	_____
10. golden	_____	_____

Name: _____ Date: ___/___/_____ Score: _____

The Reading Challenge

Lesson 5.11

Reading Multisyllable Words

✓ Lesson Check Point

Directions: Read each target word. Circle the word in the row that is divided correctly into syllables. Use a dictionary or the Internet to check your answers.

Direksyons: Li chak mo objektif. Antoure mo a ki nan ranje a ki divize an silab korèkteman yo. Itilize yon diksyonè oubyen entènèt pou tcheke repons ou yo.

Model

| megabyte | a. me-ga-byte | b. meg-a-byte | c. me-gaby-te |

| 1. amending | a. am-end-ing | b. a-mend-ing | c. am-en-ding |

| 2. extending | a. ex-tend-ing | b. ex-ten-ding | c. e-xten-ding |

| 3. systemic | a. sy-stem-ic | b. sys-te-mic | c. sys-tem-ic |

| 4. condescend | a. con-de-scend | b. cond-e-scend | c. con-des-cend |

| 5. depended | a. de-pen-ded | b. de-pend-ed | c. dep-end-ed |

| 6. expanding | a. ex-pand-ing | b. ex-pan-ding | c. exp-and-ing |

| 7. apartment | a. a-partme-nt | b. ap-art-ment | c. a-part-ment |

| 8. suspending | a. su-spend-ing | b. sus-pend-ing | c. sus-pen-ding |

Name: _____ Date: ___/___/_____ Score: _____

Lesson 5.12

Reading and Writing

Proper and Common Nouns and Adjectives

Directions: Read the words in the word box. Put an (X) on the line next to each word that is written incorrectly. Remember that all proper nouns and proper adjectives are capitalized. Use a dictionary or the Internet to check your answers.

Direksyons: Li chak mo yo ki nan bwat mo a. Met yon (X) sou ti trè a ki bò kote mo ki pa kri byen yo. Sonje ke tout non pwòp ak adjektif pwop ekri avèk yon lèt majiskil nan kòmansman yo. Itilize yon diksyonè oubyen entènèt pou tcheke repons ou yo.

Word Box		
__ East Germany	__ Estonia	__ Element
__ eliminate	__ easter	__ equator
__ Mt. everest	__ Email	__ embark
__ Efficient	__ entrance	__ england

Directions: Read each unedited sentence and underline the word that is written incorrectly. Write each sentence correctly on the line.

Direksyons: Li chak fraz ki pa edite yo epi soulinye mo ki pa ekri byen an. Ekri chak fraz korèkteman sou liy lan.

Model
All my friends are Excited about the class trip to Europe.
All my friends are excited about the class trip to Europe.

1. Eloise took a picture of the eiffel Tower.
   _____

2. In Europe, people like to eat Eggs for breakfast.
   _____

3. Eve is reading books about how eskimos survive in the Arctic.
   _____

4. Early in the morning, Beth and I will go to the english Channel.
   _____

Name: _____ Date: ___/___/_____ Score: _____

Lesson 6.1

Reading Words with the Letter F/f

✓ **Lesson Check Point**

Directions: Read each target word. Find the letter "f" and put a check (✓) in the column that identifies its position: beginning, within or end.

Direksyons: Li chak mo objektif. Jwenn lèt "f" a epi mete yon tchèck (✓) nan kolòn ki idantifye pozisyon li an: nan kòmansman, ladan oubyen nan finisman.

Target Words	Beginning (First Letter)	Within	End (Last Letter)
1. informed			
2. fox			
3. roof			
4. proof			
5. enforced			

Directions: Read each sentence and underline the words that begin with the letter "f." Write all the underlined words in alphabetical order on the lines below.

Direksyons: Li chak fraz epi soulinye mo ki kòmanse avèk lèt "f" yo. Ekri tout mo ki soulinye yo nan lòd alfabetik sou trè sa yo ki anba.

6. Fish do not have feet.

7. Frank has two big frogs.

8. My file folder is in the cabinet.

9. The fruits in the bowls are firm.

10. You can eat food with your fingers.

_____   _____   _____
_____   _____   _____
_____   _____
            _____

Name: _____ Date: ___/___/_____ Score: _____

Lesson 6.2

Reading Words with the "fr" Letter Combination

Dictionary Skills/ Vocabulary

✓ Lesson Check Point

Directions: Read each target word and its definition. Write the letter of the definition on the line of each target word. Use a dictionary or the Internet to check your answers.
Direksyons: Li chak mo objektif ak definisyon yo chak. Ekri lèt la ki koresponn ak definisyon an sou trè chak mo objektif yo. Itilize yon diksyonè oubyen entènèt pou tcheke repons ou yo.

Target Words	Definitions
1. __ fractions	a. the state of being physically free
2. __ free	b. thin, long pieces of fried potato
3. __ freedom	c. icing on a dessert
4. __ fries	d. math concept; part of a whole
5. __ frosting	e. receiving something without payment or cost

Directions: Read each sentence. Underline the word in the parentheses that correctly completes each sentence. Then, write the underlined word on the line.
Direksyons: Li chak fraz. Soulinye mo a ki nan parantèz yo ki konplete chak fraz kòrèkteman. Answit, ekri mo soulinye a sou trè a.

6. I am learning to add _____ in class. (fractions, free)

7. I ate fried chicken and _____ for lunch. (fries, frosting)

8. The nonfiction books are _____ of charge. (fractions, free)

9. I spread a thin layer of _____ on the cake. (fries, frosting)

10. Frederick Douglass fought for the _____ of enslaved people. (free, freedom)

Name: _____ Date: ___/___/_____ Score: _____

Lesson 6.3

Reading Words with the "fl" Letter Combination

Dictionary Skills/ Vocabulary

✓ Lesson Check Point

Directions: Read each target word and its definition. Write the target word on the line in front of its meaning. Use a dictionary or the Internet to check your answers.

Direksyons: Li chak mo objektif ak definisyon yo chak. Ekri mo objektif la sou trè ki devan definisyon li an. Itilize yon diksyonè oubyen entènèt pou tcheke repons ou yo.

Target Word Box				
flash	fleet	flexible	float	flooded

1. _____ vehicles owned or operated as a unit
2. _____ to stay on top of liquid without sinking
3. _____ a place full of water that is normally dry
4. _____ something that can bend easily without breaking
5. _____ a device on a camera that provides light to brighten a picture

Directions: Read each sentence. Underline the word in the parentheses that correctly completes each sentence. Then, write the underlined word on the line.

Direksyons: Li chak fraz. Soulinye mo a ki nan parantèz yo ki konplete chak fraz kòrèkteman. Answit, ekri mo soulinye a sou trè a.

6. Fred's black belt is flat and _____. (fleet, flexible)

7. Flower lilies _____ on top of the water. (float, flash)

8. The camera's built-in _____ is broken. (fleet, flash)

9. My dad's company has a new _____ of buses. (fleet, float)

10. On Friday, my den was _____ with water. (flashed, flooded)

Name: _____ Date: ___/___/_____ Score: _____

Lesson 6.3

Reading Words with the "fle" Letter Combination

 Lesson Check Point

Directions: Read each target word. Find the "fle" letter combination and put a check (✓) in the column that identifies its position: beginning, within or end.

Direksyons: Li chak mo objektif. Jwenn konbinezon lèt "fle" a epi mete yon tchèk (✓) nan kolòn nan ki idantifye pozisyon li an: nan kòmansman, ladan oubyen nan finisman.

Target Words	Beginning (First 3 Letters)	Within	End (Last 3 Letters)
1. flea			
2. baffle			
3. unfledged			
4. flexible			
5. raffle			

 Directions: Read each target word. Put a check (✓) in the "yes" column if the "fle" letter combination has the /f/ + /ə/ + /l/ sounds. Put a check (✓) in the "no" column if the "fle" letter combination does not have the /f/ + /ə/ + /l/ sounds.

Direksyons: Li chak mo objektif. Mete yon tchèk (✓) nan kolòn "yes" an si konbinezon lèt "fle" a bay sons /f/ + /ə/ + /l/. Mete yon tchèk (✓) nan kolòn "no" an si konbinezon lèt "fle" a pa bay sons /f/ + /ə/ + /l/.

Target Words	Yes	No
6. flea		
7. baffle		
8. unfledged		
9. flexible		
10. raffle		

Name: _____ Date: ___/___/_____ Score: _____

Lesson 6.4

Reading Words with the "ft," "lf" and "ff" Letter Combinations

Dictionary Skills/ Vocabulary

✓ **Lesson Check Point**

Directions: Read each target word and its definition. Write the letter of the definition on the line of each target word. Use a dictionary or the Internet to check your answers.

Direksyons: Li chak mo objektif ak definisyon yo chak. Ekri lèt la ki koresponn ak definisyon an sou trè chak mo objektif yo. Itilize yon diksyonè oubyen entènèt pou tcheke repons ou yo.

Target Words	Definitions
1. __ gift	a. a place where clerical work is conducted
2. __ office	b. the opposite of the right
3. __ left	c. something that is freely given
4. __ coffee	d. adequate; enough
5. __ sufficient	e. hot or cold drink made from coffee beans

Directions: Read each sentence and write the target word that correctly completes the sentence.

Direksyons: Li chak fraz epi ekri mo objektif ki konplete fraz la kòrèkteman.

6. I write notes with my _____ hand.

7. I always drink _____ with a toasted bagel.

8. Fred received a nice _____ for his birthday.

9. My boss had a business meeting in the _____.

10. We have a _____ amount of money to buy our books.

Unit F Lesson 6.4

Name: _____ Date: ___/___/_____ Score: _____

Lesson 6.5

Reading Words with a Silent Letter "f"

✓ **Lesson Check Point**

Directions: Read the target words in the word box. Write the words that have a silent letter "f" in the first column. Write the words that do not have a silent letter "f" in the second column.

Direksyons: Li mo objektif yo ki nan ti bwat mo a. Ekri mo yo ki genyen lèt "f" ki pa pwononse a nan premye kolòn nan. Ekri mo yo ki pa genyen lèt "f" ki pa pwononse a nan dezyèm kolòn nan.

Target Word Box				
off	stiffen	surf	life	Africa
belief	fillet	cliff	suffering	profess
staff	afford	benefit	muffin	ruffle
jiffy	bluffing	feather	prefer	confuse

Letter "f" is silent

_____
_____
_____
_____
_____
_____
_____
_____
_____

Letter "f" has the /f/ sound

_____
_____
_____
_____
_____
_____
_____
_____
_____

Learn to Read English With Directions In Haitian Creole

Name: _____ Date: ___/___/_____ Score: _____

Lesson 6.6

Reading Singular and Plural forms of Words Ending in "-f" & "-fe"

✓ **Lesson Check Point**

Directions: Read each target word. Put a check (✓) in the second column if the plural form of the target word ends with "-ves." Put a check (✓) in the third column if the plural form of the target word ends with "-s" or "-es."

Direksyons: Li chak mo objektif. Mete yon tchèck (✓) nan dezyèm kolòn nan si fòm priryèl mo objektif la fini avek "-ves." Mete yon tchèck (✓) nan twazyèm kolòn nan si fòm priryèl mo objektif la fini avek "-s" oubyen "-es."

Target Words	The plural form of the target word ends with "-ves"	The plural form of the target word ends with "-s" or "-es"
1. wife		
2. wolf		
3. proof		
4. chef		
5. life		

Directions: Read each sentence. Complete each sentence by writing the plural form of the word on the line.

Direksyons: Li chak fraz. Konplete chak fraz pandan ou ap ekri fòm priryèl korèk mo a sou trè a.

6. The cow has four _____. (hoof)

7. I received four _____ as a gift. (elf)

8. The baker is baking two _____ of bread. (loaf)

9. The _____ in the kitchen are sharp. (knife)

10. At night, I heard the _____ howling. (wolf)

Name: _____ Date: ___/___/_____ Score: _____

The Reading Challenge

Lesson 6.7

Reading Multisyllable Words

✓ **Lesson Check Point**

 Directions: Read and divide each target word into syllables. Write each word and place a hyphen (-) between the syllables in the second column. Write the number of syllables in the third column. Use a dictionary or the Internet to check your answers.

Direksyons: Li epi divize chak mo objektif an silab. Ekri chak mo epi mete yon tirè (-) ant silab yo nan dezyèm kolòn nan. Ekri kantite silab ke yo genyen an nan twazyèm kolòn nan. Itilize yon diksyonè oubyen entènèt pou tcheke repons ou yo.

Target Words	Words Divided into Syllables	Number of Syllables
1. fabric	_____	_____
2. family	_____	_____
3. factory	_____	_____
4. flamingo	_____	_____
5. featuring	_____	_____
6. feeling	_____	_____
7. formulate	_____	_____
8. flavoring	_____	_____
9. fingerprints	_____	_____
10. faithfulness	_____	_____

Name: _____ Date: ___/___/_____ Score: _____

The Reading Challenge

Lesson 6.7

Reading Multisyllable Words

✓ Lesson Check Point

 Directions: Read each target word. Circle the word in the row that is divided correctly into syllables. Use a dictionary or the Internet to check your answers.

Direksyons: Li chak mo objektif. Antoure mo a ki nan ranje a ki divize an silab korèkteman yo. Itilize yon diksyonè oubyen entènèt pou tcheke repons ou yo.

Model

| factory | a. fac-tor-y | b. fac-to-ry | c. fa-cto-ry |

| 1. factual | a. fa-ctu-al | b. fact-u-al | c. fac-tu-al |

| 2. federal | a. fe-der-al | b. fed-er-al | c. fed-e-ral |

| 3. finishing | a. fin-ish-ing | b. fi-nish-ing | c. fin-is-hing |

| 4. fascinate | a. fas-ci-nate | b. fasc-i-nate | c. fa-scin-ate |

| 5. feminine | a. fe-min-ine | b. fem-i-nine | c. fem-in-ine |

| 6. fixation | a. fi-xat-ion | b. fix-a-tion | c. fi-xa-tion |

| 7. favorite | a. fav-o-rite | b. fa-vo-rite | c. fa-vor-ite |

| 8. foundation | a. foun-da-tion | b. found-a-tion | c. foun-dat-ion |

Name: _____ Date: ___/___/_____ Score: _____

Lesson 6.8

Reading and Writing

Proper and Common Nouns and Adjectives

Directions: Read the words in the word box. Put an (X) on the line next to each word that is written incorrectly. Remember that all proper nouns and proper adjectives are capitalized. Use a dictionary or the Internet to check your answers.

Direksyons: Li chak mo yo ki nan bwat mo a. Met yon (X) sou ti trè a ki bò kote mo ki pa kri byen yo. Sonje ke tout non pwòp ak adjektif pwop ekri avèk yon lèt majiskil nan kòmansman yo. Itilize yon diksyonè oubyen entènèt pou tcheke repons ou yo.

Word Box					
__	Family	__	freshmen	__	french
__	flesh	__	finnish	__	fellow
__	Factory	__	fences	__	Florida
__	Fasten	__	Frankfort	__	Fraction

Directions: Read each unedited sentence and underline the word that is written incorrectly. Write each sentence correctly on the line.

Direksyons: Li chak fraz ki pa edite yo epi soulinye mo ki pa ekri byen an. Ekri chak fraz korèkteman sou liy lan.

Model
Fiji is my <u>Florist's</u> favorite holiday destination.
Fiji is my florist's favorite holiday destination.

1. Fred and florence are from France.
   _____

2. Flossy, the florist, has a high Fever.
   _____

3. Five flowers are Floating in the first fountain.
   _____

4. Fran is reading a book entitled "fitness Framework."
   _____

Name: _____ Date:___/___/_____ Score:_____

Lesson 7.1

Reading Words with the Letter G/g

✓ **Lesson Check Point**

Directions: Read each target word. Find the letter "g" and put a check (✓) in the column that identifies its position: beginning, within or end.

Direksyons: Li chak mo objektif. Jwenn lèt "g" a epi mete yon tchèck (✓) nan kolòn ki idantifye pozisyon li an: nan kòmansman, ladan oubyen nan finisman.

Target Words	Beginning (First Letter)	Within	End (Last Letter)
1. triangle			
2. gifted			
3. writing			
4. grandson			
5. clipping			

Directions: Read each sentence and underline the words that begin with the letter "g." Write all the underlined words in alphabetical order on the lines below.

Direksyons: Li chak fraz epi soulinye mo ki kòmanse avèk lèt "g" yo. Ekri tout mo ki soulinye yo nan lòd alfabetik sou trè sa yo ki anba.

6. The goats ran across the golf course.

7. The generous man gave everyone a new car.

8. The governor attends all the general meetings.

9. Gregg used a glass cleaner to clean the windows.

10. Andy chews bubble gum while playing board games.

_____   _____   _____
_____   _____   _____
_____   _____   _____
              _____

Name: _____   Date: ___/___/_____   Score: _____

Lesson 7.1

Reading Words with the Hard Letter "g"

✓ Lesson Check Point

Directions: Read each target word. Put a check (✓) under the correct column heading.

Direksyons: Li chak mo objektif. Mete yon tchèk (✓) anba antèt kolòn ki kòrèk la.

Target Words	Hard "g" has the /g/ sound as in the word **gum**	Soft "g" has the /j/ sound as in the word **gem**
1. golf		
2. glow		
3. ginger		
4. goats		
5. grabs		

Directions: Read each sentence and underline the words that have the hard "g" sound. The anchor word for the hard "g" sound is <u>gum</u>. Write all the underlined words in alphabetical order on the lines below.

Direksyons: Li chak fraz epi soulinye mo yo ki bay son "g" di a. Mo referans pou son "g" di a se mo, <u>gum</u>. Ekri tout mo ki soulinye yo nan lòd alfabetik sou trè sa yo ki anba.

6. Gina said, "Golf is great!"

7. In Georgia, the grass grows quickly.

8. Grandmother's gems look like glaciers.

9. The glass bottle is filled with ground ginger.

10. Generally, the boys in my group are always gossiping.

_____   _____   _____
_____   _____   _____
_____   _____   _____
                _____

Unit G Lesson 7.1

Learn to Read English With Directions In Haitian Creole

Name: _____ Date:___/___/_____ Score:_____

Lesson 7.2

Reading Words with the Soft Letter "g"

✓ Lesson Check Point

Directions: Read each target word. Put a check (✓) under the correct column heading.

Direksyons: Li chak mo objektif. Mete yon tchèk (✓) anba antèt kolòn ki kòrèk la.

Target Words	Soft "g" has the /j/ or /zh/ sound as in the words gem & massage	Hard "g" has the /g/ sound as in the word gum	Both soft "g" and hard "g" sounds as in the word gauge
1. gift			
2. grain			
3. large			
4. allergy			
5. gigantic			

Directions: Read each sentence and underline the words that have the soft "g" sound. The anchor word for the soft "g" sound is gem. Write all the underlined words in alphabetical order on the lines below.

Direksyons: Li chak fraz epi soulinye mo yo ki bay son "g" dous lan. Mo referans pou son "g" dous lan se mo, gem. Ekri tout mo ki soulinye yo nan lòd alfabetik sou trè sa yo ki anba.

6. My grandmother, Gina, was a famous gymnast.

7. The graduates studied geometry and geophysics.

8. My guests and I ate gyros after gymnastics class.

9. Gregg said, "The dirty gym floor has lots of germs."

10. In Georgia, the girls grew giant grapes in the garden.

_____   _____   _____
_____   _____   _____
_____   _____   _____
               _____

Name: _____   Date: ___/___/_____   Score: _____

Review Lessons 7.1 & 7.2

Reading Hard Letter "g" and Soft Letter "g" Words

Directions: Read each target word. Put a check (✓) under the correct column heading.

Direksyons: Li chak mo objektif. Mete yon tchèk (✓) anba antèt kolòn ki kòrèk la.

Target Words	Soft "g" has the /j/ or /zh/ sound as in the words gem & massage	Hard "g" has the /g/ sound as in the word gum	Both soft "g" and hard "g" sounds as in the word gauge
1. tiger			
2. grades			
3. gorgeous			
4. intelligent			
5. gymnastics			

Directions: Read each sentence and underline the words that have the hard "g" sound. The anchor word for the hard "g" sound is <u>gum</u>. Write all the underlined words in alphabetical order on the lines below.

Direksyons: Li chak fraz epi soulinye mo yo ki bay son "g" di a. Mo referans pou son "g" di a se mo, <u>gum</u>. Ekri tout mo ki souliye yo nan lòd alfabetik sou trè sa yo ki anba.

6. I ate a gyro and drank green tea in the garden.

7. Mr. Grant is the infamous governor of Georgia.

8. My grandparents attended General Grammar School.

9. Although Gekenna is from Ghana, he speaks Greek fluently.

10. In the morning, the giraffes and goats were eating the grass.

_____   _____   _____
_____   _____   _____
_____   _____   _____
                  _____

Name: _____ Date: ___/___/_____ Score: _____

Review Lessons 7.1 & 7.2

Reading Hard Letter "g" and Soft Letter "g" Words

Directions: Read the target words in the word box. In the first column, write the words with the letter "g" that have the /g/ sound, as in the word <u>gum</u>. In the second column, write the words with the letter "g" that have the /j/ sound, as in the word <u>gem</u>.

Direksyons: Li mo objektif yo ki nan bwat mo a. Nan premye kolòn nan, ekri mo yo ki genyen lèt "g" ki bay son /g/ a, tankou li ye nan mo <u>gum</u> nan. Nan dezyèm kolòn nan, ekri mo yo ki genyen lèt "g" ki bay son /j/ a, tankou li ye nan mo <u>gem</u> nan.

Target Word Box				
gymnast	grant	give	pigeon	glove
giraffe	get	grow	garden	gel
gift	guest	arrange	giant	got
imagine	apologize	college	goat	cage

Hard letter "g" has the /g/ sound as in the word <u>gum</u>

Soft letter "g" has the /j/ sound as in the word <u>gem</u>

Name: _____   Date: ___/___/_____   Score: _____

Lesson 7.3

Reading Words with the "gr" Letter Combination

Dictionary Skills/ Vocabulary

 Lesson Check Point

 Directions: Read each target word and its definition. Write the letter of the definition on the line of each target word. Use a dictionary or the Internet to check your answers.

Direksyons: Li chak mo objektif ak definisyon yo chak. Ekri lèt la ki koresponn ak definisyon an sou trè chak mo objektif yo. Itilize yon diksyonè oubyen entènèt pou tcheke repons ou yo.

Target Words	Definitions
1. __ graduate	a. sweet purple or green fruit that grows on a vine
2. __ gradually	b. the hard outer surface of the earth's crust
3. __ grapes	c. to earn a diploma or degree from a school
4. __ graph	d. happens over a slow period of time
5. __ ground	e. a diagram that shows data

 Directions: Read each sentence. Underline the word in the parentheses that correctly completes each sentence. Then, write the underlined word on the line.

Direksyons: Li chak fraz. Soulinye mo a ki nan parantèz yo ki konplete chak fraz kòrèkteman. Answit, ekri mo soulinye a sou trè a.

6. My grandson ran and fell on the _____. (graph, ground)

7. Today, I completed my bar _____ in class. (graduate, graph)

8. I will _____ from a graphic design program. (graduate, ground)

9. Greg will _____ learn to make griddlecakes. (graph, gradually)

10. My grandparents ate _____ and grapefruits. (grapes, gradually)

Name: _____ Date: ___/___/_____ Score: _____

Lesson 7.4

Reading Words with the "gl" Letter Combination

Dictionary Skills/ Vocabulary

✓ **Lesson Check Point**

Directions: Read each target word and its definition. Write the target word on the line in front of its meaning. Use a dictionary or the Internet to check your answers.

Direksyons: Li chak mo objektif ak definisyon yo chak. Ekri mo objektif la sou trè ki devan definisyon li an. Itilize yon diksyonè oubyen entènèt pou tcheke repons ou yo.

Target Word Box				
glad	glaring	glasses	gloomy	gloves

1. _____ protective coverings for hands
2. _____ feeling sad or depressed
3. _____ looking at someone with anger
4. _____ containers used to hold liquids
5. _____ to be happy or pleased about something or someone

Directions: Read each sentence. Underline the word in the parentheses that correctly completes each sentence. Then, write the underlined word on the line.

Direksyons: Li chak fraz. Soulinye mo a ki nan parantèz yo ki konplete chak fraz kòrèkteman. Answit, ekri mo soulinye a sou trè a.

6. The captain was _____ to see the lighthouse. (gloomy, glad)

7. The angry boys were _____ at each other. (glasses, glaring)

8. During the fight, the boxers must wear _____. (gloves, glaring)

9. The drinking _____ are in the cabinet. (glasses, gloves)

10. Usually, I feel _____ on dark, cloudy days. (gloomy, glaring)

Unit G Lesson 7.4

Learn to Read English With Directions In Haitian Creole   Copyrighted Material

 Name: _____ Date: ___/___/_____ Score: _____

Lesson 7.4

Reading Words with the "gle" Letter Combination

✓ Lesson Check Point

Directions: Read each target word. Find the "gle" letter combination and put a check (✓) in the column that identifies its position: beginning, within or end.

Direksyons: Li chak mo objektif. Jwenn konbinezon lèt "gle" a epi mete yon tchèk (✓) nan kolòn nan ki idantifye pozisyon li an: nan kòmansman, ladan oubyen nan finisman.

Target Words	Beginning (First 3 Letters)	Within	End (Last 3 Letters)
1. angled			
2. Glenn			
3. jungle			
4. gleam			
5. goggle			

Directions: Read each target word. Put a check (✓) in the "yes" column if the "gle" letter combination has the /g/ + /ə/ + /l/ sounds. Put a check (✓) in the "no" column if the "gle" letter combination does not have the /g/ + /ə/ + /l/ sounds.

Direksyons: Li chak mo objektif. Mete yon tchèk (✓) nan kolòn "yes" an si konbinezon let "gle" a bay sons /g/ + /ə/ + /l/. Mete yon tchèk (✓) nan kolòn "no" an si konbinezon let "gle" a pa bay sons /g/ + /ə/ + /l/.

Target Words	Yes	No
6. angled		
7. Glenn		
8. jungle		
9. gleam		
10. goggle		

Name: _____ Date: ___/___/_____ Score: _____

Lesson 7.5

Reading Words with the "gh" Letter Combination

✓ Lesson Check Point

Directions: Read each target word. Circle the word in the column that has the same "gh" sound as the target word.

Direksyons: Li chak mo objektif. Antoure mo a ki nan kolòn nan ki bay menm son "gh" la tankou mo objektif la.

right	a. dough
	b. cough

Ghana	a. sigh
	b. gherkin

thought	a. sight
	b. ghetto

enough	a. ought
	b. laughing

Directions: Read each target word. Put a check (✓) under the correct column heading.

Direksyons: Li chak mo objektif. Mete yon tchèk (✓) anba antèt kolòn ki kòrèk la.

Target Words	"gh" has the /g/ sound as in the word ghetto	"gh" has the /f/ sound as in the word laugh	"gh" is silent as in the word light
1. right			
2. Ghana			
3. thought			
4. enough			

 Name: _____ Date: ___/___/_____ Score: _____

Lesson 7.6

Reading Words with the "gn" Letter Combination

✓ Lesson Check Point

 Directions: Read each target word. Circle the word in the column that has the same "gn" sound(s) as the target word.

Direksyons: Li chak mo objektif. Antoure mo a ki nan kolòn nan ki bay menm son "gn" la (yo) tankou mo objektif la.

align	a. signing
	b. signify

dignify	a. eggnog
	b. foreigner

cologne	a. sovereign
	b. magnet

assignment	a. ignored
	b. lasagna

 Directions: Read each target word. Put a check (✓) under the correct column heading.

Direksyons: Li chak mo objektif. Mete yon tchèk (✓) anba antèt kolòn ki kòrèk la.

Target Words	"gn" has the /g/ + /n/ sounds as in the word <u>ignite</u>	"gn" has the silent "g" + /n/ sound as in the word <u>sign</u>
1. align		
2. dignify		
3. cologne		
4. assignment		

Name: _____ Date: ___/___/_____ Score: _____

Lesson 7.7

Reading Words with a Silent Letter "g"

✓ **Lesson Check Point**

Directions: Read the target words in the word box. Write the words that have a silent letter "g" in the first column. Write the words that do not have a silent letter "g" in the second column.

Direksyons: Li mo objektif yo ki nan ti bwat mo a. Ekri mo yo ki genyen lèt "g" ki pa pwononse a nan premye kolòn nan. Ekri mo yo ki pa genyen lèt "g" ki pa pwononse a nan dezyèm kolòn nan.

Target Word Box				
sign	wiggle	juggle	good	though
signal	light	campaign	gum	align
cologne	resign	gorillas	nag	right
greed	frog	games	gymnast	dog

Letter "g" is silent

Letter "g" has the /g/ or /j/ sound

Name: _____ Date:___/___/_____ Score:_____

The Reading Challenge

Lesson 7.8

Reading Multisyllable Words

✓ **Lesson Check Point**

Directions: Read and divide each target word into syllables. Write each word and place a hyphen (-) between the syllables in the second column. Write the number of syllables in the third column. Use a dictionary or the Internet to check your answers.

Direksyons: Li epi divize chak mo objektif an silab. Ekri chak mo epi mete yon tirè (-) ant silab yo nan dezyèm kolòn nan. Ekri kantite silab ke yo genyen an nan twazyèm kolòn nan. Itilize yon diksyonè oubyen entènèt pou tcheke repons ou yo.

Target Words	Words Divided into Syllables	Number of Syllables
1. graduate	_____	_____
2. gingerly	_____	_____
3. getaway	_____	_____
4. gigantic	_____	_____
5. golden	_____	_____
6. gourmet	_____	_____
7. galvanize	_____	_____
8. grapevine	_____	_____
9. generate	_____	_____
10. garbanzo	_____	_____

Name: _____ Date: ___/___/_____ Score: _____

The Reading Challenge

Lesson 7.8

Reading Multisyllable Words

✓ Lesson Check Point

 Directions: Read each target word. Circle the word in the row that is divided correctly into syllables. Use a dictionary or the Internet to check your answers.

Direksyons: Li chak mo objektif. Antoure mo a ki nan ranje a ki divize an silab korèkteman yo. Itilize yon diksyonè oubyen entènèt pou tcheke repons ou yo.

Model

| galaxy | a. ga-lax-y | b. gal-ax-y | c. gal-a-xy |

1. groundwork	a. gro-undwo-rk	b. ground-work	c. grou-ndwor-k
2. glorify	a. glo-ri-fy	b. glor-i-fy	c. glo-rif-y
3. governor	a. gov-er-nor	b. gov-ern-or	c. go-ver-nor
4. granola	a. gr-ano-la	b. gra-nol-a	c. gra-no-la
5. gymnastics	a. gym-nas-tics	b. gy-mnast-ics	c. gym-nast-ics
6. guarantee	a. gua-rant-ee	b. guar-an-tee	c. guar-ant-ee
7. grandchild	a. gr-andch-ild	b. gr-and-child	c. grand-child
8. guidance	a. gui-dance	b. guid-an-ce	c. guid-ance

Name: _____ Date: ___/___/_____ Score: _____

Lesson 7.9

Reading and Writing

Proper and Common Nouns and Adjectives

Directions: Read the words in the word box. Put an (X) on the line next to each word that is written incorrectly. Remember that all proper nouns and proper adjectives are capitalized. Use a dictionary or the Internet to check your answers.

Direksyons: Li chak mo yo ki nan bwat mo a. Met yon (X) sou ti trè a ki bò kote mo ki pa kri byen yo. Sonje ke tout non pwòp ak adjektif pwop ekri avèk yon lèt majiskil nan kòmansman yo. Itilize yon diksyonè oubyen entènèt pou tcheke repons ou yo.

Word Box		
__ guyanese	__ Ghetto	__ Gibraltar
__ gondola	__ governor	__ garage
__ German	__ Graduate	__ Gladiator
__ garry	__ gorilla	__ great Britain

Directions: Read each unedited sentence and underline the word that is written incorrectly. Write each sentence correctly on the line.

Direksyons: Li chak fraz ki pa edite yo epi soulinye mo ki pa ekri byen an. Ekri chak fraz korèkteman sou liy lan.

Model
Ginger and gene are going to Georgetown, Guyana.
Ginger and Gene are going to Georgetown, Guyana.

1. Dr. graham graduated from Georgetown College.
_____

2. Grandfather was a general in great Britain's army.
_____

3. Mr. and Mrs. Getter lived in the Ghetto for years.
_____

4. The governor is an active member of our Government.
_____

Name: _____ Date:___/___/_____ Score:_____

Lesson 8.1

Reading Words with the Letter H/h

✓ Lesson Check Point

Directions: Read each target word. Find the letter "h" and put a check (✓) in the column that identifies its position: beginning, within or end.
Direksyons: Li chak mo objektif. Jwenn lèt "h" a epi mete yon tchèck (✓) nan kolòn ki idantifye pozisyon li an: nan kòmansman, ladan oubyen nan finisman.

Target Words	Beginning (First Letter)	Within	End (Last Letter)
1. hair			
2. verandah			
3. helping			
4. cheeta<u>h</u>			
5. Fahrenheit			

Directions: Read each sentence and underline the words that begin with the letter "h." Write all the underlined words in alphabetical order on the lines below.
Direksyons: Li chak fraz epi soulinye mo ki kòmanse avèk lèt "h" yo. Ekri tout mo ki soulinye yo nan lòd alfabetik sou trè sa yo ki anba.

6. David's farm sells hens and hogs.

7. Hattie likes to dance to hip-hop music.

8. The hermit crab cannot climb up the hill.

9. Danny flew his helicopter to the regional airport.

10. My hairstylist, Gina, works in Harlem, New York.

_____   _____   _____
_____   _____   _____
              _____

Unit H
Lesson 8.1

Learn to Read English With Directions In Haitian Creole

Name: _____ Date: ___/___/_____ Score: _____

Lesson 8.2

Reading Words with the Letter "h" Combinations: "sh," "wh," "ch," "th," "rh," "ph" and "gh"

✓ **Lesson Check Point**

Directions: Read the target words in the word box. Identify the words with the following letter combinations: "sh," "wh," "ch," "th," "rh," "ph" and "gh." Write the word on the line that shows the position of the letter combination: beginning, within or end.

Direksyons: Li mo objektif yo ki nan ti bwat mo a. Idantifye mo yo ki genyen konbinezon lèt sa yo: "sh," "wh," "ch," "th," "rh," "ph" ak "gh". Ekri mo a sou liy ki montre pozisyon konbinezon lèt la: kòmansman, ladan oubyen finisman.

Target Word Box				
pathway	photos	things	pinwheel	cough
graph	diarrhea	rhyme	myrrh	blemished
with	triumphant	shave	Ghana	impeach
whale	cherries	caught	teachers	accomplish

	Beginning	Within	End
sh	1. _____	2. _____	3. _____
wh	4. _____	5. _____	
ch	6. _____	7. _____	8. _____
th	9. _____	10. _____	11. _____
rh	12. _____	13. _____	14. _____
ph	15. _____	16. _____	17. _____
gh	18. _____	19. _____	20. _____

Learn to Read English With Directions In Haitian Creole

Name: _____ Date: ___/___/_____ Score: _____

Lesson 8.2

Reading Words with the Letter "h" Combinations:
"sh," "wh," "ch," "th," "rh," "ph," "gh" and "sch"

✓ **Lesson Check Point**

Directions: Read the target words in the word box. Identify the words with the following letter combinations: "sh," "wh," "ch," "th," "rh," "ph," "gh" and "sch." Write the target word that correctly completes each sentence on the line.

Direksyons: Li mo objektif yo ki nan ti bwat mo a. Idantifye mo yo ki genyen konbinezon lèt sa yo: "sh," "wh," "ch," "th," "rh," "ph," "gh"ak "sch". Ekri mo objektif la ki konplete chak fraz korèkteman sou liy lan.

Target Word Box		
whistling	enough	scheduled
show	graph	Rhinos
physics		anchor
wheelchair		phone

1. _____ are large animals with two horns.

2. The captain threw the boat's _____ overboard.

3. Mr. Sherman called his brother on the _____.

4. Shelly and Bobby are _____ to the loud music.

5. The clown brought _____ balloons for all the children.

6. They used the survey information to draw a bar _____.

7. The students are _____ to start school at nine o'clock.

8. After breaking his leg, Charles had to use a _____.

9. All the children are performing in the school's talent _____.

10. Chemistry and _____ are required undergraduate courses.

Name: _____   Date: ___/___/_____   Score: _____

Lesson 8.3

Reading Words with a Silent Letter "h"

✓ Lesson Check Point

Directions: Read the target words in the word box. Write the words that have a silent letter "h" in the first column. Write the words that do not have a silent letter "h" in the second column.

Direksyons: Li mo objektif yo ki nan ti bwat mo a. Ekri mo yo ki genyen lèt "h" ki pa pwononse a nan premye kolòn nan. Ekri mo yo ki pa genyen lèt "h" ki pa pwononse a nan dezyèm kolòn nan.

Target Word Box				
exhaust	hour	hurting	helpful	statehood
inhale	rhubarb	why	honesty	Thailand
heir	unhook	exhaustion	rehearsal	ghost
hope	hammer	hairy	inhabitant	vehicle

Letter "h" is silent

Letter "h" has the /h/ sound

Name: _____ Date: ___/___/_____ Score: _____

The Reading Challenge

Lesson 8.4

Reading Multisyllable Words

✓ **Lesson Check Point**

Directions: Read and divide each target word into syllables. Write each word and place a hyphen (-) between the syllables in the second column. Write the number of syllables in the third column. Use a dictionary or the Internet to check your answers.

Direksyons: Li epi divize chak mo objektif an silab. Ekri chak mo epi mete yon tirè (-) ant silab yo nan dezyèm kolòn nan. Ekri kantite silab ke yo genyen an nan twazyèm kolòn nan. Itilize yon diksyonè oubyen entènèt pou tcheke repons ou yo.

Target Words	Words Divided into Syllables	Number of Syllables
1. hesitate	_____	_____
2. horizon	_____	_____
3. healthy	_____	_____
4. hospital	_____	_____
5. helpful	_____	_____
6. hypocrite	_____	_____
7. honestly	_____	_____
8. heavenly	_____	_____
9. hamburger	_____	_____
10. headquarters	_____	_____

Learn to Read English With Directions In Haitian Creole

 Name: _____ Date: ___/___/_____ Score: _____

The Reading Challenge

Lesson 8.4

Reading Multisyllable Words

✓ **Lesson Check Point**

Directions: Read each target word. Circle the word in the row that is divided correctly into syllables. Use a dictionary or the Internet to check your answers.

Direksyons: Li chak mo objektif. Antoure mo a ki nan ranje a ki divize an silab korèkteman yo. Itilize yon diksyonè oubyen entènèt pou tcheke repons ou yo.

Model

heroic	a. he-roi-c	b. her-o-ic	c. he-ro-ic (circled)
1. habitual	a. hab-it-u-al	b. ha-bit-u-al	c. hab-i-tu-al
2. honesty	a. hon-es-ty	b. ho-nest-y	c. hon-e-sty
3. Hispanic	a. Hi-span-ic	b. His-pa-nic	c. His-pan-ic
4. Halifax	a. Hal-if-ax	b. Hal-i-fax	c. Ha-li-fax
5. helium	a. hel-i-um	b. hel-iu-m	c. he-li-um
6. hamburger	a. hamb-ur-ger	b. ham-burg-er	c. ham-bur-ger
7. history	a. his-tor-y	b. his-to-ry	c. hi-stor-y
8. handlebar	a. han-dle-bar	b. hand-leb-ar	c. hand-le-bar

Learn to Read English With Directions In Haitian Creole

Name: _____   Date: ___/___/_____   Score: _____

Lesson 8.5

Reading and Writing

Proper and Common Nouns and Adjectives

Directions: Read the words in the word box. Put an (X) on the line next to each word that is written incorrectly. Remember that all proper nouns and proper adjectives are capitalized. Use a dictionary or the Internet to check your answers.

Direksyons: Li chak mo yo ki nan bwat mo a. Met yon (X) sou ti trè a ki bò kote mo ki pa kri byen yo. Sonje ke tout non pwòp ak adjektif pwop ekri avèk yon lèt majiskil nan kòmansman yo. Itilize yon diksyonè oubyen entènèt pou tcheke repons ou yo.

Word Box		
__ hatcHet	__ home	__ Healthy
__ Harlem	__ Hills	__ houses
__ hint	__ Haiti	__ hawaii
__ History	__ heart	__ Hotel

Directions: Read each unedited sentence and underline the word that is written incorrectly. Write each sentence correctly on the line.

Direksyons: Li chak fraz ki pa edite yo epi soulinye mo ki pa ekri byen an. Ekri chak fraz korèkteman sou liy lan.

Model
Mr. Hitt has a big house on <u>hope</u> Avenue.
<u>Mr. Hitt has a big house on Hope Avenue.</u>

1. Mrs. Harley was honored in hollywood.
   _____

2. I am Hiking up the hill to the Halifax Hotel.
   _____

3. Harriet's class went to hartway Horse Stable.
   _____

4. I am learning interesting facts about hispanic history.
   _____

Name: _____ Date: ___/___/_____ Score: _____

Lesson 9.1

Reading Words with the Letter I/i

✓ Lesson Check Point

 Directions: Read each target word. Find the letter "i" and put a check (✓) in the column that identifies its position: beginning, within or end.
Direksyons: Li chak mo objektif. Jwenn lèt "i" a epi mete yon tchèck (✓) nan kolòn ki idantifye pozisyon li an: nan kòmansman, ladan oubyen nan finisman.

Target Words	Beginning (First Letter)	Within	End (Last Letter)
1. deli			
2. bite			
3. circle			
4. impress			
5. important			

 Directions: Read each target word. Read the words in the row and circle the word that has a different vowel "i" sound.
Direksyons: Li chak mo objektif. Li mo yo ki nan ranje a epi antoure mo a ki bay yon son vwayèl "i" ki diferan an.

Target Words				
6. list	brink	dime	crick	dill
7. chip	kick	limp	disk	like
8. bill	mild	him	bring	dig
9. clip	drip	blink	grip	pint
10. miss	cling	fine	his	bin

Name: _____ Date: ___/___/_____ Score: _____

Lesson 9.2

Reading Words with the Short Vowel "i" Sound

✓ **Lesson Check Point**

Directions: Read the words in the four boxes. Circle two words with the short vowel /ĭ/ sound. The anchor word for the short vowel /ĭ/ sound is <u>insect</u>.

Direksyons: Li mo yo ki nan kat ti bwat yo. Antoure de mo ki genyen son vwayèl kout /ĭ/ a. Mo referans pou son vwayel kout /ĭ/ a se mo, <u>insect</u>.

side	kick		mine	lit		wig	tin
lice	fish		mix	rise		item	price

rim	wise		smile	lime		rip	time
idea	tip		pig	kid		drive	his

Directions: Read the words in the four boxes. Circle two words that rhyme. Rhyming words have the same ending sound, such as <u>hip</u> and <u>dip</u>.

Direksyons: Li mo yo ki nan kat ti bwat yo. Antoure de mo ki rime. De mo oubyen plizyè mo ki rime genyen menm son nan finisman yo, tankou <u>hip</u> ak <u>dip</u>.

slice	milk		hint	spite		disk	fine
silk	vine		mint	pride		risk	white

tile	site		sink	Mike		bill	hill
sick	pick		wide	pink		nine	five

Learn to Read English With Directions In Haitian Creole

Name: _____   Date: ___/___/_____   Score: _____

Lesson 9.2

Reading & Writing Words with the Short Vowel "i" Sound

✓ **Lesson Check Point**

Directions: Read each sentence and underline three words with the short vowel /ĭ/ sound. Then, write the underlined words on the lines below. The anchor word for the short vowel /ĭ/ sound is <u>insect</u>.

Direksyons: Li chak fraz epi soulinye twa mo ki genyen son vwayèl kout /ĭ/ a. Answit, ekri mo soulinye yo sou trè sa yo ki anba. Mo referans pou son vwayèl kout /ĭ/ a se mo, <u>insect</u>.

Model

<u>Jim</u> placed a <u>big</u> cup of ice on the <u>windowsill</u>.

    Jim   big   windowsill
 _____   _____   _____

1. The baby in the crib has white milk.

 _____   _____   _____

2. The wind lifted Mike's kite into the sky.

 _____   _____   _____

3. At night, the twins are in their cribs.

 _____   _____   _____

4. James will win the grand prize for swimming.

 _____   _____   _____

5. Dad said, "Be careful not to slip into the wide pit."

 _____   _____   _____

Name: _____ Date: ___/___/_____ Score: _____

Lesson 9.3

Reading Words with the Long Vowel "i" Sound

✓ Lesson Check Point

 Directions: Read the words in the four boxes. Circle two words with the long vowel /ī/ sound. The anchor word for the long vowel /ī/ sound is <u>ice</u>.

Direksyons: Li mo yo ki nan kat ti bwat yo. Antoure de mo ki genyen son vwayèl long /ī/ a. Mo referans pou son vwayel long /ī/ a se mo, <u>ice</u>.

ring	dive		vain	like		pill	jive
size	drip		wink	idea		grain	slice

crime	rice		pinch	tint		hike	lime
fish	plain		wipe	smile		dish	silk

 Directions: Read the words in the four boxes. Circle two words that rhyme. Rhyming words have the same ending sound, such as <u>rice</u> and <u>nice</u>.

Direksyons: Li mo yo ki nan kat ti bwat yo. Antoure de mo ki rime. De mo oubyen plizyè mo ki rime genyen menm son nan finisman yo, tankou <u>rice</u> ak <u>nice</u>.

fire	will		gift	rise		five	hill
tire	mint		wise	wick		dive	fist

hint	tilt		limp	wire		list	risk
wipe	pipe		mink	hire		ride	side

Name: _____ Date: ___/___/_____ Score: _____

Lesson 9.3

Reading & Writing Words with the Long Vowel "i" Sound

✓ Lesson Check Point

Directions: Read each sentence and underline three words with the long vowel /ī/ sound. Then, write the underlined words on the lines below. The anchor word for the long vowel /ī/ sound is <u>ice</u>.

Direksyons: Li chak fraz epi soulinye twa mo ki genyen son vwayèl long /ī/ a. Answit, ekri mo soulinye yo sou trè sa yo ki anba. Mo referans pou son vwayèl long /ī/ a se mo, <u>ice</u>.

Model
David and <u>I</u> flew our big, <u>white</u> <u>kite</u> along the riverbank.

    I   white   kite
_____   _____   _____

1. At night, the big island comes alive.

   _____   _____   _____

2. Timothy likes to drive his car on the highway.

   _____   _____   _____

3. Our friend will win a prize for biking six miles.

   _____   _____   _____

4. The bride will smile as she walks down the aisle.

   _____   _____   _____

5. The divers were instructed not to dive into the pool at night.

   _____   _____   _____

Name: _____ Date: ___/___/_____ Score: _____

Review Lessons 9.2 & 9.3

Reading Short Vowel and Long Vowel Words

✓ **Lesson Check Point**

Directions: Read the target words in the word box. In the first column, write the words that have the short vowel /ĭ/ sound, as in the word <u>insect</u>. In the second column, write the words that have the long vowel /ī/ sound, as in the word <u>ice</u>.

Direksyons: Li mo objektif yo ki nan bwat mo a. Nan premye kolòn nan, ekri mo ki bay son vwayèl kout /ĭ/ yo, tankou li ye nan mo <u>insect</u> la. Nan dezyèm kolòn nan, ekri mo ki bay son vwayèl long /ī/ yo, tankou li ye nan mo <u>ice</u> la.

Target Word Box				
dime	hill	lift	drip	hid
bib	tie	silent	fin	wild
clip	dip	find	pick	bite
spider	light	this	pint	like

Letter "i" has the /ĭ/ sound as in the word <u>insect</u>

Letter "i" has the /ī/ sound as in the word <u>ice</u>

Name: _____ Date: ___/___/_____ Score: _____

Lesson 9.4

Reading Words with Letter "i" Vowel Pairs

✓ Lesson Check Point

Directions: Read each target word. Circle the word in the column that has the same vowel "ia," "ie," "io" or "iu" sound(s) as the target word.

Direksyons: Li chak mo objektif. Antoure mo a ki nan kolòn nan ki bay menm son "ia," "ie," "io" oubyen "iu" la (yo) tankou mo objektif la.

dialect	a. fried
	b. liable

spacious	a. glorious
	b. tried

hierarchy	a. client
	b. dried

cried	a. allied
	b. gracious

Directions: Read each target word. Put a check (✓) under the correct column heading.

Direksyons: Li chak mo objektif. Mete yon tchèk (✓) anba antèt kolòn ki kòrèk la.

Target Words	Words have the long "i" sound as in the word <u>dial</u>	Words do not have the long "i" sound
1. dialect		
2. spacious		
3. hierarchy		
4. cried		

Name: _____ Date: ___/___/_____ Score: _____

Lesson 9.5

Reading Words with the Final Letter "i"

✓ Lesson Check Point

Directions: Read each target word. Find the letter "i" and put a check (✓) in the column that identifies its position within the syllable.
Direksyons: Li chak mo objektif. Jwenn lèt "i" a epi mete yon tchèk (✓) nan kolòn nan ki idantifye pozisyon li an nan silab la.

Target Words	"i" is at the end of a one syllable word	"i" is at the end of the first syllable	"i" is at the end of a multi-syllable word
1. hi			
2. anti			
3. bias ⁻			
4. direct			
5. Bengali			

Directions: Read each target word. Put a check (✓) under the correct column heading.
Direksyons: Li chak mo objektif. Mete yon tchèk (✓) anba antèt kolòn ki kòrèk la.

Target Words	"i" has the /ĭ/ sound as in the word insect	"i" has the /ī/ sound as in the word bike	"i" has the /ə/ sound as in the word pencil	"i" is silent as in the word maid
6. limit				
7. right				
8. mortify				
9. Jamaica				
10. utensil				

Name: _____ Date: ___/___/_____ Score: _____

Lesson 9.6

Reading Letter "i" Words with the Schwa Vowel Sound

✓ Lesson Check Point

Directions: Read each target word. Circle the word in the column that has the same "i" sound as the target word.
Direksyons: Li chak mo objektif. Antoure mo a ki nan kolòn nan ki bay menm son "i" a tankou mo objektif la.

| accessible | a. island |
| | b. nostril |

| manifold | a. beautify |
| | b. picking |

| laminate | a. unify |
| | b. insert |

| simplify | a. piles |
| | b. stencil |

Directions: Read each sentence and underline the letter "i" word that has the schwa vowel /ə/ sound. The anchor word for the letter "i" schwa vowel sound is <u>pencil</u>.
Direksyons: Li chak fraz epi soulinye mo ki genyen lèt "i" a ki bay son schwa /ə/ a. Mo referans pou son schwa lèt "i" a se mo, <u>pencil</u>.

1. My family enjoys ice skating and skiing.

2. The hotels have similar cancellation policies.

3. The five nominees have interesting points of view.

4. The warm bottle of milk will pacify the crying baby.

5. The doctor will notify the interns about the procedures.

6. The president of Mexico delivered an incredible inauguration speech.

Name: _____ Date:___/___/_____ Score:_____

Lesson 9.7

Reading Words with the "ir" Letter Combination

Dictionary Skills/ Vocabulary

✓ Lesson Check Point

Directions: Read each target word and its definition. Write the letter of the definition on the line of each target word. Use a dictionary or the Internet to check your answers.

Direksyons: Li chak mo objektif ak definisyon yo chak. Ekri lèt la ki koresponn ak definisyon an sou trè chak mo objektif yo. Itilize yon diksyonè oubyen entènèt pou tcheke repons ou yo.

Target Words	Definitions
1. __ squirms	a. having a desire to drink something
2. __ girls	b. young females
3. __ stirs	c. something hard to the touch
4. __ firm	d. to slowly move in response to something
5. __ thirsty	e. the use of circular motions to mix or blend

Directions: Read each sentence and write the target word that completes the sentence.

Direksyons: Li chak fraz epi ekri mo objektif ki konplete fraz la kòrèkteman.

6. She _____ at the sight of blood.

7. The _____ girl drank a glass of water.

8. The apples on the kitchen counter are _____.

9. All the _____ in my class are wearing pretty dresses.

10. Jane _____ thirteen chocolate chips into the ice cream.

Name: _____ Date: ___/___/_____ Score: _____

Lesson 9.8

Reading Letter "i" Words with the Long Vowel "e" Sound

✓ **Lesson Check Point**

Directions: Read each target word. Circle the word in the column that has the same "i" sound as the target word.
Direksyons: Li chak mo objektif. Antoure mo a ki nan kolòn nan ki bay menm son lèt "i" a tankou mo objektif la.

Fiji	a. pollinate
	b. mini

Haiti	a. maxi
	b. missing

multipurpose	a. Hawaii
	b. circle

taxicab	a. business
	b. chili peppers

Directions: Read each sentence and underline the letter "i" word that has the long vowel /ē/ sound. Then, write the word on the line. The anchor word, taxi has a letter "i" that has the long vowel /ē/ sound.
Direksyons: Li chak fraz epi soulinye mo ki gen lèt "i" a ki bay son vwayèl long /ē/ a. Answit, ekri mo a sou trè a. Mo referans, taxi gen yon lèt "i" ladan li ki bay son vwayèl long /ē/.

1. I am planning a fun-filled trip to Malawi. _____

2. The children like to eat broccoli with cheese. _____

3. This summer, Keith is going to Mississippi. _____

4. Since I am on a diet, I will only eat five mini muffins. _____

5. Levi will join our school's intermediate diving team. _____

6. On Saturdays, I enjoy looking at Punjabi music videos. _____

Name: _____ Date: ___/___/_____ Score: _____

Lesson 9.9

Reading Words with a Silent Letter "i"

✓ Lesson Check Point

Directions: Read the target words in the word box. Write the words that have a silent letter "i" in the first column. Write the words that do not have a silent letter "i" in the second column.

Direksyons: Li mo objektif yo ki nan ti bwat mo a. Ekri mo yo ki genyen lèt "i" ki pa pwononse a nan premye kolòn nan. Ekri mo yo ki pa genyen lèt "i" ki pa pwononse a nan dezyèm kolòn nan.

Target Word Box				
middle	digits	Jamaica	nail	obtaining
stains	bait	print	insisting	aimed
suitable	conflict	nice	suits	bills
inside	bike	details	five	business

Letter "i" is silent

Letter "i" has a letter "i" sound

Unit I Lesson 9.9

Learn to Read English With Directions In Haitian Creole

☘ Name: _____ Date: ___/___/_____ Score: _____

Unit Review - I/i

Reading Words with Vowel "i" Sounds: /ĭ/, /ī/, /ə/ & Silent

✓ Lesson Check Point

Directions: Read each target word. Circle the word in the column that has the same "i" sound as the target word.

Direksyons: Li chak mo objektif. Antoure mo a ki nan kolòn nan ki bay menm son "i" a tankou mo objektif la.

details	a. aim
	b. think

dime	a. drill
	b. bribe

child	a. Arabia
	b. sidewalk

beautify	a. things
	b. possible

Directions: Read each target word. Put a check (✓) under the correct column heading.

Direksyons: Li chak mo objektif. Mete yon tchèk (✓) anba antèt kolòn ki kòrèk la.

Target Words	"i" has the /ĭ/ sound as in the word <u>insect</u>	"i" has the /ī/ sound as in the word <u>bike</u>	"i" has the /ə/ sound as in the word <u>pencil</u>	"i" is silent as in the word <u>maid</u>
1. details				
2. dime				
3. child				
4. beautify				

Learn to Read English With Directions In Haitian Creole

Name: _____ Date: ___/___/_____ Score: _____

The Reading Challenge

Lesson 9.10

Reading Multisyllable Words

✓ Lesson Check Point

Directions: Read and divide each target word into syllables. Write each word and place a hyphen (-) between the syllables in the second column. Write the number of syllables in the third column. Use a dictionary or the Internet to check your answers.

Direksyons: Li epi divize chak mo objektif an silab. Ekri chak mo epi mete yon tirè (-) ant silab yo nan dezyèm kolòn nan. Ekri kantite silab ke yo genyen an nan twazyèm kolòn nan. Itilize yon diksyonè oubyen entènèt pou tcheke repons ou yo.

Target Words	Words Divided into Syllables	Number of Syllables
1. align	_____	_____
2. miner	_____	_____
3. notion	_____	_____
4. highly	_____	_____
5. lighting	_____	_____
6. itemized	_____	_____
7. diverting	_____	_____
8. optional	_____	_____
9. anxiously	_____	_____
10. midnight	_____	_____

 Name: _____ Date:___/___/_____ Score:_____

The Reading Challenge

Lesson 9.10

Reading Multisyllable Words

✓ Lesson Check Point

 Directions: Read each target word. Circle the word in the row that is divided correctly into syllables. Use a dictionary or the Internet to check your answers.

Direksyons: Li chak mo objektif. Antoure mo a ki nan ranje a ki divize an silab korèkteman yo. Itilize yon diksyonè oubyen entènèt pou tcheke repons ou yo.

Model

| interesting | a. in-ter-est-ing (circled) | b. int-er-est-ing | c. inte-rest-ing |

| 1. interview | a. int-e-rview | b. in-ter-view | c. int-er-view |

| 2. crazier | a. cra-zi-er | b. craz-i-er | c. cr-a-zier |

| 3. opinion | a. o-pin-ion | b. op-i-nion | c. o-pi-nion |

| 4. vacation | a. vac-at-ion | b. va-cat-ion | c. va-ca-tion |

| 5. radiate | a. rad-i-ate | b. ra-di-ate | c. ra-dia-te |

| 6. regional | a. reg-ion-al | b. re-gion-al | c. re-gio-nal |

| 7. interact | a. int-er-act | b. int-e-ract | c. in-ter-act |

| 8. tradition | a. tra-di-tion | b. tra-dit-ion | c. trad-iti-on |

Name: _____   Date: ___/___/_____   Score: _____

Lesson 9.11

Reading and Writing

Proper and Common Nouns and Adjectives

Directions: Read the words in the word box. Put an (X) on the line next to each word that is written incorrectly. Remember that all proper nouns and proper adjectives are capitalized. Use a dictionary or the Internet to check your answers.

Direksyons: Li chak mo yo ki nan bwat mo a. Met yon (X) sou ti trè a ki bò kote mo ki pa kri byen yo. Sonje ke tout non pwòp ak adjektif pwop ekri avèk yon lèt majiskil nan kòmansman yo. Itilize yon diksyonè oubyen entènèt pou tcheke repons ou yo.

Word Box		
__ impression	__ Inoperative	__ Independent
__ Intestines	__ Iron Age	__ indulgence
__ italian	__ isle of France	__ Indian
__ idealistic	__ irresponsible	__ italy

Directions: Read each unedited sentence and underline the word that is written incorrectly. Write each sentence correctly on the line.

Direksyons: Li chak fraz ki pa edite yo epi soulinye mo ki pa ekri byen an. Ekri chak fraz korèkteman sou liy lan.

Model
New Delhi and Indore are beautiful cities in <u>india</u>.
<u>New Delhi and Indore are beautiful cities in India._____</u>

1. In the afternoon, Irene Introduced me to Ian.
_____

2. Mr. iston drove along Interstate 65 to Indiana.
_____

3. Did you know that Iron was developed during the Iron Age?
_____

4. Idama is studying the industrial Revolution at the institute.
_____

Name: _____ Date: ___/___/_____ Score: _____

Lesson 10.1

Reading Words with the Letter J/j

✓ **Lesson Check Point**

Directions: Read each target word. Find the letter "j" and put a check (✓) in the column that identifies its position: beginning, within or end.
Direksyons: Li chak mo objektif. Jwenn lèt "j" a epi mete yon tchèck (✓) nan kolòn ki idantifye pozisyon li an: nan kòmansman, ladan oubyen nan finisman.

Target Words	Beginning (First Letter)	Within	End (Last Letter)
1. eject			
2. jeans			
3. join			
4. judge			
5. conjure			

Directions: Read each sentence and underline the words that begin with the letter "j." Write all the underlined words in alphabetical order on the lines below.
Direksyons: Li chak fraz epi soulinye mo ki kòmanse avèk lèt "j" yo. Ekri tout mo ki soulinye yo nan lòd alfabetik sou trè sa yo ki anba.

6. Last Friday, Jordan ate too much junk food.

7. I bought a jeweled chain at the jewelry store.

8. Ms. Jasmine always eats jerk chicken for dinner.

9. Everyone in the jazz band wore sky blue jackets.

10. Bobby is reading a book about jackals and jaguars.

_____   _____   _____
_____   _____   _____
_____   _____   _____
               _____

Name: _____ Date: ___/___/_____ Score: _____

The Reading Challenge

Lesson 10.2

Reading Multisyllable Words

✓ **Lesson Check Point**

Directions: Read and divide each target word into syllables. Write each word and place a hyphen (-) between the syllables in the second column. Write the number of syllables in the third column. Use a dictionary or the Internet to check your answers.

Direksyons: Li epi divize chak mo objektif an silab. Ekri chak mo epi mete yon tirè (-) ant silab yo nan dezyèm kolòn nan. Ekri kantite silab ke yo genyen an nan twazyèm kolòn nan. Itilize yon diksyonè oubyen entènèt pou tcheke repons ou yo.

Target Words	Words Divided into Syllables	Number of Syllables
1. java	_____	_____
2. jury	_____	_____
3. jostle	_____	_____
4. jangle	_____	_____
5. jumble	_____	_____
6. jargon	_____	_____
7. jacket	_____	_____
8. jester	_____	_____
9. justly	_____	_____
10. jockey	_____	_____

Name: _____   Date:___/___/_____   Score: _____

The Reading Challenge

Lesson 10.2

Reading Multisyllable Words

✓ Lesson Check Point

 Directions: Read each target word. Circle the word in the row that is divided correctly into syllables. Use a dictionary or the Internet to check your answers.

Direksyons: Li chak mo objektif. Antoure mo a ki nan ranje a ki divize an silab korèkteman yo. Itilize yon diksyonè oubyen entènèt pou tcheke repons ou yo.

Model

| janitor | a. ja-ni-tor | b. jan-it-or | c. jan-i-tor |

1. jocular	a. jo-cu-lar	b. joc-u-lar	c. joc-ul-ar
2. juxtapose	a. juxt-a-pose	b. jux-ta-pose	c. jux-tap-ose
3. jeopardize	a. jeo-pard-ize	b. je-opar-dize	c. jeop-ard-ize
4. jewelry	a. jew-el-ry	b. je-wel-r-y	c. jewel-ry
5. jealousy	a. jea-lou-sy	b. jeal-ous-y	c. jeal-ou-sy
6. Jupiter	a. Jup-i-ter	b. Ju-pi-ter	c. Ju-pit-er
7. jointly	a. joint-ly	b. joi-ntly	c. jo-intly
8. jokingly	a. jo-kingl-y	b. jok-ing-ly	c. jok-in-gly

Name: _____ Date: ___/___/_____ Score: _____

Lesson 10.3

Reading and Writing

Proper and Common Nouns and Adjectives

Directions: Read the words in the word box. Put an (X) on the line next to each word that is written incorrectly. Remember that all proper nouns and proper adjectives are capitalized. Use a dictionary or the Internet to check your answers.

Direksyons: Li chak mo yo ki nan bwat mo a. Met yon (X) sou ti trè a ki bò kote mo ki pa kri byen yo. Sonje ke tout non pwòp ak adjektif pwop ekri avèk yon lèt majiskil nan kòmansman yo. Itilize yon diksyonè oubyen entènèt pou tcheke repons ou yo.

Word Box		
__ Jump	__ New Jersey	__ jamaica
__ Joints	__ jumbo	__ julia
__ Johnson	__ Janitor	__ Jordan
__ july	__ Joseph	__ juggle

Directions: Read each unedited sentence and underline the word that is written incorrectly. Write each sentence correctly on the line.

Direksyons: Li chak fraz ki pa edite yo epi soulinye mo ki pa ekri byen an. Ekri chak fraz korèkteman sou liy lan.

Model
Junior has a book about <u>jupiter</u> and Earth.
Junior has a book about Jupiter and Earth.

1. John will join the Jazz band.
_____

2. Joy and jasmine saw a jellyfish.
_____

3. Joey likes to juggle his Jellybeans.
_____

4. june said, "It is not healthy to eat junk food."
_____

Name: _____ Date: ___/___/_____ Score: _____

Lesson 11.1

Reading Words with the Letter K/k

✓ Lesson Check Point

Directions: Read each target word. Find the letter "k" and put a check (✓) in the column that identifies its position: beginning, within or end.
Direksyons: Li chak mo objektif. Jwenn lèt "k" a epi mete yon tchèck (✓) nan kolòn ki idantifye pozisyon li an: nan kòmansman, ladan oubyen nan finisman.

Target Words	Beginning (First Letter)	Within	End (Last Letter)
1. joker			
2. mask			
3. keep			
4. kennel			
5. parking			

Directions: Read each sentence and underline the words that begin with the letter "k." Write all the underlined words in alphabetical order on the lines below.
Direksyons: Li chak fraz epi soulinye mo ki kòmanse avèk lèt "k" yo. Ekri tout mo ki soulinye yo nan lòd alfabetik sou trè sa yo ki anba.

6. Carolyn puts ketchup on her knish.

7. Karen said, "Kiwi is a delicious fruit."

8. The excited campers went kayaking in Key Largo.

9. Mr. Keys said to knock on the door before entering.

10. Children are not allowed to play with kitchen knives.

_____   _____   _____
_____   _____   _____
_____   _____   _____
                _____

Name: _____ Date: ___/___/_____ Score: _____

Lesson 11.2

Reading Words with the Letter "k" and "ck" Letter Combination

✓ **Lesson Check Point**

Directions: Read each target word. Put a check (✓) in the second column if the target word has one vowel. Put a check (✓) in the third column if the target word has two vowels.

Direksyons: Li chak mo objektif. Mete yon tchèk (✓) nan dezyèm kolòn nan si mo objektif la genyen yon vwayèl. Mete yon tchèk (✓) nan twazyèm kolòn nan si mo objektif la genyen de vwayèl.

Target Words	Words with 1 Vowel	Words with 2 Vowels
1. cheek		
2. joke		
3. rock		
4. rake		
5. stock		

Directions: Read each target word in the first column and write the number of vowels within the word in the second column. Read each target word in the third column and write the number of vowels within the word in the fourth column.

Direksyons: Li chak mo objektif ki nan premye kolòn nan, epi ekri kantite vwayèl la ki nan mo a nan dezyèm kolòn nan. Li chak mo objektif ki nan twazyèm kolòn nan, epi ekri kantite vwayèl la ki nan mo a nan katryèm kolòn nan.

Target Words	Number of Vowel(s)	Target Words	Number of Vowel(s)
6. stoke		stock	
7. snake		snack	
8. Luke		luck	
9. rack		rake	
10. lack		lake	

Name: _____ Date: ___/___/_____ Score: _____

Lesson 11.3

Reading Words with the "kle" Letter Combination

✓ Lesson Check Point

Directions: Read each target word. Find the "kle" letter combination and put a check (✓) in the column that identifies its position: beginning, within or end.

Direksyons: Li chak mo objektif. Jwenn konbinezon lèt "kle" a epi mete yon tchèk (✓) nan kolòn nan ki idantifye pozisyon li an: nan kòmansman, ladan oubyen nan finisman.

Target Words	Beginning (First 3 Letters)	Within	End (Last 3 Letters)
1. suckle			
2. crinkle			
3. trickled			
4. speckle			
5. kleptomaniacs			

Directions: Read each target word. Put a check (✓) in the "yes" column if the "kle" letter combination has the /k/ + /ə/ + /l/ sounds. Put a check (✓) in the "no" column if the "kle" letter combination does not have the /k/ + /ə/ + /l/ sounds.

Direksyons: Li chak mo objektif. Mete yon tchèk (✓) nan kolòn "yes" an si konbinezon lèt "kle" a bay sons /k/ + /ə/ + /l/. Mete yon tchèk (✓) nan kolòn "no" an si konbinezon lèt "kle" a pa bay sons /k/ + /ə/ + /l/.

Target Words	Yes	No
6. suckle		
7. crinkle		
8. trickled		
9. speckle		
10. kleptomaniacs		

Name: _____ Date: ___/___/_____ Score: _____

Lesson 11.4

Reading Words with a Silent Letter "k"

✓ **Lesson Check Point**

Directions: Read the target words in the word box. Write the words that have a silent letter "k" in the first column. Write the words that do not have a silent letter "k" in the second column.

Direksyons: Li mo objektif yo ki nan ti bwat mo a. Ekri mo yo ki genyen lèt "k" ki pa pwononse a nan premye kolòn nan. Ekri mo yo ki pa genyen lèt "k" ki pa pwononse a nan dezyèm kolòn nan.

Target Word Box				
silky	knack	knowledge	kitten	knife
knowingly	shirk	making	kneeling	shrink
koala	milk	knish	kicking	knot
knitting	knead	knights	knock	kebab

Letter "k" is silent

_____
_____
_____
_____
_____
_____
_____
_____

Letter "k" has the /k/ sound

_____
_____
_____
_____
_____
_____
_____
_____

Name: _____ Date: ___/___/_____ Score: _____

The Reading Challenge

Lesson 11.5

Reading Multisyllable Words

✓ Lesson Check Point

Directions: Read and divide each target word into syllables. Write each word and place a hyphen (-) between the syllables in the second column. Write the number of syllables in the third column. Use a dictionary or the Internet to check your answers.

Direksyons: Li epi divize chak mo objektif an silab. Ekri chak mo epi mete yon tirè (-) ant silab yo nan dezyèm kolòn nan. Ekri kantite silab ke yo genyen an nan twazyèm kolòn nan. Itilize yon diksyonè oubyen entènèt pou tcheke repons ou yo.

Target Words	Words Divided into Syllables	Number of Syllables
1. khaki	_____	_____
2. kebab	_____	_____
3. kidney	_____	_____
4. keynote	_____	_____
5. kayaking	_____	_____
6. knuckle	_____	_____
7. keepsake	_____	_____
8. knapsack	_____	_____
9. kaleidoscope	_____	_____
10. kindergarten	_____	_____

Learn to Read English With Directions In Haitian Creole

Name: _____ Date: ___/___/_____ Score: _____

The Reading Challenge

Lesson 11.5

Reading Multisyllable Words

✓ **Lesson Check Point**

 Directions: Read each target word. Circle the word in the row that is divided correctly into syllables. Use a dictionary or the Internet to check your answers.

Direksyons: Li chak mo objektif. Antoure mo a ki nan ranje a ki divize an silab korèkteman yo. Itilize yon diksyonè oubyen entènèt pou tcheke repons ou yo.

Model

| kangaroo | a. kang-a-roo | b. kan-ga-roo | c. kan-gar-oo |

(b. kan-ga-roo is circled)

| 1. knowingly | a. know-ing-ly | b. kno-wing-ly | c. know-in-gly |

| 2. kindle | a. ki-ndle | b. kin-dle | c. kind-le |

| 3. kickback | a. kick-back | b. ki-ckba-ck | c. ki-ck-back |

| 4. kitchenette | a. ki-tchen-ette | b. kit-chen-ette | c. kitch-en-ette |

| 5. kingdom | a. kingd-om | b. kin-gdom | c. king-dom |

| 6. Kentucky | a. Ken-tuc-ky | b. Kent-uck-y | c. Ken-tuck-y |

| 7. kindness | a. ki-ndness | b. ki-nd-ness | c. kind-ness |

| 8. kerosene | a. ker-o-sene | b. ke-ros-ene | c. ker-os-ene |

Name: _____ Date: ___/___/_____ Score: _____

Lesson 11.6

Reading and Writing

Proper and Common Nouns and Adjectives

Directions: Read the words in the word box. Put an (X) on the line next to each word that is written incorrectly. Remember that all proper nouns and proper adjectives are capitalized. Use a dictionary or the Internet to check your answers.

Direksyons: Li chak mo yo ki nan bwat mo a. Met yon (X) sou ti trè a ki bò kote mo ki pa kri byen yo. Sonje ke tout non pwòp ak adjektif pwop ekri avèk yon lèt majiskil nan kòmansman yo. Itilize yon diksyonè oubyen entènèt pou tcheke repons ou yo.

Word Box		
__ Kentucky	__ kingdom	__ kingston
__ kuwait	__ kisses	__ Keypad
__ Helen Keller	__ kilometers	__ Key West
__ Ketchup	__ Keepers	__ Mr. king

Directions: Read each unedited sentence and underline the word that is written incorrectly. Write each sentence correctly on the line.

Direksyons: Li chak fraz ki pa edite yo epi soulinye mo ki pa ekri byen an. Ekri chak fraz korèkteman sou liy lan.

Model
Helen <u>keller</u> was a kind person.
<u>Helen Keller was a kind person.</u>

1. The new karate class is being held in kingston, Kansas.
_____

2. Katie said, "The kenyan culture is rooted in history."
_____

3. My friend, Kelly, likes to fly her kite in key Largo.
_____

4. Karen and Karim always put ketchup on their Knishes.
_____

Name: _____ Date: ___/___/_____ Score: _____

Lesson 12.1

Reading Words with the Letter L/l

✓ Lesson Check Point

Directions: Read each target word. Find the letter "l" and put a check (✓) in the column that identifies its position: beginning, within or end.

Direksyons: Li chak mo objektif. Jwenn lèt "l" a epi mete yon tchèck (✓) nan kolòn ki idantifye pozisyon li an: nan kòmansman, ladan oubyen nan finisman.

Target Words	Beginning (First Letter)	Within	End (Last Letter)
1. lift			
2. garlic			
3. lounge			
4. graceful			
5. happily			

Directions: Read each sentence and underline the words that begin with the letter "l." Write all the underlined words in alphabetical order on the lines below.

Direksyons: Li chak fraz epi soulinye mo ki kòmanse avèk lèt "l" yo. Ekri tout mo ki soulinye yo nan lòd alfabetik sou trè sa yo ki anba.

6. I am late for my literature class.

7. The laundry has a lavender scent.

8. Danny drank a large glass of lemonade.

9. Today's lecture will be held in the library.

10. My lilies and lilacs are growing in the garden.

_____   _____   _____
_____   _____   _____
_____   _____   _____

Learn to Read English With Directions In Haitian Creole

 Name: _____ Date: ___/___/_____ Score: _____

Lesson 12.2

Reading Words with the Letter "l" Combinations:
"bl," "pl" & "sl"

Dictionary Skills/ Vocabulary

✓ Lesson Check Point

 Directions: Read each target word and its definition. Write the target word on the line in front of its meaning. Use a dictionary or the Internet to check your answers.

Direksyons: Li chak mo objektif ak definisyon yo chak. Ekri mo objektif la sou trè ki devan definisyon li an. Itilize yon diksyonè oubyen entènèt pou tcheke repons ou yo.

Target Word Box				
blender	plane	sled	sliced	slowly

1. _____ to have cut something with a knife
2. _____ a machine that mixes things together
3. _____ not moving quickly
4. _____ a winged vehicle that can fly
5. _____ to glide on packed snow or ice

 Directions: Read each sentence. Underline the word in the parentheses that correctly completes each sentence. Then, write the underlined word on the line.

Direksyons: Li chak fraz. Soulinye mo a ki nan parantèz yo ki konplete chak fraz kòrèkteman. Answit, ekri mo soulinye a sou trè a.

6. On snowy days, the kids _____ down the hills. (sled, sliced)

7. Mrs. Blake _____ the loaf of bread in half. (sliced, slowly)

8. Mr. Cloud took a _____ from Poland to America. (sled, plane)

9. Paul was walking _____ in the crowded hallway. (slowly, blender)

10. I placed two strawberries in the _____. (plane, blender)

Name: _____ Date: ___/___/_____ Score: _____

Lesson 12.3

Reading Words with a Silent Letter "l"

✓ **Lesson Check Point**

Directions: Read the target words in the word box. Write the words that have a silent letter "l" in the first column. Write the words that do not have a silent letter "l" in the second column.

Direksyons: Li mo objektif yo ki nan ti bwat mo a. Ekri mo yo ki genyen lèt "l" ki pa pwononse a nan premye kolòn nan. Ekri mo yo ki pa genyen lèt "l" ki pa pwononse a nan dezyèm kolòn nan.

Target Word Box				
little	balm	calves	wheel	like
could	salmon	below	dollar	listen
valley	believe	pool	half	ball
lilies	Hellenic	balloon	library	late

Letter "l" is silent

Letter "l" has the /l/ sound

_____ _____
_____ _____
_____ _____
_____ _____
_____ _____
_____ _____
_____ _____
_____ _____

Name: _____ Date:___/___/_____ Score:_____

The Reading Challenge

Lesson 12.4

Reading Multisyllable Words

✓ **Lesson Check Point**

 Directions: Read and divide each target word into syllables. Write each word and place a hyphen (-) between the syllables in the second column. Write the number of syllables in the third column. Use a dictionary or the Internet to check your answers.

Direksyons: Li epi divize chak mo objektif an silab. Ekri chak mo epi mete yon tirè (-) ant silab yo nan dezyèm kolòn nan. Ekri kantite silab ke yo genyen an nan twazyèm kolòn nan. Itilize yon diksyonè oubyen entènèt pou tcheke repons ou yo.

Target Words	Words Divided into Syllables	Number of Syllables
1. latex	_____	_____
2. logical	_____	_____
3. leopard	_____	_____
4. lingers	_____	_____
5. lawyer	_____	_____
6. lonely	_____	_____
7. linkage	_____	_____
8. leisurely	_____	_____
9. language	_____	_____
10. lemonade	_____	_____

Unit L
Lesson 12.4

Name: _____ Date: ___/___/_____ Score: _____

The Reading Challenge

Lesson 12.4

Reading Multisyllable Words

✓ **Lesson Check Point**

Directions: Read each target word. Circle the word in the row that is divided correctly into syllables. Use a dictionary or the Internet to check your answers.

Direksyons: Li chak mo objektif. Antoure mo a ki nan ranje a ki divize an silab korèkteman yo. Itilize yon diksyonè oubyen entènèt pou tcheke repons ou yo.

Model

| liberty | a. li-ber-ty | b. lib-er-ty | c. lib-ert-y |

| 1. liable | a. li-a-ble | b. li-able | c. li-ab-le |

| 2. lieutenant | a. lieut-en-ant | b. lieu-ten-ant | c. lie-uten-ant |

| 3. lineage | a. li-ne-age | b. lin-ea-ge | c. lin-e-age |

| 4. laminate | a. la-mi-nate | b. lam-i-nate | c. la-min-ate |

| 5. literate | a. li-ter-ate | b. lite-ra-te | c. lit-er-ate |

| 6. location | a. loc-a-tion | b. lo-cat-ion | c. lo-ca-tion |

| 7. logical | a. lo-gi-cal | b. log-i-cal | c. lo-gic-al |

| 8. levitate | a. lev-i-tate | b. le-vit-ate | c. lev-it-ate |

Learn to Read English With Directions In Haitian Creole

Name: _____ Date: ___/___/_____ Score: _____

Lesson 12.5

Reading and Writing

Proper and Common Nouns and Adjectives

Directions: Read the words in the word box. Put an (X) on the line next to each word that is written incorrectly. Remember that all proper nouns and proper adjectives are capitalized. Use a dictionary or the Internet to check your answers.

Direksyons: Li chak mo yo ki nan bwat mo a. Met yon (X) sou ti trè a ki bò kote mo ki pa kri byen yo. Sonje ke tout non pwòp ak adjektif pwop ekri avèk yon lèt majiskil nan kòmansman yo. Itilize yon diksyonè oubyen entènèt pou tcheke repons ou yo.

Word Box		
__ Lima, Peru	__ Lecturer	__ lithuania
__ laboratory	__ Language	__ leather
__ Lawsuit	__ literature	__ Lexington
__ london	__ Louisiana	__ League

Directions: Read each unedited sentence and underline the word that is written incorrectly. Write each sentence correctly on the line.

Direksyons: Li chak fraz ki pa edite yo epi soulinye mo ki pa ekri byen an. Ekri chak fraz korèkteman sou liy lan.

Model
last night, I read a long article about tourism in London.
Last night, I read a long article about tourism in London.

1. I drank the best lemonade on long Island.
   _____

2. Lucy was lost in Las Vegas for two Long days.
   _____

3. The Arabic language is spoken in libya and Lebanon.
   _____

4. Lydia said, "South America is also called latin America."
   _____

Name: _____ Date: ___/___/___ Score: _____

Lesson 13.1

Reading Words with the Letter M/m

✓ **Lesson Check Point**

Directions: Read each target word. Find the letter "m" and put a check (✓) in the column that identifies its position: beginning, within or end.
Direksyons: Li chak mo objektif. Jwenn lèt "m" a epi mete yon tchèck (✓) nan kolòn ki idantifye pozisyon li an: nan kòmansman, ladan oubyen nan finisman.

Target Words	Beginning (First Letter)	Within	End (Last Letter)
1. limit			
2. model			
3. helmet			
4. removal			
5. bedroom			

Directions: Read each sentence and underline the words that begin with the letter "m." Write all the underlined words in alphabetical order on the lines below.
Direksyons: Li chak fraz epi soulinye mo ki kòmanse avèk lèt "m" yo. Ekri tout mo ki soulinye yo nan lòd alfabetik sou trè sa yo ki anba.

6. Old MacDonald has a mule on his farm.

7. Every Monday, Peg drinks mineral water.

8. In March, I received a toy mouse as a gift.

9. Amber and her family moved to Missouri.

10. Did you receive the memo from Dr. Maxwell?

_____   _____   _____
_____   _____   _____
_____   _____   _____

Learn to Read English With Directions In Haitian Creole

 Name: _____ Date: ___/___/_____ Score: _____

Lesson 13.2

Reading Words with a Silent Letter "m"

✓ **Lesson Check Point**

 Directions: Read each target word. Find the letter "m" and put a check (✓) in the column that identifies its position: beginning, within or end.
Direksyons: Li chak mo objektif. Jwenn lèt "m" a epi mete yon tchèk (✓) nan kolòn ki idantifye pozisyon li an: nan kòmansman, ladan oubyen nan finisman.

Target Words	Beginning (First Letter)	Within	End (Last Letter)
1. hammer			
2. summer			
3. mnemonic			
4. bedroom			
5. compromise			

 Directions: Read each target word. Put a check (✓) in the "yes" column if the target word has a silent letter "m." Put a check (✓) in the "no" column if the target word does not have a silent letter "m."
Direksyons: Li chak mo objektif. Mete yon tchèk (✓) nan kolòn "yes" an si mo objektif la genyen yon lèt "m" ki pa pwononse. Mete yon tchèk (✓) nan kolòn "no" an si mo objektif la pa genyen yon lèt "m" ki pa pwononse.

Target Words	Yes	No
6. hammer		
7. summer		
8. mnemonic		
9. bedroom		
10. compromise		

Name: _____ Date: ___/___/_____ Score: _____

The Reading Challenge

Lesson 13.3

Reading Multisyllable Words

✓ **Lesson Check Point**

Directions: Read and divide each target word into syllables. Write each word and place a hyphen (-) between the syllables in the second column. Write the number of syllables in the third column. Use a dictionary or the Internet to check your answers.

Direksyons: Li epi divize chak mo objektif an silab. Ekri chak mo epi mete yon tirè (-) ant silab yo nan dezyèm kolòn nan. Ekri kantite silab ke yo genyen an nan twazyèm kolòn nan. Itilize yon diksyonè oubyen entènèt pou tcheke repons ou yo.

Target Words	Words Divided into Syllables	Number of Syllables
1. movies		
2. mighty		
3. mandate		
4. mariner		
5. moisture		
6. molding		
7. mutual		
8. medical		
9. microfilm		
10. maintaining		

 Name: _____ Date: ___/___/_____ Score: _____

The Reading Challenge

Lesson 13.3

Reading Multisyllable Words

✓ **Lesson Check Point**

Directions: Read each target word. Circle the word in the row that is divided correctly into syllables. Use a dictionary or the Internet to check your answers.

Direksyons: Li chak mo objektif. Antoure mo a ki nan ranje a ki divize an silab korèkteman yo. Itilize yon diksyonè oubyen entènèt pou tcheke repons ou yo.

Model

magazine	a. mag-a-zine (circled)	b. ma-ga-zine	c. mag-az-ine
1. Montana	a. Mon-tan-a	b. Mon-ta-na	c. Mont-an-a
2. memory	a. me-mo-ry	b. mem-or-y	c. mem-o-ry
3. manifold	a. man-i-fold	b. ma-ni-fold	c. man-if-old
4. meander	a. mea-n-der	b. mean-der	c. me-an-der
5. manicure	a. man-i-cure	b. ma-ni-cure	c. ma-nic-ure
6. modify	a. mo-di-fy	b. mod-i-fy	c. modif-y
7. manatee	a. ma-na-tee	b. ma-nat-ee	c. man-a-tee
8. menial	a. men-i-al	b. me-ni-al	c. men-ia-l

Name: _____ Date: ___/___/_____ Score: _____

Lesson 13.4

Reading and Writing

Proper and Common Nouns and Adjectives

Directions: Read the words in the word box. Put an (X) on the line next to each word that is written incorrectly. Remember that all proper nouns and proper adjectives are capitalized. Use a dictionary or the Internet to check your answers.

Direksyons: Li chak mo yo ki nan bwat mo a. Met yon (X) sou ti trè a ki bò kote mo ki pa kri byen yo. Sonje ke tout non pwòp ak adjektif pwop ekri avèk yon lèt majiskil nan kòmansman yo. Itilize yon diksyonè oubyen entènèt pou tcheke repons ou yo.

Word Box		
__ Myanmar	__ Mechanic	__ medicine
__ Marble	__ Memphis	__ marshall Island
__ manhattan	__ Madagascar	__ meadow
__ Maldives	__ milky Way	__ Mammals

Directions: Read each unedited sentence and underline the word that is written incorrectly. Write each sentence correctly on the line.

Direksyons: Li chak fraz ki pa edite yo epi soulinye mo ki pa ekri byen an. Ekri chak fraz korèkteman sou liy lan.

Model
My son, Mark, is going to attend MIT in <u>massachusetts</u>.
My son, Mark, is going to attend MIT in Massachusetts.

1. Does a Millipede have a million legs?
_____

2. Mom had a marvelous time in manchester.
_____

3. The town's mayor must Make an important decision.
_____

4. Max and Molly are getting married in martha's Vineyard.
_____

Name: _____ Date: ___/___/_____ Score: _____

Lesson 14.1

Reading Words with the Letter N/n

✓ Lesson Check Point

Directions: Read each target word. Find the letter "n" and put a check (✓) in the column that identifies its position: beginning, within or end.
Direksyons: Li chak mo objektif. Jwenn lèt "n" a epi mete yon tchèck (✓) nan kolòn ki idantifye pozisyon li an: nan kòmansman, ladan oubyen nan finisman.

Target Words	Beginning (First Letter)	Within	End (Last Letter)
1. muffin			
2. friend			
3. needle			
4. modern			
5. dancing			

Directions: Read each sentence and underline the words that begin with the letter "n." Write all the underlined words in alphabetical order on the lines below.
Direksyons: Li chak fraz epi soulinye mo ki kòmanse avèk lèt "n" yo. Ekri tout mo ki soulinye yo nan lòd alfabetik sou trè sa yo ki anba.

6. Margaret said, "The nighthawks hunt at night."

7. The nature trails along the Niagara River are very clean.

8. My best friend, Nathan, was invited to Northern Africa.

9. Newton and the kids are eating chicken nuggets and fries.

10. The award-winning North Dakota newspaper is informative.

_____   _____   _____
_____   _____   _____
_____   _____   _____
                _____

 Name: _____ Date: ___/___/_____ Score: _____

Lesson 14.2

Reading Words with the "ng" Letter Combination

✓ **Lesson Check Point**

 Directions: Read each target word. Circle the word in the column that has the same "ng" sound(s) as the target word.

Direksyons: Li chak mo objektif. Antoure mo a ki nan kolòn nan ki bay menm son "ng" la (yo) tankou mo objektif la.

congratulation	a. ingredient
	b. change

Congo	a. ranger
	b. finger

triangle	a. singer
	b. Singapore

stranger	a. England
	b. manger

 Directions: Read each target word. Put a check (✓) under the correct column heading.

Direksyons: Li chak mo objektif. Mete yon tchèk (✓) anba antèt kolòn ki kòrèk la.

Target Words	"ng" has the /n/ + /g/ sounds as in the word <u>ingrain</u>	"ng" has the /n/ + /j/ sounds as in the word <u>ginger</u>	"ng" has the /ng/ sound as in the word <u>bang</u>	"ng" has the /ng/ + /g/ sounds as in the word <u>congress</u>
1. Congo				
2. triangle				
3. stranger				
4. congratulation				

Name: _____ Date: ___/___/_____ Score: _____

Lesson 14.3

Reading Words with a Silent Letter "n"

✓ **Lesson Check Point**

Directions: Read the target words in the word box. Write the words that have a silent letter "n" in the first column. Write the words that do not have a silent letter "n" in the second column.

Direksyons: Li mo objektif yo ki nan ti bwat mo a. Ekri mo yo ki genyen lèt "n" ki pa pwononse a nan premye kolòn nan. Ekri mo yo ki pa genyen lèt "n" ki pa pwononse a nan dezyèm kolòn nan.

Target Word Box				
partners	chimney	expand	channel	ringing
column	machine	autumn	annex	manners
ribbons	hornet	hymn	romantic	columns
network	penny	solemn	condemn	nonsense

Letter "n" **Letter "n" has the**
is silent **/n/ sound**

_____ _____
_____ _____
_____ _____
_____ _____
_____ _____
_____ _____
_____ _____
_____ _____

Name: _____ Date: ___/___/_____ Score: _____

The Reading Challenge

Lesson 14.4

Reading Multisyllable Words

✓ **Lesson Check Point**

Directions: Read and divide each target word into syllables. Write each word and place a hyphen (-) between the syllables in the second column. Write the number of syllables in the third column. Use a dictionary or the Internet to check your answers.

Direksyons: Li epi divize chak mo objektif an silab. Ekri chak mo epi mete yon tirè (-) ant silab yo nan dezyèm kolòn nan. Ekri kantite silab ke yo genyen an nan twazyèm kolòn nan. Itilize yon diksyonè oubyen entènèt pou tcheke repons ou yo.

Target Words	Words Divided into Syllables	Number of Syllables
1. neon		
2. needle		
3. necktie		
4. natural		
5. naughty		
6. nautilus		
7. November		
8. nourishing		
9. Netherlands		
10. networking		

Unit N
Lesson 14.4

Name: _____ Date: ___/___/_____ Score: _____

The Reading Challenge

Lesson 14.4

Reading Multisyllable Words

✓ Lesson Check Point

 Directions: Read each target word. Circle the word in the row that is divided correctly into syllables. Use a dictionary or the Internet to check your answers.

Direksyons: Li chak mo objektif. Antoure mo a ki nan ranje a ki divize an silab korèkteman yo. Itilize yon diksyonè oubyen entènèt pou tcheke repons ou yo.

Model

| napkin | a. na-pkin | b. napk-in | c. nap-kin (circled) |

1. numeral	a. num-er-al	b. nu-mer-al	c. nu-me-ral
2. nominal	a. nom-i-nal	b. no-mi-nal	c. no-min-al
3. navigate	a. nav-i-gate	b. na-vi-gate	c. na-vig-ate
4. nectarine	a. nect-ar-ine	b. nec-ta-rine	c. nec-tar-ine
5. negotiate	a. ne-go-ti-ate	b. ne-got-iate	c. neg-o-ti-ate
6. national	a. nat-ion-al	b. na-tion-al	c. na-tio-nal
7. numerate	a. nu-mer-ate	b. num-er-ate	c. nu-me-rate
8. nursery	a. nur-ser-y	b. nurs-e-ry	c. nurs-er-y

Name: _____ Date: ___/___/_____ Score: _____

Lesson 14.5

Reading and Writing

Proper and Common Nouns and Adjectives

Directions: Read the words in the word box. Put an (X) on the line next to each word that is written incorrectly. Remember that all proper nouns and proper adjectives are capitalized. Use a dictionary or the Internet to check your answers.

Direksyons: Li chak mo yo ki nan bwat mo a. Met yon (X) sou ti trè a ki bò kote mo ki pa kri byen yo. Sonje ke tout non pwòp ak adjektif pwop ekri avèk yon lèt majiskil nan kòmansman yo. Itilize yon diksyonè oubyen entènèt pou tcheke repons ou yo.

Word Box		
__ Nevada	__ network	__ november
__ nile River	__ Nebraska	__ nurse
__ Newspaper	__ Neckbone	__ Name
__ Nantucket	__ new Orleans	__ North Dakota

Directions: Read each unedited sentence and underline the word that is written incorrectly. Write each sentence correctly on the line.

Direksyons: Li chak fraz ki pa edite yo epi soulinye mo ki pa ekri byen an. Ekri chak fraz korèkteman sou liy lan.

Model
In <u>november</u>, Newton would like to visit Nantucket.
<u>In November, Newton would like to visit Nantucket.</u>

1. My Neighbor's name is Nathan.
_____

2. nancy's new nanny is from Nepal.
_____

3. The Newscasters reported from the Netherlands.
_____

4. Nathalie said, "Newark is the capital of new Jersey."
_____

Name: _____ Date:___/___/_____ Score:_____

Lesson 15.1

Reading Words with the Letter O/o

✓ Lesson Check Point

Directions: Read each target word. Find the letter "o" and put a check (✓) in the column that identifies its position: beginning, within or end.
Direksyons: Li chak mo objektif. Jwenn lèt "o" a epi mete yon tchèck (✓) nan kolòn ki idantifye pozisyon li an: nan kòmansman, ladan oubyen nan finisman.

Target Words	Beginning (First Letter)	Within	End (Last Letter)
1. once			
2. zero			
3. ghetto			
4. mostly			
5. loving			

Directions: Read each target word. Read the words in the row and circle the word that has a different vowel "o" sound.
Direksyons: Li chak mo objektif. Li mo yo ki nan ranje a epi antoure mo a ki bay yon son vwayèl "o" ki diferan an.

Target Words				
6. poster	goats	rope	work	foam
7. plotting	spots	hop	not	tote
8. mommy	do	rob	blot	pot
9. enrolled	pony	yo-yo	crop	hotel
10. hoping	both	born	road	loan

Learn to Read English With Directions In Haitian Creole

Name: _____ Date: ___/___/_____ Score: _____

Lesson 15.2

Reading Words with the Short Vowel "o" Sound

✓ **Lesson Check Point**

Directions: Read the words in the four boxes. Circle two words with the short vowel /ŏ/ or /ô/ sound. The anchor word for the short vowel /ŏ/ and /ô/ sounds is frog.

Direksyons: Li mo yo ki nan kat ti bwat yo. Antoure de mo ki genyen son vwayèl kout /ŏ/ oubyen /ô/ a. Mo referans pou son vwayèl kout /ŏ/ ak /ô/ a se mo, frog.

jolt	Bob
rod	info

post	both
cop	mob

do	jog
cove	got

hop	over
to	ox

most	droll
cod	not

stock	bold
ghost	rob

Directions: Read the words in the four boxes. Circle two words that rhyme. Rhyming words have the same ending sound, such as hot and not.

Direksyons: Li mo yo ki nan kat ti bwat yo. Antoure de mo ki rime. De mo oubyen plizyè mo ki rime genyen menm son nan finisman yo, tankou hot ak not.

code	sock
hole	rock

cross	dross
dole	bone

go	mom
oval	Tom

top	home
hose	mop

job	lone
hope	rob

Ron	con
coat	coast

Name: _____   Date: ___/___/_____   Score: _____

Lesson 15.2

Reading & Writing Words with the Short Vowel "o" Sound

✓ **Lesson Check Point**

Directions: Read each sentence and underline three words with the short vowel /ŏ/ or /ô/ sound. Then, write the underlined words on the lines below. The anchor word for the short vowel /ŏ/ and /ô/ sounds is <u>frog</u>.

Direksyons: Li chak fraz epi soulinye twa mo ki genyen son vwayèl kout /ŏ/ oubyen /ô/ a. Answit, ekri mo soulinye yo sou trè sa yo ki anba. Mo referans pou son vwayèl kout /ŏ/ ak /ô/ a se mo, <u>frog</u>.

Model
Everyone saw the <u>frog</u> <u>hop</u> close to the <u>rock</u>.

    frog   hop   rock

1. Mommy lost my doll in the house.

   _____   _____   _____

2. Today, Bob's socks were floating in the pond.

   _____   _____   _____

3. Owen tossed the cod back into the cold pond.

   _____   _____   _____

4. My mom and Todd cooked spicy octopus soup.

   _____   _____   _____

5. When I was outside, I saw frogs with lots of spots.

   _____   _____   _____

Name: _____ Date: ___/___/_____ Score: _____

Lesson 15.3

Reading Words with the Long Vowel "o" Sound

✓ **Lesson Check Point**

 Directions: Read the words in the four boxes. Circle two words with the long vowel /ō/ sound. The anchor word for the long vowel /ō/ sound is <u>open</u>.

Direksyons: Li mo yo ki nan kat ti bwat yo. Antoure de mo ki genyen son vwayèl long /ō/ a. Mo referans pou son vwayèl long /ō/ a se mo, <u>open</u>.

loft	boast	rose	stomp	goat	fond
knock	vote	cloth	coal	pose	stock

smock	robe	frog	most	knob	prom
loan	font	snob	stroll	hope	coast

 Directions: Read the words in the four boxes. Circle two words that rhyme. Rhyming words have the same ending sound, such as <u>hope</u> and <u>soap</u>.

Direksyons: Li mo yo ki nan kat ti bwat yo. Antoure de mo ki rime. De mo oubyen plizyè mo ki rime genyen menm son nan finisman yo, tankou <u>hope</u> ak <u>soap</u>.

zone	cone	knot	tone	yoke	woke
shot	mole	bone	ago	over	smog

no	doze	gold	fold	open	crop
go	shop	coach	flock	rode	toad

Name: _____ Date: ___/___/_____ Score: _____

Lesson 15.3

Reading & Writing Words with the Long Vowel "o" Sound

✓ Lesson Check Point

Directions: Read each sentence and underline three words with the long vowel /ō/ sound. Then, write the underlined words on the lines below. The anchor word for the long vowel /ō/ sound is <u>open</u>.

Direksyons: Li chak fraz epi soulinye twa mo ki genyen son vwayèl long /ō/ a. Answit, ekri mo soulinye yo sou trè sa yo ki anba. Mo referans pou son vwayèl long /ō/ a se mo, <u>open</u>.

Model

We will <u>go</u> to the <u>rodeo</u> and <u>limbo</u> competitions for fun.

     go   rodeo   limbo

1. Owen said, "The robots operate with two tokens."

   _____   _____   _____

2. The group of students is focused on the yodeler's show.

   _____   _____   _____

3. Leo said, "The motel will serve donuts in the morning."

   _____   _____   _____

4. The poet will write a poem about sailing on the Atlantic Ocean.

   _____   _____   _____

5. The yellow envelope has information about the car's turbocharger.

   _____   _____   _____

Name: _____ Date: ___/___/_____ Score: _____

Review Lessons 15.2 & 15.3

Reading Short Vowel and Long Vowel Words

Directions: Read the target words in the word box. In the first column, write the words that have the short vowel /ŏ/ or /ô/ sound, as in the word <u>frog</u>. In the second column, write the words that have the long vowel /ō/ sound, as in the word <u>open</u>.

Direksyons: Li mo objektif yo ki nan bwat mo a. Nan premye kolòn nan, ekri mo yo ki bay son vwayèl kout /ŏ/ oubyen /ô/ a, tankou li ye nan mo <u>frog</u> la. Nan dezyèm kolòn nan, ekri mo yo ki bay son vwayèl long /ō/ a, tankou li ye nan mo <u>open</u> la.

Target Word Box				
pony	chopping	hotel	poet	knock
lockers	mocking	blotch	flopping	ago
odd	stroller	piano	scotch	total
moment	utmost	octopus	boldest	softer

Letter "o" has the /ŏ/ or /ô/ sound as in the word <u>frog</u>

Letter "o" has the /ō/ sound as in the word <u>open</u>

Name: _____ Date: ___/___/_____ Score: _____

Lesson 15.4

Reading Words with Letter "o" Vowel Pairs

✓ **Lesson Check Point**

Directions: Read each target word. Circle the word in the column that has the same vowel "oa," "oe," "oo" or "ou" sound(s) as the target word.

Direksyons: Li chak mo objektif. Antoure mo a ki nan kolòn nan ki bay menm son vwayèl "oa," "oe," "oo" oubyen "ou" la (yo) tankou mo objektif la.

aloe	a. book		cocoa	a. loans
	b. toast			b. amount

banjoes	a. approach		moody	a. wooden
	b. noun			b. smoothie

Directions: Read each target word. Put a check (✓) under the correct column heading.

Direksyons: Li chak mo objektif. Mete yon tchèk (✓) anba antèt kolòn ki kòrèk la.

Target Words	Words have the long "o" sound as in the word <u>coat</u>	Words do not have the long "o" sound
1. aloe		
2. cocoa		
3. banjoes		
4. moody		

Name: _____ Date: ___/___/_____ Score: _____

Lesson 15.5

Reading Words with the Final Letter "o"

✓ Lesson Check Point

 Directions: Read each target word. Find the letter "o" and put a check (✓) in the column that identifies its position within the syllable.

Direksyons: Li chak mo objektif. Jwenn lèt "o" a epi mete yon tchèck (✓) nan kolòn nan ki idantifye pozisyon li an nan silab la.

Target Words	"o" is at the end of a one syllable word	"o" is at the end of the first syllable	"o" is at the end of a multi-syllable word
1. motel			
2. info			
3. go			
4. also			
5. probate			

 Directions: Read each target word. Put a check (✓) under the correct column heading.

Direksyons: Li chak mo objektif. Mete yon tchèk (✓) anba antèt kolòn ki kòrèk la.

Target Words	"o" has the /ŏ/ sound as in the word <u>frog</u>	"o" has the /ō/ sound as in the word <u>go</u>	"o" has the /ə/ sound as in the word <u>carrot</u>	"o" is silent as in the word <u>people</u>
6. second				
7. foxes				
8. coach				
9. poker				
10. victory				

Name: _____ Date: ___/___/_____ Score: _____

Lesson 15.6

Reading Letter "o" Words with the Schwa Vowel Sound

✓ **Lesson Check Point**

Directions: Read each target word. Circle the word in the column that has the same "o" sound as the target word.

Direksyons: Li chak mo objektif. Antoure mo a ki nan kolòn nan ki bay menm son "o" a tankou mo objektif la.

inspector	a. topping
	b. comfort

other	a. omega
	b. company

seldom	a. nothing
	b. janitor

wonder	a. done
	b. parrot

Directions: Read each sentence and underline the letter "o" word that has the schwa vowel /ə/ sound or short vowel /ŭ/ sound. The anchor word for the letter "o" schwa vowel /ə/ sound is <u>carrot</u> and the letter "o" short vowel /ŭ/ sound is <u>dove</u>.

Direksyons: Li chak fraz epi soulinye mo ki genyen lèt "o" a ki bay son schwa /ə/ oubyen son /ŭ/ a. Mo referans pou son schwa /ə/ lèt "o" a se <u>carrot</u> epi son lèt "o" /ŭ/ kout la se <u>dove</u>.

1. The oldest parrot has great oral skills.

2. After the storm, Dad will shovel the snow.

3. On Mother's Day, I bought a flower bouquet.

4. Oscar's homemade lemonade costs one dollar.

5. The janitor opened the door and cleaned the room.

6. The actors and actresses are in an outstanding comedy.

Name: _____ Date:___/___/_____ Score:_____

Lesson 15.7

Reading Words with Vowel "o" Sounds: /ŏ/, /ō/ & /o͞o/

✓ **Lesson Check Point**

 Directions: Read each target word. Put a check (✓) under the correct column heading.
Direksyons: Li chak mo objektif. Mete yon tchèk (✓) anba antèt kolòn ki kòrèk la.

Target Words	"o" has the /ŏ/ sound as in the word <u>frog</u>	"o" has the /ō/ sound as in the word <u>go</u>	"o" has the /o͞o/ sound as in the word <u>to</u>
1. spot			
2. omit			
3. proof			
4. profess			
5. movies			

 Directions: Read each sentence and underline the word that has a letter "o" that has the vowel /o͞o/ sound, as in the word <u>two</u>.
Direksyons: Li chak fraz epi soulinye mo a ki genyen let "o" a ki bay son /o͞o/ an, tankou li ye nan mo <u>two</u> la.

6. Can you tell me how yodelers yodel?

7. An explorer proved that Earth is round.

8. In October, I plan to visit Grandma's house.

9. Who placed the colorful rocks in the boxes?

10. The large moving van will arrive at one o'clock.

Name: _____ Date: ___/___/_____ Score: _____

Lesson 15.8

Reading Words with the "or" Letter Combination

✓ **Lesson Check Point**

Directions: Read each target word. Circle the word in the column that has the same "o" + "r" sounds as the target word.

Direksyons: Li chak mo objektif. Antoure mo a ki nan kolòn nan ki bay menm son "o" + "r" yo tankou mo objektif la.

razor	a. corrects
	b. lord

dormant	a. horse
	b. mirror

color	a. normal
	b. tailor

storm	a. visitor
	b. hornet

Directions: Read each target word. Put a check (✓) under the correct column heading.

Direksyons: Li chak mo objektif. Mete yon tchèk (✓) anba antèt kolòn ki kòrèk la.

Target Words	"or" has the /ô/ + /r/ sounds as in the word <u>door</u>	"or" has the /ə/ + /r/ sounds as in the word <u>doctor</u>
1. store		
2. horse		
3. correct		
4. formal		

Name: _____ Date:___/___/_____ Score:_____

Lesson 15.8

Reading Words with the "or" Letter Combination

Dictionary Skills/ Vocabulary

✓ Lesson Check Point

Directions: Read each target word and its definition. Write the target word on the line in front of its meaning. Use a dictionary or the Internet to check your answers.

Direksyons: Li chak mo objektif ak definisyon yo chak. Ekri mo objektif la sou trè ki devan definisyon li an. Itilize yon diksyonè oubyen entènèt pou tcheke repons ou yo.

Target Word Box				
dorm	cork	floor	cords	north

1. _____ the upward direction
2. _____ the lowest surface in a room
3. _____ rope-like objects that are conduits of electricity
4. _____ a one-inch wide wooden cylinder used to seal a bottle
5. _____ a living space for students at a college/university campus

Directions: Read each sentence and write the target word that correctly completes the sentence.

Direksyons: Li chak fraz epi ekri mo objektif ki konplete fraz la kòrèkteman.

6. The antique compass rose is pointing _____.

7. Ashley is going to mop the kitchen _____.

8. It is difficult to remove the bottle's _____.

9. Children are not allowed to plug in electric _____.

10. The college students are living in small _____ rooms.

Name: _____ Date:___/___/_____ Score:_____

Lesson 15.9

Reading Words with a Silent Letter "o"

✓ **Lesson Check Point**

 Directions: Read the target words in the word box. Write the words that have a silent letter "o" in the first column. Write the words that do not have a silent letter "o" in the second column.

Direksyons: Li mo objektif yo ki nan ti bwat mo a. Ekri mo yo ki genyen lèt "o" ki pa pwononse a nan premye kolòn nan. Ekri mo yo ki pa genyen lèt "o" ki pa pwononse a nan dezyèm kolòn nan.

Target Word Box				
phoenix	holds	leopard	Phoenician	Leonard
jeopardy	people	tops	locker	costly
come	short	phone	grown	subpoena
long	colonel	subpoenas	jeopardize	town

Letter "o" is silent	Letter "o" has a letter "o" sound
_____	_____
_____	_____
_____	_____
_____	_____
_____	_____
_____	_____
_____	_____
_____	_____

Name: _____ Date: ___/___/_____ Score: _____

Unit Review - O/o

Reading Words with Vowel "o" Sounds: /ŏ/, /ō/, /ə/ & Silent

✓ **Lesson Check Point**

Directions: Read each target word. Circle the word in the column that has the same "o" sound as the target word.

Direksyons: Li chak mo objektif. Antoure mo a ki nan kolòn nan ki bay menm son "o" a tankou mo objektif la.

| shopping | a. document |
| | b. phone |

| oldest | a. poster |
| | b. join |

| propel | a. rocking |
| | b. produce |

| leopard | a. jeopardy |
| | b. jockey |

Directions: Read each target word. Put a check (✓) under the correct column heading.

Direksyons: Li chak mo objektif. Mete yon tchèk (✓) anba antèt kolòn ki kòrèk la.

Target Words	"o" has the /ŏ/ sound as in the word <u>frog</u>	"o" has the /ō/ sound as in the word <u>go</u>	"o" has the /ə/ sound as in the word <u>carrot</u>	"o" is silent as in the word <u>people</u>
1. oldest				
2. propel				
3. leopard				
4. shopping				

Name: _____ Date: ___/___/_____ Score: _____

The Reading Challenge

Lesson 15.10

Reading Multisyllable Words

✓ **Lesson Check Point**

 Directions: Read and divide each target word into syllables. Write each word and place a hyphen (-) between the syllables in the second column. Write the number of syllables in the third column. Use a dictionary or the Internet to check your answers.

Direksyons: Li epi divize chak mo objektif an silab. Ekri chak mo epi mete yon tirè (-) ant silab yo nan dezyèm kolòn nan. Ekri kantite silab ke yo genyen an nan twazyèm kolòn nan. Itilize yon diksyonè oubyen entènèt pou tcheke repons ou yo.

Target Words	Words Divided into Syllables	Number of Syllables
1. aloe	_____	_____
2. poetry	_____	_____
3. cohort	_____	_____
4. pointer	_____	_____
5. toiletry	_____	_____
6. border	_____	_____
7. forestry	_____	_____
8. normal	_____	_____
9. looking	_____	_____
10. avoiding	_____	_____

Unit O
Lesson 15.10

Learn to Read English With Directions In Haitian Creole

Name: _____ Date: ___/___/_____ Score: _____

The Reading Challenge

Lesson 15.10

Reading Multisyllable Words

✓ Lesson Check Point

Directions: Read each target word. Circle the word in the row that is divided correctly into syllables. Use a dictionary or the Internet to check your answers.

Direksyons: Li chak mo objektif. Antoure mo a ki nan ranje a ki divize an silab korèkteman yo. Itilize yon diksyonè oubyen entènèt pou tcheke repons ou yo.

Model

| proposal | a. prop-o-sal | b. pro-po-sal | c. pro-pos-al |

| 1. conductor | a. cond-u-ctor | b. con-duc-tor | c. con-duct-or |

| 2. emperor | a. em-pe-ror | b. em-per-or | c. e-mper-or |

| 3. northerner | a. nor-ther-ner | b. north-e-rner | c. north-ern-er |

| 4. counselor | a. cou-nsel-or | b. coun-sel-or | c. couns-e-lor |

| 5. janitor | a. jan-i-tor | b. jan-it-or | c. ja-nit-or |

| 6. discover | a. di-scov-er | b. dis-cov-er | c. dis-co-ver |

| 7. royalty | a. roy-al-ty | b. roy-alt-y | c. ro-yal-ty |

| 8. jeopardy | a. jeo-par-dy | b. je-opar-dy | c. jeop-ard-y |

Name: _____ Date: ___/___/_____ Score: _____

Lesson 15.11

Reading and Writing

Proper and Common Nouns and Adjectives

Directions: Read the words in the word box. Put an (X) on the line next to each word that is written incorrectly. Remember that all proper nouns and proper adjectives are capitalized. Use a dictionary or the Internet to check your answers.

Direksyons: Li chak mo yo ki nan bwat mo a. Met yon (X) sou ti trè a ki bò kote mo ki pa kri byen yo. Sonje ke tout non pwòp ak adjektif pwop ekri avèk yon lèt majiskil nan kòmansman yo. Itilize yon diksyonè oubyen entènèt pou tcheke repons ou yo.

Word Box		
__ oman	__ oregon Trail	__ Old French
__ Olympian	__ oceanside, NY	__ oort cloud
__ opening	__ occupant	__ otherwise
__ october	__ Omelet	__ observant

Directions: Read each unedited sentence and underline the word that is written incorrectly. Write each sentence correctly on the line.

Direksyons: Li chak fraz ki pa edite yo epi soulinye mo ki pa ekri byen an. Ekri chak fraz korèkteman sou liy lan.

Model
At <u>One</u> o'clock, the Owens family went to Onega Bay.
<u>At one o'clock, the Owens family went to Onega Bay.</u>

1. My friend, Odessa, is reading an Outstanding book.
_____

2. Dr. Orin's objective is to strengthen Olivia's Optic nerves.
_____

3. The governor of oregon had a meeting at the Oval Office.
_____

4. In October, Mr. O'Keeffe's class will read about the Indian ocean.
_____

Name: _____ Date: ___/___/_____ Score: _____

Lesson 16.1

Reading Words with the Letter P/p

✓ Lesson Check Point

Directions: Read each target word. Find the letter "p" and put a check (✓) in the column that identifies its position: beginning, within or end.
Direksyons: Li chak mo objektif. Jwenn lèt "p" a epi mete yon tchèck (✓) nan kolòn ki idantifye pozisyon li an: nan kòmansman, ladan oubyen nan finisman.

Target Words	Beginning (First Letter)	Within	End (Last Letter)
1. tap			
2. stop			
3. parrots			
4. captain			
5. napkin			

Directions: Read each sentence and underline the words that begin with the letter "p." Write all the underlined words in alphabetical order on the lines below.
Direksyons: Li chak fraz epi soulinye mo ki kòmanse avèk lèt "p" yo. Ekri tout mo ki soulinye yo nan lòd alfabetik sou trè sa yo ki anba.

6. Grandma is packing her purple suitcase.

7. The young girls have pretty pink dresses.

8. My report is in a clear plastic folder for protection.

9. Janice is buying peppers at Pathmark Supermarket.

10. The people are eating chicken and corn at the picnic.

_____   _____   _____
_____   _____   _____
_____   _____   _____
              _____

Name: _____ Date: ___/___/_____ Score: _____

Lesson 16.2

Reading Words with the "ph" Letter Combination

✓ Lesson Check Point

Directions: Read each target word. Circle the word in the column that has the same "ph" sound(s) as the target word.

Direksyons: Li chak mo objektif. Antoure mo a ki nan kolòn nan ki bay menm son "ph" la (yo) tankou mo objektif la.

pamphlet	a. phrases
	b. upheaval

phonics	a. shepherd
	b. phobia

biographical	a. upholstery
	b. phony

haphazard	a. uphold
	b. physicist

Directions: Read each target word. Put a check (✓) under the correct column heading.

Direksyons: Li chak mo objektif. Mete yon tchèk (✓) anba antèt kolòn ki kòrèk la.

Target Words	"ph" has the /f/ sound as in the word <u>phone</u>	"ph" has the /p/ +/h/ sounds as in the word <u>uphill</u>
1. pamphlet		
2. phonics		
3. biographical		
4. haphazard		

Name: _____ Date:___/___/_____ Score:_____

Lesson 16.3

Reading Words with the "pr" Letter Combination

Dictionary Skills/ Vocabulary

✓ Lesson Check Point

Directions: Read each target word and its definition. Write the letter of the definition on the line of each target word. Use a dictionary or the Internet to check your answers.

Direksyons: Li chak mo objektif ak definisyon yo chak. Ekri lèt la ki koresponn ak definisyon an sou trè chak mo objektif yo. Itilize yon diksyonè oubyen entènèt pou tcheke repons ou yo.

Target Words	Definitions
1. __ predict	a. a school for students from the age of 3 to 5
2. __ preschool	b. a difficult situation or conflict
3. __ prepare	c. the amount of money something costs
4. __ price	d. to get ready
5. __ problem	e. to say or guess that something will happen

Directions: Read each sentence and write the target word that correctly completes the sentence.
Direksyons: Li chak fraz epi ekri mo objektif ki konplete fraz la kòrèkteman.

6. After ten absences, Pat developed an attendance _____.

7. Good readers _____ the events of a story.

8. During the sale, Pat bought the car for half _____.

9. The _____ students are on a class trip.

10. Peter has to _____ dinner for the presidential ball.

Name: _____   Date: ___/___/_____   Score: _____

Lesson 16.4

Reading Words with the "pl" Letter Combination

Dictionary Skills/ Vocabulary

✓ **Lesson Check Point**

Directions: Read each target word and its definition. Write the target word on the line in front of its meaning. Use a dictionary or the Internet to check your answers.

Direksyons: Li chak mo objektif ak definisyon yo chak. Ekri mo objektif la sou trè ki devan definisyon li an. Itilize yon diksyonè oubyen entènèt pou tcheke repons ou yo.

Target Word Box				
players	platinum	plentiful	pluck	plywood

1. _____ a valuable silvery-white transition metal
2. _____ a large amount of something
3. _____ to pull and release strings on an instrument
4. _____ individuals involved in a game or sport
5. _____ pressed wood that forms a solid piece of wood

Directions: Read each sentence. Underline the word in the parentheses that correctly completes each sentence. Then, write the underlined word on the line.

Direksyons: Li chak fraz. Soulinye mo a ki nan parantèz yo ki konplete chak fraz kòrèkteman. Answit, ekri mo soulinye a sou trè a.

6. The house was built with _____. (platinum, plywood)

7. I will buy a _____ chain as a gift for Peter. (pluck, platinum)

8. The plums are _____ at harvest time. (players, plentiful)

9. My school's baseball team has six strong _____. (players, pluck)

10. The violinists will _____ their strings in harmony. (pluck, platinum)

 Name: _____ Date: ___/___/_____ Score: _____

Lesson 16.4

Reading Words with the "ple" Letter Combination

✓ **Lesson Check Point**

Directions: Read each target word. Find the "ple" letter combination and put a check (✓) in the column that identifies its position: beginning, within or end.

Direksyons: Li chak mo objektif. Jwenn konbinezon lèt "ple" a epi mete yon tchèk (✓) nan kolòn nan ki idantifye pozisyon li an: nan kòmansman, ladan oubyen nan finisman.

Target Words	Beginning (First 3 Letters)	Within	End (Last 3 Letters)
1. people			
2. ripple			
3. pledge			
4. deplete			
5. temple			

Directions: Read each target word. Put a check (✓) in the "yes" column if the "ple" letter combination has the /p/ + /ə/ + /l/ sounds. Put a check (✓) in the "no" column if the "ple" letter combination does not have the /p/ + /ə/ + /l/ sounds.

Direksyons: Li chak mo objektif. Mete yon tchèk (✓) nan kolòn "yes" an si konbinezon let "ple" a bay sons /p/ + /ə/ + /l/. Mete yon tchèk (✓) nan kolòn "no" an si konbinezon let "ple" a pa bay sons /p/ + /ə/ + /l/.

Target Words	Yes	No
6. people		
7. ripple		
8. pledge		
9. deplete		
10. temple		

Name: _____ Date: ___/___/_____ Score: _____

Lesson 16.5

Reading Words with a Silent Letter "p"

✓ **Lesson Check Point**

Directions: Read the target words in the word box. Write the words that have a silent letter "p" in the first column. Write the words that do not have a silent letter "p" in the second column.

Direksyons: Li mo objektif yo ki nan ti bwat mo a. Ekri mo yo ki genyen lèt "p" ki pa pwononse a nan premye kolòn nan. Ekri mo yo ki pa genyen lèt "p" ki pa pwononse a nan dezyèm kolòn nan.

Target Word Box				
maps	receipt	period	raspberry	depot
psychology	adapt	camping	flips	rapid
happy	cupboard	psycho	comprised	coup
psychotic	places	approach	pneumonia	repeat

Letter "p" is silent

_____
_____
_____
_____
_____
_____
_____
_____

Letter "p" has the /p/ sound

_____
_____
_____
_____
_____
_____
_____
_____

Name: _____ Date: ___/___/_____ Score: _____

The Reading Challenge

Lesson 16.6

Reading Multisyllable Words

✓ **Lesson Check Point**

Directions: Read and divide each target word into syllables. Write each word and place a hyphen (-) between the syllables in the second column. Write the number of syllables in the third column. Use a dictionary or the Internet to check your answers.

Direksyons: Li epi divize chak mo objektif an silab. Ekri chak mo epi mete yon tirè (-) ant silab yo nan dezyèm kolòn nan. Ekri kantite silab ke yo genyen an nan twazyèm kolòn nan. Itilize yon diksyonè oubyen entènèt pou tcheke repons ou yo.

Target Words	Words Divided into Syllables	Number of Syllables
1. plaza	_____	_____
2. partner	_____	_____
3. printer	_____	_____
4. plentiful	_____	_____
5. permit	_____	_____
6. poem	_____	_____
7. procedure	_____	_____
8. perfection	_____	_____
9. program	_____	_____
10. prodigy	_____	_____

Name: _____ Date:___/___/_____ Score: _____

The Reading Challenge

Lesson 16.6

Reading Multisyllable Words

✓ **Lesson Check Point**

 Directions: Read each target word. Circle the word in the row that is divided correctly into syllables. Use a dictionary or the Internet to check your answers.

Direksyons: Li chak mo objektif. Antoure mo a ki nan ranje a ki divize an silab korèkteman yo. Itilize yon diksyonè oubyen entènèt pou tcheke repons ou yo.

Model

paragraph	a. par-a-graph (circled)	b. pa-ra-graph	c. par-ag-raph

1. potato	a. po-tat-o	b. pot-a-to	c. po-ta-to
2. papaya	a. pa-pa-ya	b. pa-pay-a	c. pap-a-ya
3. parachute	a. pa-ra-chute	b. par-a-chute	c. par-ach-ute
4. principal	a. princ-i-pal	b. prin-cip-al	c. prin-ci-pal
5. politics	a. pol-i-tics	b. po-li-ti-cs	c. pol-it-ics
6. pendulum	a. pend-u-lum	b. pen-du-lum	c. pen-dul-um
7. percentage	a. per-cen-tage	b. perc-ent-age	c. per-cent-age
8. pesticide	a. pes-ti-cide	b. pest-i-cide	c. pes-tic-ide

Learn to Read English With Directions In Haitian Creole

Name: _____ Date:___/___/_____ Score:_____

Lesson 16.7

Reading and Writing

Proper and Common Nouns and Adjectives

Directions: Read the words in the word box. Put an (X) on the line next to each word that is written incorrectly. Remember that all proper nouns and proper adjectives are capitalized. Use a dictionary or the Internet to check your answers.

Direksyons: Li chak mo yo ki nan bwat mo a. Met yon (X) sou ti trè a ki bò kote mo ki pa kri byen yo. Sonje ke tout non pwòp ak adjektif pwop ekri avèk yon lèt majiskil nan kòmansman yo. Itilize yon diksyonè oubyen entènèt pou tcheke repons ou yo.

Word Box		
__ Principal	__ Port of Spain	__ plumber
__ Poland	__ Plaintiff	__ princess Grace
__ Pilot	__ pitcher	__ pedestrian
__ puerto Rico	__ President	__ Paris

Directions: Read each unedited sentence and underline the word that is written incorrectly. Write each sentence correctly on the line.

Direksyons: Li chak fraz ki pa edite yo epi soulinye mo ki pa ekri byen an. Ekri chak fraz korèkteman sou liy lan.

Model
The poem, "puddles," was written by Patrick Parker.
The poem, "Puddles," was written by Patrick Parker.

1. Pat has a panamanian passport in her handbag.
   _____

2. peter will bring plums and peaches to the picnic.
   _____

3. Mr. Paul is the President of the perfume company.
   _____

4. The Palmer family is having a picnic in Prospect park.
   _____

Name: _____   Date: ___/___/_____   Score: _____

Lesson 17.1

Reading Words with the Letter Q/q

✓ Lesson Check Point

Directions: Read each target word. Find the letter "q" and put a check (✓) in the column that identifies its position: beginning, within or end.
Direksyons: Li chak mo objektif. Jwenn lèt "q" a epi mete yon tchèck (✓) nan kolòn ki idantifye pozisyon li an: nan kòmansman, ladan oubyen nan finisman.

Target Words	Beginning (First Letter)	Within	End (Last Letter)
1. Iraq			
2. tranquil			
3. requested			
4. conquest			
5. quicksand			

Directions: Read each sentence and underline the words that begin with the letter "q." Write all the underlined words in alphabetical order on the lines below.
Direksyons: Li chak fraz epi soulinye mo ki kòmanse avèk lèt "q" yo. Ekri tout mo ki soulinye yo nan lòd alfabetik sou trè sa yo ki anba.

6. Quincy ran quickly across the finish line.

7. It is quicker to travel to Qatar by plane than by boat.

8. The coaches quarreled about the quarterback's penalty.

9. We completed a questionnaire about the joy of quilting.

10. The supervisor asked Quinn about his qualifications for the job.

_____   _____   _____
_____   _____   _____
_____   _____   _____
                _____

Name: _____ Date:___/___/_____ Score:_____

Lesson 17.2

Reading Words with the Letter "q" and "qu" Letter Combination

✓ **Lesson Check Point**

Directions: Read each target word. Circle the word in the column that has the same "q" or "qu" sound(s) as the target word.

Direksyons: Li chak mo objektif. Antoure mo a ki nan kolòn nan ki bay menm son "q" oubyen "qu" a (yo) tankou mo objektif la.

antique	a. quit
	b. opaque

aquatic	a. equator
	b. Qatar

opaque	a. boutique
	b. quicken

question	a. Iraq
	b. quarterly

Directions: Read each target word. Put a check (✓) under the correct column heading.

Direksyons: Li chak mo objektif. Mete yon tchèk (✓) anba antèt kolòn ki kòrèk la.

Target Words	"qu" has the /k/ sound as in the word <u>plaque</u>	"qu" has the /k/ + /w/ sounds as in the word <u>queen</u>
1. antique		
2. aquatic		
3. opaque		
4. question		

Name: _____ Date: ___/___/_____ Score: _____

Lesson 17.2

Reading Words with the "qu" Letter Combination

✓ Lesson Check Point

Directions: Read each target word. Circle the word in the column that has the same "qu" sound(s) as the target word.

Direksyons: Li chak mo objektif. Antoure mo a ki nan kolòn nan ki bay menm son "qu" a (yo) tankou mo objektif la.

antiquity	a. bequest
	b. antiques

uniquely	a. boutiques
	b. inquiry

lacquer	a. racquet
	b. consequent

squeeze	a. equalized
	b. opaque

Directions: Read each target word. Put a check (✓) under the correct column heading.

Direksyons: Li chak mo objektif. Mete yon tchèk (✓) anba antèt kolòn ki kòrèk la.

Target Words	"qu" has the /k/ + /w/ sounds as in the word **queen**	"qu" has the /k/ sound as in the word **plaque**	"qu" is silent as in the word **racquet**
1. antiquity			
2. uniquely			
3. lacquer			
4. squeeze			

Name: _____ Date: ___/___/_____ Score: _____

The Reading Challenge

Lesson 17.3

Reading Multisyllable Words

✓ **Lesson Check Point**

Directions: Read and divide each target word into syllables. Write each word and place a hyphen (-) between the syllables in the second column. Write the number of syllables in the third column. Use a dictionary or the Internet to check your answers.

Direksyons: Li epi divize chak mo objektif an silab. Ekri chak mo epi mete yon tirè (-) ant silab yo nan dezyèm kolòn nan. Ekri kantite silab ke yo genyen an nan twazyèm kolòn nan. Itilize yon diksyonè oubyen entènèt pou tcheke repons ou yo.

Target Words	Words Divided into Syllables	Number of Syllables
1. quoting	_____	_____
2. quietly	_____	_____
3. qualifies	_____	_____
4. quandary	_____	_____
5. quarterly	_____	_____
6. questioned	_____	_____
7. quenching	_____	_____
8. quarterback	_____	_____
9. qualifying	_____	_____
10. quadriplegic	_____	_____

Name: _____ Date:___/___/_____ Score:_____

The Reading Challenge

Lesson 17.3

Reading Multisyllable Words

✓ **Lesson Check Point**

 Directions: Read each target word. Circle the word in the row that is divided correctly into syllables. Use a dictionary or the Internet to check your answers.

Direksyons: Li chak mo objektif. Antoure mo a ki nan ranje a ki divize an silab korèkteman yo. Itilize yon diksyonè oubyen entènèt pou tcheke repons ou yo.

Model

| quarter | a. quart-er | b. quar-ter | c. qu-arter |

| 1. qualify | a. qua-li-fy | b. qual-i-fy | c. qua-lif-y |

| 2. quartet | a. quar-tet | b. qu-ar-tet | c. quar-t-et |

| 3. quantity | a. qua-nti-ty | b. quan-ti-ty | c. quan-tit-y |

| 4. quickly | a. quick-ly | b. qui-ck-ly | c. qu-ick-ly |

| 5. quandary | a. quan-da-ry | b. quan-dar-y | c. quand-a-ry |

| 6. queasy | a. qu-ea-sy | b. que-a-sy | c. quea-sy |

| 7. quintet | a. quin-tet | b. quint-et | c. qu-intet |

| 8. quintuple | a. quin-tu-ple | b. quin-tup-le | c. quint-u-ple |

Name: _____ Date: ___/___/_____ Score: _____

Lesson 17.4

Reading and Writing

Proper and Common Nouns and Adjectives

Directions: Read the words in the word box. Put an (X) on the line next to each word that is written incorrectly. Remember that all proper nouns and proper adjectives are capitalized. Use a dictionary or the Internet to check your answers.

Direksyons: Li chak mo yo ki nan bwat mo a. Met yon (X) sou ti trè a ki bò kote mo ki pa kri byen yo. Sonje ke tout non pwòp ak adjektif pwop ekri avèk yon lèt majiskil nan kòmansman yo. Itilize yon diksyonè oubyen entènèt pou tcheke repons ou yo.

Word Box		
__ quintet	__ Quizzed	__ Qatar
__ Quebec	__ Queen	__ queen Anne
__ Quilted	__ quesadilla	__ quickened
__ queens, NY	__ Quarterly	__ quirky

Directions: Read each unedited sentence and underline the word that is written incorrectly. Write each sentence correctly on the line.

Direksyons: Li chak fraz ki pa edite yo epi soulinye mo ki pa ekri byen an. Ekri chak fraz korèkteman sou liy lan.

Model
Today's quiz is about the <u>queen</u> of England and her monarchy.
<u>Today's quiz is about the Queen of England and her monarchy.</u>

1. The quarterly payments were made by quincy.
   _____

2. I heard the ducks quack loudly at the queens Zoo.
   _____

3. queenie puts a question mark at the end of her sentence.
   _____

4. Mr. and Mrs. quill are eating quiche and quail for dinner.
   _____

Name: _____ Date: ___/___/_____ Score: _____

Lesson 18.1

Reading Words with the Letter R/r

✓ Lesson Check Point

Directions: Read each target word. Find the letter "r" and put a check (✓) in the column that identifies its position: beginning, within or end.
Direksyons: Li chak mo objektif. Jwenn lèt "r" a epi mete yon tchèck (✓) nan kolòn ki idantifye pozisyon li an: nan kòmansman, ladan oubyen nan finisman.

Target Words	Beginning (First Letter)	Within	End (Last Letter)
1. rabbit			
2. lawyer			
3. hammer			
4. converse			
5. deodorant			

Directions: Read each sentence and underline the words that begin with the letter "r." Write all the underlined words in alphabetical order on the lines below.
Direksyons: Li chak fraz epi soulinye mo ki kòmanse avèk lèt "r" yo. Ekri tout mo ki soulinye yo nan lòd alfabetik sou trè sa yo ki anba.

6. The long rope is in George's rowboat.

7. The park rangers are listening to the radio.

8. At the restaurant, I ate pasta and roast beef.

9. Josiah and his friends ran up the ramp quickly.

10. The residents of Georgetown recycle their plastic bottles.

_____   _____   _____
_____   _____   _____
_____   _____   _____
               _____

Name: _____ Date:___/___/_____ Score:_____

Lesson 18.2

Reading Words with the Letter "r" Combinations: "br," "cr," "dr," "fr," "gr," "pr" and "tr"

✓ Lesson Check Point

Directions: Read the target words in the word box. Identify the words with the following letter combinations: "br," "cr," "dr," "fr," "gr," "pr" and "tr." Write the target word on the line that correctly completes each sentence.

Direksyons: Li chak mo objektif yo ki nan bwat mo a. Idantifye mo yo ki gen konbinezon lèt: "br," "cr," "dr," "fr," "gr," "pr" ak "tr" yo. Ekri mo objektif la sou liy nan ki konplete korèkteman fraz la.

Target Word Box			
traded	group	project	fries
trace	fragrance		grocery
breakfast	crossing		drive

1. Mary brushes her teeth after eating _____.

2. Troy and Brandon _____ their baseball cards.

3. This month, Trevor is learning to _____ a car.

4. Brenda and Francis are _____ the street safely.

5. Brad's science _____ received the first place prize.

6. Brenda smells the _____ of the expensive perfume.

7. Trisha can _____ her ancestry back two hundred years.

8. Grace's food truck serves hamburgers and French _____.

9. The _____ of students went on an exciting school trip.

10. Last night, Gloria and Fred had bread and grapes in their _____ cart.

Name: _____ Date: ___/___/_____ Score: _____

The Reading Challenge

Lesson 18.3

Reading Multisyllable Words

✓ Lesson Check Point

Directions: Read and divide each target word into syllables. Write each word and place a hyphen (-) between the syllables in the second column. Write the number of syllables in the third column. Use a dictionary or the Internet to check your answers.

Direksyons: Li epi divize chak mo objektif an silab. Ekri chak mo epi mete yon tirè (-) ant silab yo nan dezyèm kolòn nan. Ekri kantite silab ke yo genyen an nan twazyèm kolòn nan. Itilize yon diksyonè oubyen entènèt pou tcheke repons ou yo.

Target Words	Words Divided into Syllables	Number of Syllables
1. rebel	_____	_____
2. recess	_____	_____
3. razors	_____	_____
4. radar	_____	_____
5. rocker	_____	_____
6. revision	_____	_____
7. reason	_____	_____
8. rainfall	_____	_____
9. recently	_____	_____
10. righteously	_____	_____

Name: _____ Date: ___/___/_____ Score: _____

The Reading Challenge

Lesson 18.3

Reading Multisyllable Words

✓ Lesson Check Point

Directions: Read each target word. Circle the word in the row that is divided correctly into syllables. Use a dictionary or the Internet to check your answers.

Direksyons: Li chak mo objektif. Antoure mo a ki nan ranje a ki divize an silab korèkteman yo. Itilize yon diksyonè oubyen entènèt pou tcheke repons ou yo.

Model

| runaway | a. ru-na-way | b. run-a-way (circled) | c. run-aw-ay |

| 1. retainer | a. re-tain-er | b. ret-ain-er | c. re-tai-ner |

| 2. revolting | a. re-volt-ing | b. rev-olt-ing | c. rev-ol-ting |

| 3. radio | a. ra-di-o | b. rad-i-o | c. ra-dio |

| 4. royalty | a. roya-lt-y | b. roy-al-ty | c. ro-ya-lty |

| 5. rewarding | a. rew-ard-ing | b. re-war-ding | c. re-ward-ing |

| 6. routinely | a. rou-tine-ly | b. rout-ine-ly | c. rout-in-ely |

| 7. radiate | a. rad-i-ate | b. ra-dia-te | c. ra-di-ate |

| 8. refugee | a. ref-ug-ee | b. re-fug-ee | c. ref-u-gee |

Name: _____ Date: ___/___/_____ Score: _____

Lesson 18.4

Reading and Writing

Proper and Common Nouns and Adjectives

Directions: Read the words in the word box. Put an (X) on the line next to each word that is written incorrectly. Remember that all proper nouns and proper adjectives are capitalized. Use a dictionary or the Internet to check your answers.

Direksyons: Li chak mo yo ki nan bwat mo a. Met yon (X) sou ti trè a ki bò kote mo ki pa kri byen yo. Sonje ke tout non pwòp ak adjektif pwop ekri avèk yon lèt majiskil nan kòmansman yo. Itilize yon diksyonè oubyen entènèt pou tcheke repons ou yo.

Word Box		
__ Rapid City	__ King ramses	__ Racetrack
__ romania	__ Road	__ Rembrandt
__ romeo and Juliet	__ redemption	__ receptionist
__ river	__ Rome	__ Rectangle

Directions: Read each unedited sentence and underline the word that is written incorrectly. Write each sentence correctly on the line.

Direksyons: Li chak fraz ki pa edite yo epi soulinye mo ki pa ekri byen an. Ekri chak fraz korèkteman sou liy lan.

Model
We saw two <u>Retired</u> racehorses at Richardson Ranch.
<u>We saw two retired racehorses at Richardson Ranch.</u>

1. I met rosalind at Rutherford's Roller Rink.
_____

2. Mr. and Mrs. remfort bought a new Rolls Royce.
_____

3. raymond is the chief radiologist at Rock Hospital.
_____

4. Did you know ronald Reagan was an American president?
_____

Name: _____ Date: ___/___/_____ Score: _____

Lesson 19.1

Reading Words with the Letter S/s

✓ Lesson Check Point

Directions: Read each target word. Find the letter "s" and put a check (✓) in the column that identifies its position: beginning, within or end.
Direksyons: Li chak mo objektif. Jwenn lèt "s" a epi mete yon tchèck (✓) nan kolòn ki idantifye pozisyon li an: nan kòmansman, ladan oubyen nan finisman.

Target Words	Beginning (First Letter)	Within	End (Last Letter)
1. seven			
2. astonish			
3. pockets			
4. consider			
5. signify			

Directions: Read each sentence and underline the words that begin with the letter "s." Write all the underlined words in alphabetical order on the lines below.
Direksyons: Li chak fraz epi soulinye mo ki kòmanse avèk lèt "s" yo. Ekri tout mo ki soulinye yo nan lòd alfabetik sou trè sa yo ki anba.

6. I am shopping for a silk dress.

7. Randy is singing at the seaport.

8. Jim and Samuel are eating sandwiches.

9. The students stood in the long line for lunch.

10. The senators are working in the state office building.

_____   _____   _____

_____   _____   _____

_____   _____   _____

_____

Unit S
Lesson 19.1

Name: _____ Date: ___/___/_____ Score: _____

Lesson 19.1

Reading Words with the Letter S/s

✓ Lesson Check Point

Directions: Read each target word. Circle the word in the column that has the same "s" sound as the target word.

Direksyons: Li chak mo objektif. Antoure mo a ki nan kolòn nan ki bay menm son "s" a tankou mo objektif la.

boys	a. delicious
	b. busy

television	a. story
	b. pleasure

issued	a. computers
	b. assuring

increase	a. resident
	b. impulse

Directions: Read each target word. Put a check (✓) under the correct column heading.

Direksyons: Li chak mo objektif. Mete yon tchèk (✓) anba antèt kolòn ki kòrèk la.

Target Words	"s" has the /s/ sound as in the word <u>sun</u>	"s" has the /sh/ sound as in the word <u>sugar</u>	"s" has the /z/ sound as in the word <u>his</u>	"s" has the /zh/ sound as in the word <u>vision</u>
1. boys				
2. television				
3. issued				
4. increase				

Name: _____ Date:___/___/_____ Score:_____

Lesson 19.2

Reading Words with the "sion," "sial" & "scious" Suffixes

✓ Lesson Check Point

 Directions: Read each target word. Circle the word in the column that has the same "sion," "sial" or "scious" sound as the target word.

Direksyons: Li chak mo objektif. Antoure mo a ki nan kolòn nan ki bay menm son "sion", "sial" oubyen "scious" yo tankou mo objektif la.

| profession | a. extension |
| | b. division |

| admission | a. television |
| | b. impression |

| luscious | a. controversial |
| | b. conscious |

| inclusion | a. mansion |
| | b. decision |

 Directions: Read each target word. Put a check (✓) under the correct column heading.

Direksyons: Li chak mo objektif. Mete yon tchèk (✓) anba antèt kolòn ki kòrèk la.

Target Words	"sion" has the /sh/ +/ə/+/n/ sounds as in the word <u>passion</u>	"sion" has the /zh/ +/ə/+/n/ sounds as in the word <u>vision</u>	"scious" has the /sh/ +/ə/+/s/ sounds as in the word <u>conscious</u>
1. profession			
2. admission			
3. luscious			
4. inclusion			

Name: _____ Date: ___/___/_____ Score: _____

Lesson 19.3

Reading Words with the "sch" Letter Combination

✓ Lesson Check Point

Directions: Read each target word. Circle the word in the column that has the same "sch" sound(s) as the target word.
Direksyons: Li chak mo objektif. Antoure mo a ki nan kolòn nan ki bay menm son "sch" la (yo) tankou mo objektif la.

schmooze	a. schematic
	b. schillings

scholarly	a. schooner
	b. schmuck

schematic	a. school
	b. schilling

schwa	a. scholar
	b. schmear

Directions: Read each target word. Put a check (✓) under the correct column heading.
Direksyons: Li chak mo objektif. Mete yon tchèk (✓) anba antèt kolòn ki kòrèk la.

Target Words	"sch" has the /s/ + /k/ sounds as in the word school	"sch" has the /sh/ sound as in the word schilling
1. schmooze		
2. scholarly		
3. schematic		
4. schwa		

Name: _____ Date:___/___/_____ Score:_____

Lesson 19.4

Reading Words with the "scr," "shr," "spr" & "str" Letter Combinations

Dictionary Skills/ Vocabulary

✓ **Lesson Check Point**

Directions: Read each target word and its definition. Write the letter of the definition on the line of each target word. Use a dictionary or the Internet to check your answers.

Direksyons: Li chak mo objektif ak definisyon yo chak. Ekri lèt la ki koresponn ak definisyon an sou trè chak mo objektif yo. Itilize yon diksyonè oubyen entènèt pou tcheke repons ou yo.

Target Words	Definitions
1. __ sprout	a. the process of becoming smaller
2. __ screamed	b. the physical ability to carry or lift heavy objects
3. __ shrink	c. a tiny, shelled sea animal
4. __ strong	d. the early stage of a plant
5. __ shrimp	e. to have made a loud piercing sound

Directions: Read each sentence. Underline the word in the parentheses that correctly completes each sentence. Then, write the underlined word on the line.

Direksyons: Li chak fraz. Soulinye mo a ki nan parantèz yo ki konplete chak fraz kòrèkteman. Answit, ekri mo soulinye a sou trè a.

6. In the spring, my seeds will start to _____. (sprout, strong)

7. The excess heat caused my sweater to _____. (sprout, shrink)

8. Sam's seafood platter has _____ and lobster. (strong, shrimp)

9. She _____ when the patient fell off the bed. (screamed, shrink)

10. The _____ girl lifted a sixty-pound weight. (screamed, strong)

Name: _____ Date: ___/___/_____ Score: _____

Lesson 19.5

Reading Words with the "sl" & "sle" Letter Combinations

Dictionary Skills/ Vocabulary

✓ Lesson Check Point

Directions: Read each target word and its definition. Write the target word on the line in front of its meaning. Use a dictionary or the Internet to check your answers.

Direksyons: Li chak mo objektif ak definisyon yo chak. Ekri mo objektif la sou trè ki devan definisyon li an. Itilize yon diksyonè oubyen entènèt pou tcheke repons ou yo.

Target Word Box				
slapped	slash	slender	slipped	slur

1. _____ to speak unclearly
2. _____ the past tense of the verb, to slip
3. _____ small, thin or slim
4. _____ to have put something down quickly with force
5. _____ to make a major reduction; to make prices lower

Directions: Read each sentence. Underline the word in the parentheses that correctly completes each sentence. Then, write the underlined word on the line.

Direksyons: Li chak fraz. Soulinye mo a ki nan parantèz yo ki konplete chak fraz kòrèkteman. Answit, ekri mo soulinye a sou trè a.

6. Sue started to _____ her words before falling asleep. (slender, slur)

7. During the holidays, prices are _____ in half. (slapped, slashed)

8. She won the election by a _____ margin. (slipped, slender)

9. Yesterday, a student _____ on the wet floor. (slipped, slashed)

10. Stan _____ the slip of paper on the table. (slapped, slur)

Name: _____   Date: ___/___/_____   Score: _____

Lesson 19.5

Reading Words with the "sle" Letter Combination

✓ Lesson Check Point

Directions: Read each target word. Find the "sle" letter combination and put a check (✓) in the column that identifies its position: beginning, within or end.

Direksyons: Li chak mo objektif. Jwenn konbinezon lèt "sle" a epi mete yon tchèk (✓) nan kolòn nan ki idantifye pozisyon li an: nan kòmansman, ladan oubyen nan finisman.

Target Words	Beginning (First 3 Letters)	Within	End (Last 3 Letters)
1. aisle			
2. asleep			
3. sleet			
4. hassle			
5. tussle			

Directions: Read each target word. Put a check (✓) in the "yes" column if the "sle" letter combination has the /s/ + /ə/ + /l/ or /z/ + /ə/ + /l/ sounds. Put a check (✓) in the "no" column if the "sle" letter combination does not have the /s/ + /ə/ + /l/ or /z/ + /ə/ + /l/ sounds.

Direksyons: Li chak mo objektif. Mete yon tchèk (✓) nan kolòn "yes" an si konbinezon lèt "sle" a bay sons /s/ + /ə/ + /l/ oubyen /z/ + /ə/ + /l/ sounds. Mete yon tchèk (✓) nan kolòn "no" an si konbinezon lèt "sle" a pa bay sons /s/ + /ə/ + /l/ oubyen /z/ + /ə/ + /l/ sounds.

Target Words	Yes	No
6. aisle		
7. asleep		
8. sleet		
9. hassle		
10. tussle		

Name: _____ Date: ___/___/_____ Score: _____

Lesson 19.6

Reading Words with the "sm" Letter Combination

✓ Lesson Check Point

Directions: Read each target word. Circle the word in the column that has the same "sm" sounds as the target word.

Direksyons: Li chak mo objektif. Antoure mo a ki nan kolòn nan ki bay menm son "sm" yo tankou mo objektif la.

tourism	a. bilingualism
	b. cosmetology

newsman	a. cynicism
	b. bridesmaid

capitalism	a. charismatic
	b. enthusiasm

dismember	a. bridesmaid
	b. mismatch

Directions: Read each target word. Put a check (✓) under the correct column heading.

Direksyons: Li chak mo objektif. Mete yon tchèk (✓) anba antèt kolòn ki kòrèk la.

Target Words	"sm" has the /s/ + /m/ sounds as in the word smell	"sm" has the /z/ + /m/ sounds as in the word cosmic	"sm" has the /z/ + /ə/ + /m/ sounds as in the word autism
1. tourism			
2. newsman			
3. capitalism			
4. dismember			

Name: _____ Date: ___/___/_____ Score: _____

Lesson 19.7

Reading Words with the "ss" Letter Combination

✓ Lesson Check Point

Directions: Read each target word. Circle the word in the column that has the same "ss" sound(s) as the target word.

Direksyons: Li chak mo objektif. Antoure mo a ki nan kolòn nan ki bay menm son "ss" la (yo) tankou mo objektif la.

concussion	a. expressing
	b. expression

compassion	a. aggression
	b. aggressive

misstated	a. dissatisfaction
	b. massive

Missouri	a. dissolve
	b. concession

Directions: Read each target word. Put a check (✓) under the correct column heading.

Direksyons: Li chak mo objektif. Mete yon tchèk (✓) anba antèt kolòn ki kòrèk la.

Target Words	"ss" has the /sh/ sound as in the word tissue	"ss" has the /s/ + /s/ sounds as in the word misspell	"ss" has the /z/ sound as in the word dissolve
1. concussion			
2. compassion			
3. misstated			
4. Missouri			

Name: _____ Date: ___/___/_____ Score: _____

Lesson 19.8

Reading Words with a Silent Letter "s"

✓ **Lesson Check Point**

Directions: Read the target words in the word box. Write the words that have a silent letter "s" in the first column. Write the words that do not have a silent letter "s" in the second column.

Direksyons: Li mo objektif yo ki nan ti bwat mo a. Ekri mo yo ki genyen lèt "s" ki pa pwononse a nan premye kolòn nan. Ekri mo yo ki pa genyen lèt "s" ki pa pwononse a nan dezyèm kolòn nan.

Target Word Box				
bless	apropos	bunches	fossil	debris
extends	islet	houses	actress	shower
ears	smooth	likes	graders	wipes
isle	comprise	aisle	assert	islands

Letter "s" is silent

_____
_____
_____
_____
_____
_____
_____
_____

Letter "s" has the /s/, /z/ or /sh/ sound

_____
_____
_____
_____
_____
_____
_____
_____

Name: _____   Date: ___/___/_____   Score: _____

The Reading Challenge

Lesson 19.9

Reading Multisyllable Words

✓ Lesson Check Point

Directions: Read and divide each target word into syllables. Write each word and place a hyphen (-) between the syllables in the second column. Write the number of syllables in the third column. Use a dictionary or the Internet to check your answers.

Direksyons: Li epi divize chak mo objektif an silab. Ekri chak mo epi mete yon tirè (-) ant silab yo nan dezyèm kolòn nan. Ekri kantite silab ke yo genyen an nan twazyèm kolòn nan. Itilize yon diksyonè oubyen entènèt pou tcheke repons ou yo.

Target Words	Words Divided into Syllables	Number of Syllables
1. single		
2. setup		
3. secretly		
4. Scotland		
5. servicing		
6. secondary		
7. sculpture		
8. sectional		
9. saturated		
10. slenderized		

Name: _____ Date: ___/___/_____ Score: _____

The Reading Challenge

Lesson 19.9

Reading Multisyllable Words

✓ **Lesson Check Point**

Directions: Read each target word. Circle the word in the row that is divided correctly into syllables. Use a dictionary or the Internet to check your answers.

Direksyons: Li chak mo objektif. Antoure mo a ki nan ranje a ki divize an silab korèkteman yo. Itilize yon diksyonè oubyen entènèt pou tcheke repons ou yo.

Model

| Saturday | a. Sa-tur-day | b. Sat-ur-day | c. Sa-turd-ay |

| 1. signify | a. sig-nif-y | b. sig-ni-fy | c. sign-i-fy |

| 2. solution | a. sol-u-tion | b. so-lut-ion | c. so-lu-tion |

| 3. secular | a. se-cul-ar | b. sec-u-lar | c. se-cu-lar |

| 4. simulate | a. si-mu-late | b. sim-u-late | c. si-mul-ate |

| 5. solitude | a. sol-i-tude | b. so-li-tude | c. so-lit-ude |

| 6. saliva | a. sa-liv-a | b. sa-l-iva | c. sa-li-va |

| 7. selection | a. se-lect-ion | b. sel-ect-ion | c. se-lec-tion |

| 8. satiate | a. sa-ti-ate | b. sat-i-ate | c. sa-tia-te |

Name: _____ Date:___/___/_____ Score:_____

Lesson 19.10

Reading and Writing

Proper and Common Nouns and Adjectives

Directions: Read the words in the word box. Put an (X) on the line next to each word that is written incorrectly. Remember that all proper nouns and proper adjectives are capitalized. Use a dictionary or the Internet to check your answers.

Direksyons: Li chak mo yo ki nan bwat mo a. Met yon (X) sou ti trè a ki bò kote mo ki pa kri byen yo. Sonje ke tout non pwòp ak adjektif pwop ekri avèk yon lèt majiskil nan kòmansman yo. Itilize yon diksyonè oubyen entènèt pou tcheke repons ou yo.

Word Box		
__ september	__ Sergeant sam	__ san Francisco
__ siamese cat	__ sunday	__ sextuplet
__ semester	__ senator	__ Saturn
__ Senegal	__ scotland	__ San Jose

Directions: Read each unedited sentence and underline the word that is written incorrectly. Write each sentence correctly on the line.

Direksyons: Li chak fraz ki pa edite yo epi soulinye mo ki pa ekri byen an. Ekri chak fraz korèkteman sou liy lan.

Model
The <u>Seafood</u> is sensational at Salton Restaurant!
<u>The seafood is sensational at Salton Restaurant!</u>

1. silverfish is a staple in the Senegalese diet.
_____

2. In science class, I am studying the planet saturn.
_____

3. The local silversmith, Sam, is moving to san Juan.
_____

4. My sister, Cindy, is the newly elected State senator.
_____

Name: _____ Date: ___/___/_____ Score: _____

Lesson 20.1

Reading Words with the Letter T/t

✓ **Lesson Check Point**

Directions: Read each target word. Find the letter "t" and put a check (✓) in the column that identifies its position: beginning, within or end.

Direksyons: Li chak mo objektif. Jwenn lèt "t" a epi mete yon tchèck (✓) nan kolòn ki idantifye pozisyon li an: nan kòmansman, ladan oubyen nan finisman.

Target Words	Beginning (First Letter)	Within	End (Last Letter)
1. today			
2. drift			
3. jacket			
4. partner			
5. telephone			

Directions: Read each sentence and underline the words that begin with the letter "t." Write all the underlined words in alphabetical order on the lines below.

Direksyons: Li chak fraz epi soulinye mo yo ki kòmanse avèk lèt "t" a. Ekri tout mo ki souliye yo nan lòd alfabetik sou trè sa yo ki anba.

6. Tonight, Susan has a very painful toothache.

7. My art teacher drew baby turtles on canvas.

8. My teammate, Fred, received an athletic trophy.

9. Stacey is brushing her teeth with a new toothbrush.

10. In Santo Domingo, a major thunderstorm is scheduled for Tuesday.

_____   _____   _____
_____   _____   _____
_____   _____   _____
                _____

Learn to Read English With Directions In Haitian Creole

Name: _____ Date: ___/___/_____ Score: _____

Lesson 20.2

Reading Words with the "thm" Letter Combination

✓ Lesson Check Point

 Directions: Read each target word. Circle the word in the column that has the same "thm" sound(s) as the target word.

Direksyons: Li chak mo objektif. Antoure mo a ki nan kolòn nan ki bay menm son "thm" la (yo) tankou mo objektif la.

biorhythm	a. logarithm
	b. birthmarks

isthmus	a. asthma
	b. rhythms

birthmark	a. asthmatic
	b. bathmats

algorithm	a. antilogarithm
	b. isthmian

 Directions: Read each target word. Put a check (✓) under the correct column heading.

Direksyons: Li chak mo objektif. Mete yon tchèk (✓) anba antèt kolòn ki kòrèk la.

Target Words	"thm" has the /th/ + /ə/ + /m/ sounds as in the word rhythm	"thm" has the /th/ + /m/ sounds as in the word bathmat	"thm" silent "th" + /m/ sound as in the word asthma
1. biorhythm			
2. birthmark			
3. isthmus			
4. algorithm			

Name: _____ Date: ___/___/_____ Score: _____

Lesson 20.3

Reading Words with the "tion," "tial" & "tious" Suffixes

✓ Lesson Check Point

Directions: Read each target word. Circle the word in the column that has the same "tion," "tial" or "tious" sound as the target word.

Direksyons: Li chak mo objektif. Antoure mo a ki nan kolòn nan ki bay menm son "tion", "tial" oubyen "tious" yo tankou mo objektif la.

essential	a. initially
	b. election

competition	a. audition
	b. ambitious

equation	a. bumptious
	b. compilation

cautious	a. inflation
	b. conscientious

Directions: Read each target word. Put a check (✓) under the correct column heading.

Direksyons: Li chak mo objektif. Mete yon tchèk (✓) anba antèt kolòn ki kòrèk la.

Target Words	"tion" has the /sh/ +/ə/+/n/ sounds as in the word <u>education</u>	"tial" has the /sh/ +/ə/+/l/ sounds as in the word <u>partial</u>	"tious" has the /sh/ +/ə/+/s/ sounds as in the word <u>ambitious</u>
1. essential			
2. competition			
3. equation			
4. cautious			

Name: _____ Date:___/___/_____ Score:_____

Lesson 20.4

Reading Words with the "tr" Letter Combination

Dictionary Skills/ Vocabulary

✓ **Lesson Check Point**

Directions: Read each target word and its definition. Write the letter of the definition on the line of each target word. Use a dictionary or the Internet to check your answers.

Direksyons: Li chak mo objektif ak definisyon yo chak. Ekri lèt la ki koresponn ak definisyon an sou trè chak mo objektif yo. Itilize yon diksyonè oubyen entènèt pou tcheke repons ou yo.

Target Words	Definitions
1. __ transcript	a. doctor's care designed to relieve or cure a disease
2. __ tray	b. performance designed to display athletic skills
3. __ treatment	c. a record of grades and classes taken at a school
4. __ trouble	d. a firm surface used to carry things
5. __ tryouts	e. to go out of one's way, to do a little extra

Directions: Read each sentence. Underline the word in the parentheses that correctly completes each sentence. Then, write the underlined word on the line.

Direksyons: Li chak fraz. Soulinye mo a ki nan parantèz yo ki konplete chak fraz kòrèkteman. Answit, ekri mo soulinye a sou trè a.

6. I requested my college _____. (treatment, transcript)

7. Trent placed his food on a clean _____. (tray, tryouts)

8. She is scheduled to have a medical _____. (treatment, tray)

9. The team is having _____ for new players. (tryouts, trouble)

10. I took the _____to write the names on tags. (transcript, trouble)

 Name: _____ Date: ___/___/_____ Score: _____

Lesson 20.5

Reading Words with the "tle" Letter Combination

✓ **Lesson Check Point**

 Directions: Read each target word. Find the "tle" letter combination and put a check (✓) in the column that identifies its position: beginning, within or end.

Direksyons: Li chak mo objektif. Jwenn konbinezon lèt "tle" a epi mete yon tchèk (✓) nan kolòn nan ki idantifye pozisyon li an: nan kòmansman, ladan oubyen nan finisman.

Target Words	Beginning (First 3 Letters)	Within	End (Last 3 Letters)
1. turtle			
2. little			
3. cutlet			
4. bustle			
5. heartless			

 Directions: Read each target word. Put a check (✓) in the "yes" column if the "tle" letter combination has the /t/ + /ə/ + /l/ sounds. Put a check (✓) in the "no" column if the "tle" letter combination does not have the /t/ + /ə/ + /l/ sounds.

Direksyons: Li chak mo objektif. Mete yon tchèk (✓) nan kolòn "yes" an si konbinezon let "tle" a bay sons /t/ + /ə/ + /l/. Mete yon tchèk (✓) nan kolòn "no" an si konbinezon let "tle" a pa bay sons /t/ + /ə/ + /l/.

Target Words	Yes	No
6. turtle		
7. little		
8. cutlet		
9. bustle		
10. heartless		

Name: _____ Date: ___/___/_____ Score: _____

Lesson 20.6

Reading Words with the Letter "t" Sounds

✓ **Lesson Check Point**

Directions: Read each target word. Circle the word in the column that has the same "t" sound as the target word.

Direksyons: Li chak mo objektif. Antoure mo a ki nan kolòn nan ki bay menm son "t" a tankou mo objektif la.

agriculture	a. acting
	b. immature

adjunct	a. connect
	b. denture

expectancy	a. factor
	b. action

unrighteous	a. acting
	b. actuality

Directions: Read each target word. Put a check (✓) under the correct column heading.

Direksyons: Li chak mo objektif. Mete yon tchèk (✓) anba antèt kolòn ki kòrèk la.

Target Words	"t" has the /t/ sound as in the word <u>multiply</u>	"t" has the /ch/ sound as in the word <u>picture</u>	"t" has the /sh/ sound as in the word <u>position</u>
1. agriculture			
2. adjunct			
3. expectancy			
4. unrighteous			

Name: _____ Date: ___/___/_____ Score: _____

Lesson 20.7

Reading Words with a Silent Letter "t"

✓ **Lesson Check Point**

Directions: Read the target words in the word box. Write the words that have a silent letter "t" in the first column. Write the words that do not have a silent letter "t" in the second column.

Direksyons: Li mo objektif yo ki nan ti bwat mo a. Ekri mo yo ki genyen lèt "t" ki pa pwononse a nan premye kolòn nan. Ekri mo yo ki pa genyen lèt "t" ki pa pwononse a nan dezyèm kolòn nan.

Target Word Box				
appointment	listeners	conflict	depot	cutting
debut	dependent	testing	empty	gourmet
mortgage	tactile	soften	different	street
decorate	castle	moisten	little	transform

Letter "t" is silent

_____
_____
_____
_____
_____
_____
_____
_____

Letter "t" has the /t/ sound

_____
_____
_____
_____
_____
_____
_____
_____

Name: _____ Date: ___/___/_____ Score: _____

The Reading Challenge

Lesson 20.8

Reading Multisyllable Words

✓ **Lesson Check Point**

Directions: Read and divide each target word into syllables. Write each word and place a hyphen (-) between the syllables in the second column. Write the number of syllables in the third column. Use a dictionary or the Internet to check your answers.

Direksyons: Li epi divize chak mo objektif an silab. Ekri chak mo epi mete yon tirè (-) ant silab yo nan dezyèm kolòn nan. Ekri kantite silab ke yo genyen an nan twazyèm kolòn nan. Itilize yon diksyonè oubyen entènèt pou tcheke repons ou yo.

Target Words	Words Divided into Syllables	Number of Syllables
1. ticket	_____	_____
2. table	_____	_____
3. twinkle	_____	_____
4. textual	_____	_____
5. totality	_____	_____
6. takeover	_____	_____
7. trumpeting	_____	_____
8. teenagers	_____	_____
9. Thursday	_____	_____
10. throughout	_____	_____

Name: _____ Date:___/___/_____ Score:_____

The Reading Challenge

Lesson 20.8

Reading Multisyllable Words

✓ **Lesson Check Point**

 Directions: Read each target word. Circle the word in the row that is divided correctly into syllables. Use a dictionary or the Internet to check your answers.

Direksyons: Li chak mo objektif. Antoure mo a ki nan ranje a ki divize an silab korèkteman yo. Itilize yon diksyonè oubyen entènèt pou tcheke repons ou yo.

Model

| telephone | a. te-lep-hone | b. tel-e-phone | c. te-le-phone |

| 1. talkative | a. ta-lka-tive | b. talk-at-ive | c. talk-a-tive |

| 2. tolerance | a. to-ler-ance | b. tol-er-ance | c. tol-e-rance |

| 3. therapy | a. ther-ap-y | b. the-rap-y | c. ther-a-py |

| 4. tabletop | a. ta-ble-top | b. tab-le-top | c. ta-blet-op |

| 5. thermostat | a. ther-mo-stat | b. the-rmos-tat | c. ther-mos-tat |

| 6. trimester | a. tri-mes-ter | b. tri-mest-er | c. trim-es-ter |

| 7. telecast | a. te-le-cast | b. te-lec-ast | c. tel-e-cast |

| 8. trainable | a. trai-nab-le | b. train-a-ble | c. tra-ina-ble |

Name: _____ Date: ___/___/_____ Score: _____

Lesson 20.9

Reading and Writing

Proper and Common Nouns and Adjectives

Directions: Read the words in the word box. Put an (X) on the line next to each word that is written incorrectly. Remember that all proper nouns and proper adjectives are capitalized. Use a dictionary or the Internet to check your answers.

Direksyons: Li chak mo yo ki nan bwat mo a. Met yon (X) sou ti trè a ki bò kote mo ki pa kri byen yo. Sonje ke tout non pwòp ak adjektif pwop ekri avèk yon lèt majiskil nan kòmansman yo. Itilize yon diksyonè oubyen entènèt pou tcheke repons ou yo.

Word Box		
__ Trunk	__ trinidad	__ track
__ traffic	__ Texas	__ Thailand
__ truck	__ towel	__ Train
__ togo	__ Trick	__ thursday

Directions: Read each unedited sentence and underline the word that is written incorrectly. Write each sentence correctly on the line.

Direksyons: Li chak fraz ki pa edite yo epi soulinye mo ki pa ekri byen an. Ekri chak fraz korèkteman sou liy lan.

Model
Tracy named her beautiful <u>Twin</u> daughters Tia and Tina.
Tracy named her beautiful twin daughters Tia and Tina.

1. this year, thousands of tourists will visit Turkey.
   _____

2. My favorite television show is "The twilight Zone."
   _____

3. The assigned Textbook is entitled "Today's Technology".
   _____

4. I ordered a Tender T-bone steak at the Turkish restaurant.
   _____

Name: _____ Date:___/___/_____ Score:_____

Lesson 21.1

Reading Words with the Letter U/u

✓ Lesson Check Point

 Directions: Read each target word. Find the letter "u" and put a check (✓) in the column that identifies its position: beginning, within or end.
Direksyons: Li chak mo objektif. Jwenn lèt "u" a epi mete yon tchèck (✓) nan kolòn ki idantifye pozisyon li an: nan kòmansman, ladan oubyen nan finisman.

Target Words	Beginning (First Letter)	Within	End (Last Letter)
1. upper			
2. Hindu			
3. subject			
4. umpire			
5. haiku			

 Directions: Read each target word. Read the words in the row and circle the word that has a different vowel "u" sound.
Direksyons: Li chak mo objektif. Li mo yo ki nan ranje a epi antoure mo a ki bay yon son vwayèl "u" ki diferan an.

Target Words				
6. plunk	yuck	lull	dung	tune
7. snuff	hunk	cute	chug	hut
8. slung	used	bunt	cud	tub
9. husk	muck	snug	prune	bunk
10. buses	under	jump	quick	unzip

Name: _____ Date: ___/___/_____ Score: _____

Lesson 21.2

Reading Words with the Short Vowel "u" Sound

✓ Lesson Check Point

Directions: Read the words in the four boxes. Circle two words with the short vowel /ŭ/ sound. The anchor word for the short vowel /ŭ/ sound is up.

Direksyons: Li mo yo ki nan kat ti bwat yo. Antoure de mo ki genyen son vwayèl kout /ŭ/ a. Mo referans pou son vwayèl kout /ŭ/ a se mo, up.

lute	club		elude	pulp		dupe	nude
shut	flume		jute	rump		drum	thus

mush	dude		club	fun		plume	plug
spruce	musk		fume	Luke		bus	prude

Directions: Read the words in the four boxes. Circle two words that rhyme. Rhyming words have the same ending sound, such as just and must.

Direksyons: Li mo yo ki nan kat ti bwat yo. Antoure de mo ki rime. De mo oubyen plizyè mo ki rime genyen menm son nan finisman yo, tankou just ak must.

tune	gum		shun	stun		cup	shush
Peru	sum		menu	pluck		ruler	pup

flung	trunk		struck	lunch		truck	guest
sunk	rust		bluff	bunch		chuck	clung

Name: _____ Date: ___/___/_____ Score: _____

Lesson 21.2

Reading & Writing Words with the Short Vowel "u" Sound

✓ **Lesson Check Point**

Directions: Read each sentence and underline three words with the short vowel /ŭ/ sound. Then, write the underlined words on the lines below. The anchor word for the short vowel /ŭ/ sound is <u>up</u>.

Direksyons: Li chak fraz epi soulinye twa mo ki genyen son vwayèl kout /ŭ/ a. Answit, ekri mo soulinye yo sou trè sa yo ki anba. Mo referans pou son vwayèl kout /ŭ/a se mo, <u>up</u>.

Model
Ulysses, the <u>drummer</u>, <u>jumps</u> when he plays the <u>drums</u>.

    drummer   jumps   drums
    _____   _____   _____

1. Do not run with a mug or cup in your hands.

    _____   _____   _____

2. In June, it is fun to take the bus to the reading club.

    _____   _____   _____

3. Duke's puppy used to run up and down the ramp.

    _____   _____   _____

4. I noticed that my student's muffin had crushed nuts.

    _____   _____   _____

5. As Luke rushed for the bus, he started to run very fast.

    _____   _____   _____

Learn to Read English With Directions In Haitian Creole

Name: _____ Date: ___/___/_____ Score: _____

Lesson 21.3

Reading Words with the Long Vowel "u" Sound

✓ Lesson Check Point

 Directions: Read the words in the four boxes. Circle two words with the long vowel /yoo/ or /oo/ sound. The anchor word for the long vowel /yoo/ and /oo/ sounds is <u>tube</u>.

Direksyons: Li mo yo ki nan kat ti bwat yo. Antoure de mo ki genyen son vwayèl long /yoo/ oubyen /oo/ a. Mo referans pou son vwayèl long /yoo/ ak /oo/ es la palabra, <u>tube</u>.

trunk	hue		argue	circuit		hutch	Luke
attitude	jumper		such	mule		skull	ritual

avenue	fuse		plush	costume		annual	punch
flush	guess		flung	perfume		surely	commute

 Directions: Read the words in the four boxes. Circle two words that rhyme. Rhyming words have the same ending sound, such as <u>rule</u> and <u>mule</u>.

Direksyons: Li mo yo ki nan kat ti bwat yo. Antoure de mo ki rime. De mo oubyen plizyè mo ki rime genyen menm son nan finisman yo, tankou <u>rule</u> ak <u>mule</u>.

cube	pluck		spruce	truce		chuck	rescue
chunk	tube		skunk	slung		crush	avenue

consume	shush		usual	gradual		abuse	strung
presume	bluff		pushing	struck		suckling	amuse

Name: _____   Date: ___/___/_____   Score: _____

Lesson 21.3

Reading & Writing Words with the Long Vowel "u" Sound

✓ Lesson Check Point

Directions: Read each sentence and underline three words with the long vowel /y$\overline{oo}$/ or /$\overline{oo}$/ sound. Then, write the underlined words on the lines below. The anchor word for the long vowel /y$\overline{oo}$/ and /$\overline{oo}$/ sounds is tube.

Direksyons: Li chak fraz epi soulinye twa mo ki genyen son vwayèl long /y$\overline{oo}$/ oubyen /$\overline{oo}$/ yo. Answit, ekri mo soulinye yo sou trè sa yo ki anba. Mo referans pou son vwayèl long /y$\overline{oo}$/ ak /$\overline{oo}$/ es la palabra, tube.

Model

Bruce is going to play the tuba and drums in Uganda.

　　Bruce　　　　　　　tuba　　　　　　　Uganda
　_____　　_____　　_____

1. My trees usually produce an abundance of fruits.

　_____　　_____　　_____

2. In June, Eugene and his family will have fun in Yugoslavia.

　_____　　_____　　_____

3. Sue was fortunate to ride the cute mule around the farm.

　_____　　_____　　_____

4. It is unacceptable to have a rude, crude attitude with adults.

　_____　　_____　　_____

5. Destiny told Ursula to reduce the amount of perfume she uses.

　_____　　_____　　_____

Name: _____   Date: ___/___/_____   Score: _____

Review Lessons 21.2 & 21.3

Reading Short Vowel and Long Vowel Words

Directions: Read the target words in the word box. In the first column, write the words that have the short vowel /ŭ/ sound, as in the word <u>up</u>. In the second column, write the words that have the long vowel /yōō/ or /ōō/ sound, as in the word <u>tube</u>.

Direksyons: Li mo yoobjektif yo ki nan bwat mo a. Nan premye kolòn nan, ekri mo ki bay son vwayèl kout /ŭ/ yo, tankou li ye nan mo <u>up</u> la. Nan dezyèm kolòn nan, ekri mo ki bay son vwayèl long /yōō/ oubyen /ōō/, yo, tankou li ye nan mo <u>tube</u> la.

Target Word Box				
absolute	dispute	gradual	bluffing	hunch
crushing	produce	punch	bugle	duel
slushy	munch	exclude	sucking	include
consume	skunk	much	avenue	stump

Letter "u" has the /ŭ/ sound as in the word <u>up</u>	Letter "u" has the /yōō/ or /ōō/ sound as in the word <u>tube</u>

Name: _____ Date: ___/___/_____ Score: _____

Lesson 21.4

Reading Words with Letter "u" Vowel Pairs

✓ **Lesson Check Point**

Directions: Read each target word. Circle the word in the column that has the same vowel "ua," "ue" or "ui" sound(s) as the target word.

Direksyons: Li chak mo objektif. Antoure mo a ki nan kolòn nan ki bay menm son vwayèl "ua," "ue" oubyen "ui" la (yo) tankou mo objektif la.

pursuit	a. blue
	b. individual

avenue	a. visual
	b. suitor

virtually	a. punctual
	b. nuisance

suitcase	a. flue
	b. residual

Directions: Read each target word. Put a check (✓) under the correct column heading.

Direksyons: Li chak mo objektif. Mete yon tchèk (✓) anba antèt kolòn ki kòrèk la.

Target Words	Words have the long "u" sound as in the word <u>blue</u>	Words do not have the long "u" sound
1. dual		
2. built		
3. suite		
4. influence		

Name: _____ Date: ___/___/_____ Score: _____

Lesson 21.5

Reading Words with the Final Letter "u"

✓ Lesson Check Point

Directions: Read each target word. Find the letter "u" and put a check (✓) in the column that identifies its position within the syllable.
Direksyons: Li chak mo objektif. Jwenn lèt "u" a epi mete yon tchèck (✓) nan kolòn nan ki idantifye pozisyon li an nan silab la.

Target Words	"u" is at the end of a one syllable word	"u" is at the end of the first syllable	"u" is at the end of a multi-syllable word
1. flu			
2. dual			
3. unify			
4. usual			
5. mutual			

Directions: Read each target word. Put a check (✓) under the correct column heading.
Direksyons: Li chak mo objektif. Mete yon tchèk (✓) anba antèt kolòn ki kòrèk la.

Target Words	"u" has the /ŭ/ sound as in the word tub	"u" has the /yōō/ sound as in the word tube	"u" has the /ə/ sound as in the word circus	"u" is silent as in the word build
6. built				
7. mule				
8. jump				
9. until				
10. surprise				

Name: _____ Date: ___/___/_____ Score: _____

Lesson 21.6

Reading Letter "u" Words with the Schwa Vowel Sound

✓ Lesson Check Point

Directions: Read each target word. Circle the word in the column that has the same "u" sound as the target word.

Direksyons: Li chak mo objektif. Antoure mo a ki nan kolòn nan ki bay menm son "u" a tankou mo objektif la.

adjust	a. murmur
	b. umbrella

supply	a. suggest
	b. subject

radius	a. playful
	b. until

lawful	a. surround
	b. true

Directions: Read each sentence and underline the letter "u" word that has the schwa vowel /ə/ sound. The anchor word for the letter "u" schwa vowel sound is <u>campus</u>.

Direksyons: Li chak fraz epi soulinye mo ki genyen lèt "u" a ki bay son schwa /ə/. Mo referans pou son schwa lèt "u" a se mo, <u>campus</u>.

1. The popular students attend Utah University.

2. The beautiful flowers enhance the house's value.

3. Gus was unable to determine the radius of a circle.

4. My family and I used to visit the Yucatan Peninsula.

5. My university professor worked in the music industry.

6. The security guards monitor the cameras on a regular basis.

Name: _____ Date:___/___/_____ Score:_____

Lesson 21.7

Reading Words with the "ur" Letter Combination

Dictionary Skills/ Vocabulary

✓ Lesson Check Point

Directions: Read each target word and its definition. Write the letter of the definition on the line of each target word. Use a dictionary or the Internet to check your answers.

Direksyons: Li chak mo objektif ak definisyon yo chak. Ekri lèt la ki koresponn ak definisyon an sou trè chak mo objektif yo. Itilize yon diksyonè oubyen entènèt pou tcheke repons ou yo.

Target Words	Definitions
1. __ curls	a. destroyed and/or consumed by fire
2. __ burned	b. something of high importance
3. __ curse	c. the act of not succeeding
4. __ urgent	d. the act of twisting something into coils
5. __ failure	e. to say bad words or swear

Directions: Read each sentence and write the target word on the line that correctly completes the sentence.
Direksyons: Li chak fraz epi ekri mo objektif ki konplete fraz la kòrèkteman.

6. At two o'clock, I received an _____ phone call.

7. Successful people believe _____ is not an option.

8. My hair _____ up when the weather is humid.

9. It is not acceptable to _____ in class.

10. We are going out for dinner because Dad _____ the chicken.

Name: _____ Date: ___/___/_____ Score: _____

Lesson 21.8

Reading Words with a Silent Letter "u"

✓ **Lesson Check Point**

Directions: Read the target words in the word box. Write the words that have a silent letter "u" in the first column. Write the words that do not have a silent letter "u" in the second column.

Direksyons: Li mo objektif yo ki nan ti bwat mo a. Ekri mo yo ki genyen lèt "u" ki pa pwononse a nan premye kolòn nan. Ekri mo yo ki pa genyen lèt "u" ki pa pwononse anan dezyèm kolòn nan.

Target Word Box				
intrigue	student	guest	individual	guardian
continual	guilty	antique	occupy	prologue
argument	brushing	dumpster	guard	drummers
guarded	confusion	technique	lunch	guide

Letter "u" is silent	Letter "u" has a letter "u" sound
_____	_____
_____	_____
_____	_____
_____	_____
_____	_____
_____	_____
_____	_____
_____	_____

Name: _____   Date: ___/___/_____   Score: _____

Unit Review - U/u

Reading Words with Vowel "u" Sounds: /ŭ/, /oo/, /ə/ & Silent

✓ **Lesson Check Point**

Directions: Read each target word. Circle the word in the column that has the same "u" sound as the target word.

Direksyons: Li chak mo objektif. Antoure mo a ki nan kolòn nan ki bay menm son vwayèl "u" atankou mo objektif la.

summer	a. pumping
	b. tissue

Tuesday	a. suitcase
	b. plague

vague	a. cruel
	b. league

support	a. circus
	b. building

Directions: Read each target word. Put a check (✓) under the correct column heading.

Direksyons: Li chak mo objektif. Mete yon tchèk (✓) anba antèt kolòn ki kòrèk la.

Target Words	"u" has the /ŭ/ sound as in the word <u>tub</u>	"u" has the /oo/ sound as in the word <u>tube</u>	"u" has the /ə/ sound as in the word <u>circus</u>	"u" is silent as in the word <u>build</u>
1. summer				
2. Tuesday				
3. vague				
4. support				

Name: _____ Date:___/___/_____ Score:_____

The Reading Challenge

Lesson 21.9

Reading Multisyllable Words

 Lesson Check Point

Directions: Read and divide each target word into syllables. Write each word and place a hyphen (-) between the syllables in the second column. Write the number of syllables in the third column. Use a dictionary or the Internet to check your answers.

Direksyons: Li epi divize chak mo objektif an silab. Ekri chak mo epi mete yon tirè (-) ant silab yo nan dezyèm kolòn nan. Ekri kantite silab ke yo genyen an nan twazyèm kolòn nan. Itilize yon diksyonè oubyen entènèt pou tcheke repons ou yo.

Target Words	Words Divided into Syllables	Number of Syllables
1. juicy	_____	_____
2. album	_____	_____
3. bushes	_____	_____
4. rushing	_____	_____
5. perfume	_____	_____
6. shoulder	_____	_____
7. building	_____	_____
8. tribunal	_____	_____
9. disputing	_____	_____
10. dumpster	_____	_____

Name: _____ Date: ___/___/_____ Score: _____

The Reading Challenge

Lesson 21.9

Reading Multisyllable Words

✓ Lesson Check Point

Directions: Read each target word. Circle the word in the row that is divided correctly into syllables. Use a dictionary or the Internet to check your answers.

Direksyons: Li chak mo objektif. Antoure mo a ki nan ranje a ki divize an silab korèkteman yo. Itilize yon diksyonè oubyen entènèt pou tcheke repons ou yo.

Model

| visualize | a. vis-ua-lize | b. vi-su-al-ize (circled) | c. vis-u-a-lize |

| 1. inclusion | a. in-clu-sion | b. in-clus-ion | c. incl-u-sion |

| 2. excusing | a. ex-cus-ing | b. exc-u-sing | c. ex-cu-sing |

| 3. producing | a. prod-u-cing | b. pro-duc-ing | c. prod-uc-ing |

| 4. residual | a. res-id-ual | b. re-sid-u-al | c. re-sid-ual |

| 5. publishing | a. publ-ish-ing | b. pu-blish-ing | c. pub-lish-ing |

| 6. exclusive | a. e-xclu-sive | b. ex-clu-sive | c. ex-clus-ive |

| 7. presuming | a. pre-sum-ing | b. pres-u-ming | c. pr-esum-ing |

| 8. consonant | a. con-son-ant | b. cons-o-nant | c. con-so-nant |

Name: _____ Date: ___/___/_____ Score: _____

Lesson 21.10

Reading and Writing

Proper and Common Nouns and Adjectives

Directions: Read the words in the word box. Put an (X) on the line next to each word that is written incorrectly. Remember that all proper nouns and proper adjectives are capitalized. Use a dictionary or the Internet to check your answers.

Direksyons: Li chak mo yo ki nan bwat mo a. Met yon (X) sou ti trè a ki bò kote mo ki pa kri byen yo. Sonje ke tout non pwòp ak adjektif pwop ekri avèk yon lèt majiskil nan kòmansman yo. Itilize yon diksyonè oubyen entènèt pou tcheke repons ou yo.

Word Box		
___ Umbria	___ upbringing	___ Ace university
___ upper Canada	___ Ultimately	___ UFO
___ united	___ Uganda	___ Unblock
___ umbrella	___ universal Time	___ Umpire

Directions: Read each unedited sentence and underline the word that is written incorrectly. Write each sentence correctly on the line.

Direksyons: Li chak fraz ki pa edite yo epi soulinye mo ki pa ekri byen an. Ekri chak fraz korèkteman sou liy lan.

Model
Mrs. Ubangi usually has union meetings at a local <u>University</u>.
<u>Mrs. Ubangi usually has union meetings at a local university.</u>

1. Oxford University is located in the united Kingdom.
   _____

2. Last summer, Uncle moved from uganda to the USA.
   _____

3. Did you know that Uncle Udell speaks urdu and Hindi fluently?
   _____

4. Ulric said, "The united States of America has excellent universities."
   _____

Name: _____ Date: ___/___/_____ Score: _____

Lesson 22.1

Reading Words with the Letter V/v

✓ **Lesson Check Point**

Directions: Read each target word. Find the letter "v" and put a check (✓) in the column that identifies its position: beginning, within or end.
Direksyons: Li chak mo objektif. Jwenn lèt "v" a epi mete yon tchèck (✓) nan kolòn ki idantifye pozisyon li an: nan kòmansman, ladan oubyen nan finisman.

Target Words	Beginning (First Letter)	Within	End (Last Letter)
1. vapor			
2. server			
3. violet			
4. violins			
5. provided			

Directions: Read each sentence and underline the words that begin with the letter "v." Write all the underlined words in alphabetical order on the lines below.
Direksyons: Li chak fraz epi soulinye mo ki kòmanse avèk lèt "v" yo. Ekri tout mo ki soulinye yo nan lòd alfabetik sou trè sa yo ki anba.

6. Mr. Samuel was voted volunteer of the month.

7. Ryan placed all the valuables in his bank vault.

8. This fall, Teresa and Bobby plan to visit Vienna.

9. The antagonist in the story, "Vampire's Heart," is vain.

10. My challenging vocabulary words are vertebrate and invertebrate.

_____   _____   _____
_____   _____   _____
_____   _____   _____
                 _____

Name: _____ Date: ___/___/_____ Score: _____

The Reading Challenge

Lesson 22.2

Reading Multisyllable Words

✓ **Lesson Check Point**

Directions: Read and divide each target word into syllables. Write each word and place a hyphen (-) between the syllables in the second column. Write the number of syllables in the third column. Use a dictionary or the Internet to check your answers.

Direksyons: Li epi divize chak mo objektif an silab. Ekri chak mo epi mete yon tirè (-) ant silab yo nan dezyèm kolòn nan. Ekri kantite silab ke yo genyen an nan twazyèm kolòn nan. Itilize yon diksyonè oubyen entènèt pou tcheke repons ou yo.

Target Words	Words Divided into Syllables	Number of Syllables
1. very	_____	_____
2. velvet	_____	_____
3. visible	_____	_____
4. Viking	_____	_____
5. vertical	_____	_____
6. valuable	_____	_____
7. vibrantly	_____	_____
8. voltage	_____	_____
9. visionary	_____	_____
10. validation	_____	_____

Unit V
Lesson 22.2

Name: _____ Date: ___/___/_____ Score: _____

The Reading Challenge

Lesson 22.2

Reading Multisyllable Words

✓ **Lesson Check Point**

Directions: Read each target word. Circle the word in the row that is divided correctly into syllables. Use a dictionary or the Internet to check your answers.

Direksyons: Li chak mo objektif. Antoure mo a ki nan ranje a ki divize an silab korèkteman yo. Itilize yon diksyonè oubyen entènèt pou tcheke repons ou yo.

Model

| volcano | a. vo-lcan-o | b. vol-can-o | c. vol-ca-no (circled) |

1. vehicle	a. ve-hi-cle	b. ve-hic-le	c. veh-i-cle
2. various	a. va-rio-us	b. va-ri-ous	c. var-i-ous
3. vinegar	a. vi-neg-ar	b. vi-ne-gar	c. vin-e-gar
4. ventilate	a. vent-i-late	b. ven-ti-late	c. ven-til-ate
5. violence	a. vi-ol-ence	b. vio-le-nce	c. vi-o-lence
6. vindicate	a. vin-di-cate	b. vin-dic-ate	c. vin-dica-te
7. volition	a. vo-li-tion	b. vol-i-tion	c. vol-it-ion
8. vaporize	a. vap-o-rize	b. va-por-ize	c. vap-or-ize

Name: _____ Date:___/___/_____ Score:_____

Lesson 22.3

Reading and Writing

Proper and Common Nouns and Adjectives

Directions: Read the words in the word box. Put an (X) on the line next to each word that is written incorrectly. Remember that all proper nouns and proper adjectives are capitalized. Use a dictionary or the Internet to check your answers.

Direksyons: Li chak mo yo ki nan bwat mo a. Met yon (X) sou ti trè a ki bò kote mo ki pa kri byen yo. Sonje ke tout non pwòp ak adjektif pwop ekri avèk yon lèt majiskil nan kòmansman yo. Itilize yon diksyonè oubyen entènèt pou tcheke repons ou yo.

Word Box		
__ virgin Islands	__ Verse	__ Venice
__ vibrant	__ Volcano	__ valley Forge
__ Vintage	__ Vermont	__ Vienna
__ Vietnamese	__ villager	__ Visiting

Directions: Read each unedited sentence and underline the word that is written incorrectly. Write each sentence correctly on the line.

Direksyons: Li chak fraz ki pa edite yo epi soulinye mo ki pa ekri byen an. Ekri chak fraz korèkteman sou liy lan.

Model
The villagers in Vienna love to receive Visitors.
The villagers in Vienna love to receive visitors.

1. Valerie Volunteers at General Veterans Hospital.
   _____

2. On Tuesday, vice President Vernon voted on the bill.
   _____

3. My music Video features Voldoff, the professional violinist.
   _____

4. Historians record that the Vikings made strong, seafaring Vessels.
   _____

Name: _____ Date: ___/___/_____ Score: _____

Lesson 23.1

Reading Words with the Letter W/w

✓ Lesson Check Point

Directions: Read each target word. Find the letter "w" and put a check (✓) in the column that identifies its position: beginning, within or end.
Direksyons: Li chak mo objektif. Jwenn lèt "w" a epi mete yon tchèck (✓) nan kolòn ki idantifye pozisyon li an: nan kòmansman, ladan oubyen nan finisman.

Target Words	Beginning (First Letter)	Within	End (Last Letter)
1. unwilling			
2. overview			
3. wishbone			
4. weather			
5. trustworthy			

Directions: Read each sentence and underline the words that begin with the letter "w." Write all the underlined words in alphabetical order on the lines below.
Direksyons: Li chak fraz epi soulinye mo ki kòmanse avèk lèt "w" yo. Ekri tout mo ki soulinye yo nan lòd alfabetik sou trè sa yo ki anba.

6. It is cold and windy in the winter.

7. On Tuesday, they ate watermelon and waffles.

8. The wheelbarrow has a pile of dirt and worms.

9. Samuel bought his watch from the local wholesale store.

10. The weather in Los Angeles, California is generally warm.

_____ _____ _____

_____ _____ _____

_____ _____ _____

_____

Name: _____ Date: ___/___/_____ Score: _____

Lesson 23.2

Reading Words with a Vowel before the Letter "w"

✓ Lesson Check Point

Directions: Read each target word. Circle the word in the column that has the same "aw," "ew" or "ow" sound as the target word.

Direksyons: Li chak mo objektif. Antoure mo a ki nan kolòn nan ki bay menm son vwayèl "aw," "ew" oubyen "ow" la (yo) tankou mo objektif la.

awaiting	a. lawyer
	b. awareness

flowing	a. glowing
	b. plowing

towels	a. powder
	b. throwing

sewn	a. knew
	b. rowing

Directions: Read each target word. Put a check (✓) under the correct column heading.

Direksyons: Li chak mo objektif. Mete yon tchèk (✓) anba antèt kolòn ki kòrèk la.

Target Words	Underlined letters have /o͞o/ sound as in the word <u>few</u>	Underlined letters have /ô/ sound as in the word <u>law</u>	Underlined letters have /ō/ sound as in the word <u>sew</u>	Underlined letters have /ou/ sound as in the word <u>cow</u>
1. f<u>aw</u>n				
2. fl<u>ow</u>ing				
3. t<u>ow</u>els				
4. s<u>ew</u>n				

Name: _____ Date: ___/___/_____ Score: _____

Lesson 23.3

Reading Words with a Silent "w" and "wr" Letter Combination

Dictionary Skills/ Vocabulary

✓ Lesson Check Point

Directions: Read each target word and its definition. Write the letter of the definition on the line of each target word. Use a dictionary or the Internet to check your answers.

Direksyons: Li chak mo objektif ak definisyon yo chak. Ekri lèt la ki koresponn ak definisyon an sou trè chak mo objektif yo. Itilize yon diksyonè oubyen entènèt pou tcheke repons ou yo.

Target Words	Definitions
1. __ wrap	a. incorrect or erroneous
2. __ wrench	b. to move or squirm
3. __ wriggles	c. a tool used to tighten or loosen an object
4. __ wrong	d. to have printed words on a surface or paper
5. __ wrote	e. to fold in a tight covering

Directions: Read each sentence. Underline the word in the parentheses that correctly completes each sentence. Then, write the underlined word on the line.

Direksyons: Li chak fraz. Soulinye mo a in an parantèz yo ki konplete chak fraz kòrèkteman. Answit, ekri mo soulinye a sou trè a.

6. Wendell has a _____ in his toolbox. (wrench, wrote)

7. My favorite author _____ five books. (wrapped, wrote)

8. I accidentally rang the _____ doorbell. (wrong, wrench)

9. I will _____ my sandwich in foil paper. (wriggles, wrap)

10. My baby _____ her fingers when she is happy. (wrong, wriggles)

Name: _____ Date: ___/___/_____ Score: _____

Lesson 23.3

Reading Words with a Silent Letter "w"

✓ **Lesson Check Point**

Directions: Read the target words in the word box. Write the words that have a silent letter "w" in the first column. Write the words that do not have a silent letter "w" in the second column.

Direksyons: Li mo objektif yo in an ti bwat mo a. Ekri mo yo ki genyen lèt "w" ki pa pwononse a nan premye kolòn nan. Ekri mo yo ki pa genyen lèt "w" ki pa pwononse anan dezyèm kolòn nan.

Target Word Box				
two	crow	firewood	waiters	farewell
dwelling	writing	wrap	beware	answering
earwax	biweekly	wreck	window	freeway
tow	sword	driveway	backward	wrote

Letter "w" is silent

_____
_____
_____
_____
_____
_____
_____
_____

Letter "w" has the /w/ sound

_____
_____
_____
_____
_____
_____
_____
_____

Name: _____ Date: ___/___/_____ Score: _____

The Reading Challenge

Lesson 23.4

Reading Multisyllable Words

✓ **Lesson Check Point**

Directions: Read and divide each target word into syllables. Write each word and place a hyphen (-) between the syllables in the second column. Write the number of syllables in the third column. Use a dictionary or the Internet to check your answers.

Direksyons: Li epi divize chak mo objektif an silab. Ekri chak mo epi mete yon tirè (-) ant silab yo nan dezyèm kolòn nan. Ekri kantite silab ke yo genyen an nan twazyèm kolòn nan. Itilize yon diksyonè oubyen entènèt pou tcheke repons ou yo.

Target Words	Words Divided into Syllables	Number of Syllables
1. walrus	_____	_____
2. working	_____	_____
3. wisdom	_____	_____
4. wholesaling	_____	_____
5. wastefulness	_____	_____
6. Washington	_____	_____
7. wanderer	_____	_____
8. watermelon	_____	_____
9. wraparound	_____	_____
10. weatherize	_____	_____

Name: _____ Date: ___/___/_____ Score: _____

The Reading Challenge

Lesson 23.4

Reading Multisyllable Words

✓ **Lesson Check Point**

 Directions: Read each target word. Circle the word in the row that is divided correctly into syllables. Use a dictionary or the Internet to check your answers.

Direksyons: Li chak mo objektif. Antoure mo a ki nan ranje a ki divize an silab korèkteman yo. Itilize yon diksyonè oubyen entènèt pou tcheke repons ou yo.

Model

| wonderful | a. wo-nder-ful | b. won-der-ful | c. won-derf-ul |

| 1. winery | a. wi-ner-y | b. win-er-y | c. win-e-ry |

| 2. Wisconsin | a. Wi-scon-sin | b. Wis-con-sin | c. Wis-cons-in |

| 3. westerner | a. west-er-ner | b. wes-ter-ner | c. west-ern-er |

| 4. whenever | a. whe-nev-er | b. when-ev-er | c. when-e-ver |

| 5. whimsical | a. whim-si-cal | b. whi-msic-al | c. whim-sic-al |

| 6. wilderness | a. wil-der-ness | b. wil-dern-ess | c. wild-er-ness |

| 7. wonderful | a. wond-er-ful | b. won-derf-ul | c. won-der-ful |

| 8. woefulness | a. woef-u-lness | b. woe-ful-ness | c. woe-fuln-ess |

Unit W Lesson 23.4

Learn to Read English With Directions In Haitian Creole   Copyrighted Material

Name: _____ Date: ___/___/_____ Score: _____

Lesson 23.5

Reading and Writing

Proper and Common Nouns and Adjectives

Directions: Read the words in the word box. Put an (X) on the line next to each word that is written incorrectly. Remember that all proper nouns and proper adjectives are capitalized. Use a dictionary or the Internet to check your answers.

Direksyons: Li chak mo yo ki nan bwat mo a. Met yon (X) sou ti trè a ki bò kote mo ki pa kri byen yo. Sonje ke tout non pwòp ak adjektif pwop ekri avèk yon lèt majiskil nan kòmansman yo. Itilize yon diksyonè oubyen entènèt pou tcheke repons ou yo.

Word Box		
__ Window	__ wasteland	__ Walachia
__ West Indies	__ Washington	__ weddell Sea
__ wales	__ whatever	__ Wedding
__ Welsh	__ White rice	__ Webpage

Directions: Read each unedited sentence and underline the word that is written incorrectly. Write each sentence correctly on the line.

Direksyons: Li chak fraz ki pa edite yo epi soulinye mo ki pa ekri byen an. Ekri chak fraz korèkteman sou liy lan.

Model

We walked along the winding path that led to the Waterfalls.
We walked along the winding path that led to the waterfalls.

1. We check the Weather forecast on the World Wide Web.
   _____

2. Warren is wearing a Wool sweater and a pair of gloves.
   _____

3. We saw a walrus and two wildcats at the west Virginia Zoo.
   _____

4. On wednesday, Whitney and her family are going to the water park.
   _____

Name: _____ Date: ___/___/_____ Score: _____

Lesson 24.1

Reading Words with the Letter X/x

✓ **Lesson Check Point**

Directions: Read each target word. Find the letter "x" and put a check (✓) in the column that identifies its position: beginning, within or end.
Direksyons: Li chak mo objektif. Jwenn lèt "x" a epi mete yon tchèck (✓) nan kolòn ki idantifye pozisyon li an: nan kòmansman, ladan oubyen nan finisman.

Target Words	Beginning (First Letter)	Within	End (Last Letter)
1. x-ray			
2. boxer			
3. duplex			
4. examine			
5. xylograph			

Directions: Read each sentence and underline the words that begin with the letter "x." Write all the underlined words in alphabetical order on the lines below.
Direksyons: Li chak fraz epi soulinye mo ki kòmanse avèk lèt "x" yo. Ekri tout mo ki soulinye in an lòd alfabetik sou trè in a ki anba.

6. The xylophonist skillfully plays the xylophone.

7. Xavier said, "The x-axis is perpendicular to the y-axis."

8. I am reading historical details about Xining and Xanthus.

9. There are two brown bottles of xanthine and xanthene in the lab.

10. Xenophilia and xenophily refer to love for people from different cultures.

_____ _____ _____

_____ _____ _____

_____ _____ _____

_____

Learn to Read English With Directions In Haitian Creole

Name: _____ Date: ____/___/____ Score: _____

Lesson 24.1

Reading Words with the Letter X/x

 Lesson Check Point

Directions: Read each target word. Circle the word in the column that has the same "x" sound(s) as the target word.
Direksyons: Li chak mo objektif. Antoure mo a ki nan kolòn nan ki bay menm son "x" yo tankou mo objektif la.

xylography	a. xylophone
	b. relaxation

complexion	a. exhilarate
	b. obnoxious

Oxford	a. saxophone
	b. Malcolm X

exhaustion	a. examination
	b. anxious

 Directions: Read each target word. Put a check (✓) under the correct column heading.
Direksyons: Li chak mo objektif. Mete yon tchèk (✓) anba antèt kolòn ki kòrèk la.

Target Words	"x" has the /k/ + /s/ sounds as in the word <u>box</u>	"x" has the /z/ sound as in the word <u>xylophone</u>	"x" has the /g/ + /z/ sounds as in the word <u>exhibit</u>	"x" has the /k/ + /sh/ sounds as in the word <u>anxious</u>
1. xylography				
2. complexion				
3. Oxford				
4. exhaustion				

Name: _____ Date: ___/___/_____ Score: _____

The Reading Challenge

Lesson 24.2

Reading Multisyllable Words

✓ Lesson Check Point

Directions: Read and divide each target word into syllables. Write each word and place a hyphen (-) between the syllables in the second column. Write the number of syllables in the third column. Use a dictionary or the Internet to check your answers.

Direksyons: Li epi divize chak mo objektif an silab. Ekri chak mo epi mete yon tirè (-) ant silab yo nan dezyèm kolòn nan. Ekri kantite silab ke yo genyen an nan twazyèm kolòn nan. Itilize yon diksyonè oubyen entènèt pou tcheke repons ou yo.

Target Words	Words Divided into Syllables	Number of Syllables
1. climax	_____	_____
2. anxiety	_____	_____
3. waxing	_____	_____
4. fixation	_____	_____
5. expectant	_____	_____
6. remixing	_____	_____
7. xylophone	_____	_____
8. textbooks	_____	_____
9. expanded	_____	_____
10. toxicology	_____	_____

Name: _____ Date:___/___/_____ Score: _____

The Reading Challenge

Lesson 24.2

Reading Multisyllable Words

✓ Lesson Check Point

Directions: Read each target word. Circle the word in the row that is divided correctly into syllables. Use a dictionary or the Internet to check your answers.

Direksyons: Li chak mo objektif. Antoure mo a ki nan ranje a ki divize an silab korèkteman yo. Itilize yon diksyonè oubyen entènèt pou tcheke repons ou yo.

Model

oxidized	a. ox-i-dized (circled)	b. oxi-d-ized	c. o-xi-dized

1. complexion	a. com-plex-ion	b. com-ple-xion	c. co-mple-xion
2. auxiliary	a. au-xi-liary	b. aux-i-liary	c. aux-il-ia-ry
3. excitement	a. exci-te-ment	b. ex-cite-ment	c. exc-ite-ment
4. taxation	a. ta-xa-tion	b. tax-a-tion	c. tax-at-ion
5. examining	a. ex-am-in-ing	b. exam-i-ning	c. exa-min-ing
6. lexicon	a. le-xi-con	b. le-xic-on	c. lex-i-con
7. exporting	a. exp-o-rting	b. exp-or-ting	c. ex-port-ing
8. exclusive	a. excl-u-sive	b. ex-clu-sive	c. ex-clus-ive

Unit X
Lesson 24.2

Name: _____ Date: ___/___/_____ Score: _____

Lesson 24.3

Reading and Writing

Proper and Common Nouns and Adjectives

Directions: Read the words in the word box. Put an (X) on the line next to each word that is written incorrectly. Remember that all proper nouns and proper adjectives are capitalized. Use a dictionary or the Internet to check your answers.

Direksyons: Li chak mo yo ki nan bwat mo a. Met yon (X) sou ti trè a ki bò kote mo ki pa kri byen yo. Sonje ke tout non pwòp ak adjektif pwop ekri avèk yon lèt majiskil nan kòmansman yo. Itilize yon diksyonè oubyen entènèt pou tcheke repons ou yo.

Word Box		
__ Dr. xavier	__ Xingu River	__ xanthus
__ Xerox	__ Xylograph	__ xebec
__ X-rays	__ xanadu	__ xenophiles
__ x-axis	__ Xylophonist	__ xylem

Directions: Read each unedited sentence and underline the word that is written incorrectly. Write each sentence correctly on the line.

Direksyons: Li chak fraz ki pa edite yo epi soulinye mo ki pa ekri byen an. Ekri chak fraz korèkteman sou liy lan.

Model
Xia said, "The population of xankandi is 33,000 people."
Xia said, "The population of Xankandi is 33,000 people."

1. The article noted that Mr. Xavier is a professional Xylophonist.
_____

2. The xingu River in Brazil flows north into the Amazon River.
_____

3. I noticed that Xanthan gum is an ingredient in marshmallows.
_____

4. Mr. and Mrs. xing work for Xerox in the printing department.
_____

Name: _____ Date: ___/___/_____ Score: _____

Lesson 25.1

Reading Words with the Letter Y/y

Directions: Read each target word. Find the letter "y" and put a check (✓) in the column that identifies its position: beginning, within or end.
Direksyons: Li chak mo objektif. Jwenn lèt "y" a epi mete yon tchèck (✓) nan kolòn ki idantifye pozisyon li an: nan kòmansman, ladan oubyen nan finisman.

Target Words	Beginning (First Letter)	Within	End (Last Letter)
1. yeast			
2. factory			
3. deeply			
4. crystals			
5. gymnastic			

Directions: Read each sentence and underline the words that begin with the letter "y." Write all the underlined words in alphabetical order on the lines below.
Direksyons: Li chak fraz epi soulinye mo ki kòmanse avèk lèt "y" yo. Ekri tout mo ki soulinye in an lòd alfabetik sou trè in a ki anba.

6. I bought a roll of yellow yarn.

7. Yesterday, Isaiah was caught yawning in class.

8. Did James watch the New York Yankees' game?

9. All the youngsters are playing in the large yard.

10. Yusef used the yardstick to measure the area of his bedroom.

_____ _____ _____
_____ _____ _____
_____ _____ _____
          _____

Name: _____ Date:___/___/_____ Score:_____

Lesson 25.1

Reading Words with the Letter Y/y

✓ Lesson Check Point

 Directions: Read each target word. Circle the word in the row that has a different "y" sound than the target word.
Direksyons: Li chak mo objektif. Antoure mo a in an ranje a ki bay yon son vwayèl "y" ki diferan an.

Target Words				
1. sycamore	catalyst	analytic	hypnosis	gigabyte
2. yesterday	yielded	papaya	symphony	yonder
3. Kenya	Malaya	yogurt	bicycles	Maya
4. typhoon	typical	types	tycoon	tyrant
5. youngster	baby	yellow	yarn	years

 Directions: Read the words in the four boxes. Circle two words that have the same "y" sound.
Direksyons: Li mo yo in an kat kat ti bwat yo. Antoure de mo ki bay menm son "y" yo.

goodbye	mystery
styling	today

young	argyle
baby	yogurt

syntax	youth
eyelids	analyze

rhyme	hypnosis
you'll	calypso

Kenya	Maya
hype	hyssop

windy	yellow
yardage	syntax

Learn to Read English With Directions In Haitian Creole

Name: _____ Date: ___/___/_____ Score: _____

Lesson 25.2

Reading Words with a Vowel before the Letter "y"

✓ Lesson Check Point

Directions: Read each target word. Circle the word in the column that has the same "y" sound as the target word.

Li chak mo objektif. Antoure mo a ki nan kolòn nan ki bay menm son "y" la tankou mo objektif la.

employed	a. annoying
	b. baby

parley	a. jersey
	b. younger

spraying	a. disobey
	b. yielding

Guyana	a. buying
	b. soliloquy

Directions: Read each target word. Put a check (✓) under the correct column heading.

Direksyons: Li chak mo objektif. Mete yon tchèk (✓) anba antèt kolòn ki kòrèk la.

Target Words	"y" has the /y/ sound as in the word <u>yes</u>	"oy" has the /oi/ sound as in the word <u>boy</u>	"y" has the /ī/ sound as in the word <u>by</u>	"y" is silent as in the word <u>day</u>
1. employed				
2. parley				
3. spraying				
4. Guyana				

Learn to Read English With Directions In Haitian Creole

 Name: _____ Date:___/___/_____ Score:_____

Lesson 25.3

Reading Words with the "cy" Letter Combination

✓ **Lesson Check Point**

 Directions: Read each target word. Find the "cy" letter combination and put a check (✓) in the column to identify its position in the word: beginning, within or end.

Direksyons : Li chak mo objektif. Jwenn konbinezon lèt "cy" laepi mete yon tchèk (✓) nan kolòn nan ki idantifye pozisyon li an : nan kòmansman, ladan oubyen nan finisman.

Target Words	Beginning (First 2 Letters)	Within	End (Last 2 Letters)
1. cystic			
2. Cynthia			
3. Cyprus			
4. currency			
5. policyholder			

 Directions: Read each target word. Put a check (✓) under the correct column heading.

Direksyons: Li chak mo objektif. Mete yon tchèk (✓) anba antèt kolòn ki kòrèk la.

Target Words	"cy" has the /s/ + /ĭ/ sounds as in the word <u>cylinder</u>	"cy" has the /s/ + /ī/ sounds as in the word <u>cycle</u>	"cy" has the /s/ + /ē/ sounds as in the word <u>agency</u>
6. cystic			
7. Cynthia			
8. Cyprus			
9. currency			
10. policyholder			

Name: _____ Date: ___/___/_____ Score: _____

Lesson 25.4

Reading Words with the Final Letter "y"

✓ **Lesson Check Point**

 Directions: Read each target word. Find the letter "y" and put a check (✓) in the column that identifies its position within the word.
Direksyons: Li chak mo objektif. Jwenn lèt "y" la epi mete yon tchèck (✓) nan kolòn nan ki idantifye pozisyon li an nan mo a.

Target Words	"y" is at the end of a one syllable word	"y" is at the end of the first syllable	"y" is at the end of a multi-syllable word
1. fry			
2. happy			
3. melody			
4. cyclone			
5. hydrometer			

 Directions: Read each target word. Put a check (✓) under the correct column heading.
Direksyons: Li chak mo objektif. Mete yon tchèk (✓) anba antèt kolòn ki kòrèk la.

Target Words	"y" has the /ē/ sound as in the word <u>agency</u>	"y" has the /ī/ sound as in the word <u>flying</u>
6. fry		
7. happy		
8. melody		
9. cyclone		
10. hydrometer		

Name: _____ Date: ___/___/_____ Score: _____

Lesson 25.5

Reading Words with the "yr" Letter Combination

✓ Lesson Check Point

 Directions: Read each target word. Circle the word in the column that has the same "yr" sounds as the target word.
Direksyons : Li chak mo objektif. Antoure mo a ki nan kolòn nan ki bay menm son "yr" yo tankou mo objektif la.

| pyrometer | a. tyrannize |
| | b. papyrus |

| myrrh | a. tyranny |
| | b. myrtle |

| syringe | a. gyros |
| | b. martyr |

| lyricist | a. syrup |
| | b. hyrax |

 Directions: Read each target word. Put a check (✓) under the correct column heading.
Direksyons: Li chak mo objektif. Mete yon tchèk (✓) anba antèt kolòn ki kòrèk la.

Target Words	"yr" has the /û/ + /r/ sounds as in the word myrtle	"yr" has the /ĭ/ + /r/ sounds as in the word pyramid	"yr" has the /ī/ + /r/ sounds as in the word gyro	"yr" has the /ə/ + /r/ sounds as in the word martyr
1. myrrh				
2. lyricist				
3. syringe				
4. pyrometer				

Name: _____ Date: ___/___/_____ Score: _____

Lesson 25.6

Reading Letter "y" Words with the Schwa Vowel Sound

✓ Lesson Check Point

Directions: Read each target word. Circle the word in the column that has the same "y" sound as the target word.

Direksyons: Li chak mo objektif. Antoure mo a ki nan kolòn nan ki bay menm son "y" la tankou mo objektif la.

Polynesian	a. beryl
	b. money

vinyl	a. polymer
	b. facility

Polynesia	a. vinyl
	b. eyesore

sibyl	a. multiply
	b. Pennsylvania

Directions: Read each target word. Put a check (✓) under the correct column heading.

Direksyons: Li chak mo objektif. Mete yon tchèk (✓) anba antèt kolòn ki kòrèk la.

Target Words	"y" has the /ə/ sound as in the word <u>syringe</u>	"y" does not have the /ə/ sound
1. Polynesian		
2. vinyl		
3. Polynesia		
4. sibyl		

Name: _____ Date: ___/___/_____ Score: _____

Lesson 25.7

Reading Words with a Silent Letter "y"

✓ **Lesson Check Point**

Directions: Read the target words in the word box. Write the words that have a silent letter "y" in the first column. Write the words that do not have a silent letter "y" in the second column.

Direksyons: Li mo objektif yo ki nan ti bwat mo a. Ekri mo yo ki genyen lèt "y" ki pa pwononse a nan premye kolòn nan. Ekri mo yo ki pa genyen lèt "y" ki pa pwononse anan dezyèm kolòn nan.

Target Word Box				
layers	obey	survey	jersey	today
years	youngster	hay	yellow	yourself
Sunday	cruelty	yummy	yours	medley
yonder	convey	yolk	Friday	youth

Letter "y" is silent

_____
_____
_____
_____
_____
_____
_____
_____
_____

Letter "y" has the /y/ or /ē/ sound

_____
_____
_____
_____
_____
_____
_____
_____
_____

Name: _____ Date:___/___/_____ Score:_____

The Reading Challenge

Lesson 25.8

Reading Multisyllable Words

✓ **Lesson Check Point**

Directions: Read and divide each target word into syllables. Write each word and place a hyphen (-) between the syllables in the second column. Write the number of syllables in the third column. Use a dictionary or the Internet to check your answers.

Direksyons: Li epi divize chak mo objektif an silab. Ekri chak mo epi mete yon tirè (-) ant silab yo nan dezyèm kolòn nan. Ekri kantite silab ke yo genyen an nan twazyèm kolòn nan. Itilize yon diksyonè oubyen entènèt pou tcheke repons ou yo.

Target Words	Words Divided into Syllables	Number of Syllables
1. yanking	_____	_____
2. yogurt	_____	_____
3. younger	_____	_____
4. yearling	_____	_____
5. yeasty	_____	_____
6. yielded	_____	_____
7. yesterday	_____	_____
8. youngest	_____	_____
9. yourselves	_____	_____
10. yardsticks	_____	_____

Name: _____ Date: ____/____/____ Score: _____

The Reading Challenge

Lesson 25.8

Reading Multisyllable Words

 Lesson Check Point

 Directions: Read each target word. Circle the word in the row that is divided correctly into syllables. Use a dictionary or the Internet to check your answers.
Direksyons: Li chak mo objektif. Antoure mo a ki nan ranje a ki divize an silab korèkteman yo. Itilize yon diksyonè oubyen entènèt pou tcheke repons ou yo.

Model

| yesterday | a. ye-ster-day | b. yest-er-day | c. yes-ter-day |

| 1. yodeling | a. yod-e-ling | b. yod-el-ing | c. yo-del-ing |

| 2. Yakima | a. Ya-ki-ma | b. Ya-kim-a | c. Yak-im-a |

| 3. youngster | a. young-ster | b. you-ngst-er | c. yo-ung-ster |

| 4. yarmulke | a. yarm-ul-ke | b. yar-mul-ke | c. ya-rmul-ke |

| 5. yeastier | a. yeast-i-er | b. yea-sti-er | c. yeas-ti-er |

| 6. yardstick | a. yard-stick | b. yards-tick | c. yardst-ick |

| 7. yearly | a. yearl-y | b. yea-rly | c. year-ly |

| 8. yogurt | a. yo-gurt | b. yog-urt | c. yo-gu-rt |

Name: _____ Date: _____/___/_____ Score: _____

Lesson 25.9

Reading and Writing

Proper and Common Nouns and Adjectives

Directions: Read the words in the word box. Put an (X) on the line next to each word that is written incorrectly. Remember that all proper nouns and proper adjectives are capitalized. Use a dictionary or the Internet to check your answers.

Direksyons: Li chak mo yo ki nan bwat mo a. Met yon (X) sou ti trè a ki bò kote mo ki pa kri byen yo. Sonje ke tout non pwòp ak adjektif pwop ekri avèk yon lèt majiskil nan kòmansman yo. Itilize yon diksyonè oubyen entènèt pou tcheke repons ou yo.

Word Box		
__ Yemen	__ yourself	__ yonkers
__ yippee	__ yosemite Falls	__ yearlong
__ yogyakarta	__ Yoruba	__ Yugoslavia
__ Yesterday	__ Yonder	__ Youngsters

Directions: Read each unedited sentence and underline the word that is written incorrectly. Write each sentence correctly on the line.

Direksyons: Li chak fraz ki pa edite yo epi soulinye mo ki pa ekri byen an. Ekri chak fraz korèkteman sou liy lan.

Model
Is the New York <u>yankees</u> your favorite baseball team?
<u>Is the New York Yankees your favorite baseball team?</u>

1. Can You locate the Yucatan Peninsula on the map?
_____

2. Yes, Yvette speaks both yoruba and English fluently.
_____

3. yesterday, I went to a Yugoslavian restaurant for lunch.
_____

4. Yolanda said, "William Butler yeats was a famous poet and playwright."
_____

Name: _____ Date:___/___/_____ Score:_____

Lesson 26.1

Reading Words with the Letter Z/z

✓ Lesson Check Point

Directions: Read each target word. Find the letter "z" and put a check (✓) in the column that identifies its position: beginning, within or end.
Direksyons: Li chak mo objektif. Jwenn lèt "z" a epi mete yon tchèck (✓) nan kolòn ki idantifye pozisyon li an: nan kòmansman, ladan oubyen nan finisman.

Target Words	Beginning (First Letter)	Within	End (Last Letter)
1. waltz			
2. whiz			
3. zenith			
4. zealous			
5. Switzerland			

Directions: Read each sentence and underline the words that begin with the letter "z." Write all the underlined words in alphabetical order on the lines below.
Direksyons: Li chak fraz epi soulinye mo ki kòmanse avèk lèt "z" yo. Ekri tout mo ki soulinye yo nan lòd alfabetik sou trè sa yo ki anba.

6. The zebra in the cartoon is zany.

7. Samuel stored the zucchini in two Ziploc bags.

8. The zookeeper is feeding the zebras and horses.

9. Alexander and Zoë went to Zimbabwe on vacation.

10. The Zulu warriors proclaimed the war chants with great zeal.

_____   _____   _____

_____   _____   _____

_____   _____   _____

_____

Name: _____ Date: ___/___/_____ Score: _____

Lesson 26.1

Reading Words with the Letter Z/z

✓ Lesson Check Point

 Directions: Read each target word. Circle the word in the column that has the same "z" sound as the target word.
Direksyons: Li chak mo objektif. Antoure mo a ki nan kolòn nan ki bay menm son "z" la tankou mo objektif la.

bronze	a. computerize
	b. blitz

emphasizes	a. futz
	b. Byzantine

Lutz	a. hazardous
	b. quartz

criticized	a. bar mitzvah
	b. magnetize

 Directions: Read each target word. Put a check (✓) under the correct column heading.
Direksyons: Li chak mo objektif. Mete yon tchèk (✓) anba antèt kolòn ki kòrèk la.

Target Words	"z" has the /z/ sound as in the word <u>zipper</u>	"z" has the /s/ sound as in the word <u>quartz</u>
1. bronze		
2. emphasizes		
3. Lutz		
4. criticized		

Name: _____   Date: ___/___/____   Score: _____

Lesson 26.2

Reading Words with a Silent Letter "z"

✓ **Lesson Check Point**

Directions: Read the target words in the word box. Write the words that have a silent letter "z" in the first column. Write the words that do not have a silent letter "z" in the second column.

Direksyons: Li mo objektif yo ki nan ti bwat mo a. Ekri mo yo ki genyen lèt "z" ki pa pwononse a nan premye kolòn nan. Ekri mo yo ki pa genyen lèt "z" ki pa pwononse anan dezyèm kolòn nan.

Target Word Box				
embezzled	normalize	laziness	dazzling	frazzle
colonized	dizzy	fizzles	agonizing	zipper
puzzled	verbalized	nozzle	bronze	Byzantine
squeeze	jazz	amazing	dazzle	nuzzled

Letter "z" is silent	Letter "z" has the /z/ or /s/ sound
_____	_____
_____	_____
_____	_____
_____	_____
_____	_____
_____	_____
_____	_____
_____	_____

Name: _____ Date: ___/___/_____ Score: _____

The Reading Challenge

Lesson 26.3

Reading Multisyllable Words

✓ **Lesson Check Point**

Directions: Read and divide each target word into syllables. Write each word and place a hyphen (-) between the syllables in the second column. Write the number of syllables in the third column. Use a dictionary or the Internet to check your answers.

Direksyons: Li epi divize chak mo objektif an silab. Ekri chak mo epi mete yon tirè (-) ant silab yo nan dezyèm kolòn nan. Ekri kantite silab ke yo genyen an nan twazyèm kolòn nan. Itilize yon diksyonè oubyen entènèt pou tcheke repons ou yo.

Target Words	Words Divided into Syllables	Number of Syllables
1. zinger	_____	_____
2. Zurich	_____	_____
3. zonal	_____	_____
4. Zaire	_____	_____
5. zooming	_____	_____
6. Zambia	_____	_____
7. Zululand	_____	_____
8. zigzags	_____	_____
9. Zimbabwe	_____	_____
10. zealousness	_____	_____

Name: _____ Date: ___/___/_____ Score: _____

The Reading Challenge

Lesson 26.3

Reading Multisyllable Words

✓ **Lesson Check Point**

 Directions: Read each target word. Circle the word in the row that is divided correctly into syllables. Use a dictionary or the Internet to check your answers.

Direksyons: Li chak mo objektif. Antoure mo a ki nan ranje a ki divize an silab korèkteman yo. Itilize yon diksyonè oubyen entènèt pou tcheke repons ou yo.

Model

zoology	a. zo-ol-o-gy (circled)	b. zoo-lo-gy	c. zool-o-gy
1. Zanzibar	a. Zanz-i-bar	b. Zan-zib-ar	c. Zan-zi-bar
2. zealously	a. zea-lousl-y	b. zeal-ous-ly	c. zea-lous-ly
3. zygotic	a. zyg-o-tic	b. zyg-ot-ic	c. zy-got-ic
4. zestfulness	a. ze-stful-ness	b. zest-ful-ness	c. zes-tful-ness
5. zodiac	a. zo-di-ac	b. zod-i-ac	c. zo-dia-c
6. zenith	a. zen-i-th	b. ze-nith	c. z-en-ith
7. zoning	a. zo-ning	b. zon-ing	b. zo-n-ing
8. zookeeper	a. zooke-eper	b. zook-eep-er	c. zoo-keep-er

Name: _____ Date: ___/___/_____ Score: _____

Lesson 26.4

Reading and Writing

Proper and Common Nouns and Adjectives

Directions: Read the words in the word box. Put an (X) on the line next to each word that is written incorrectly. Remember that all proper nouns and proper adjectives are capitalized. Use a dictionary or the Internet to check your answers.

Direksyons: Li chak mo yo ki nan bwat mo a. Met yon (X) sou ti trè a ki bò kote mo ki pa kri byen yo. Sonje ke tout non pwòp ak adjektif pwop ekri avèk yon lèt majiskil nan kòmansman yo. Itilize yon diksyonè oubyen entènèt pou tcheke repons ou yo.

Word Box		
__ zebu	__ zebra	__ zurich
__ Zambian	__ Zoology	__ zygote
__ zeus	__ zombie	__ zero
__ Zipper	__ Zenith	__ Zillion

Directions: Read each unedited sentence and underline the word that is written incorrectly. Write each sentence correctly on the line.

Direksyons: Li chak fraz ki pa edite yo epi soulinye mo ki pa ekri byen an. Ekri chak fraz korèkteman sou liy lan.

Model
The steep path zigzags through the <u>zagros</u> Mountains.
<u>The steep path zigzags through the Zagros Mountains.</u>

1. Do you know that Zeanna's zip code ends with a Zero?
   _____

2. On Wednesday, Zachary is going to zambia on vacation.
   _____

3. In the morning, Zoey Zapped her breakfast in the microwave.
   _____

4. Mr. zebulon said that Zealand is the largest island in Denmark.
   _____

Name: _____ Date:___/___/_____ Score:_____

Appendix 1.0

Introduction of the Letter A/a

✓ **Lesson Check Point**

 Directions: Circle the correct letter "a" pair: uppercase and lowercase letters.
Direksyons: Antoure lèt ki kòrèk "a" pè: lèt majiskil ak lèt miniskil.

    Ae   Ao   Ea   Aa   Oa

 Directions: The uppercase letter "A" is in the first column. Look at the four letters in the row and circle the lowercase letter that matches the uppercase letter "A."
Direksyons: Lèt majiskil "A" se nan premye kolòn nan. Gade kat lèt ki nan ranje a epi antoure lèt miniskil ki koresponn ak lèt majiskil "A".

A	a	e	c	o
A	x	u	q	a
A	c	o	a	u
A	e	a	u	c

 Directions: The lowercase letter "a" is in the first column. Look at the four letters in the row and circle the uppercase letter that matches the lowercase letter "a."
Direksyons: Lèt miniskil "a" se nan premye kolòn nan. Gade kat lèt ki nan ranje a epi antoure lèt majiskil ki koresponn ak lèt miniskil "a".

a	E	A	X	V
a	R	U	O	A
a	A	E	G	Z
a	U	J	A	E

Name: _____ Date: ___/___/___ Score: _____

Appendix 2.0

Introduction of the Letter B/b

✓ **Lesson Check Point**

Directions: Circle the correct letter "b" pair: uppercase and lowercase letters.

Direksyons: Antoure lèt ki kòrèk "b" pè: lèt majiskil ak lèt miniskil.

    Bb   bD   Fb   Bp   Bd

Directions: The uppercase letter "B" is in the first column. Look at the four letters in the row and circle the lowercase letter that matches the uppercase letter "B."

Direksyons: Lèt majiskil "B" se nan premye kolòn nan. Gade kat lèt ki nan ranje a epi antoure lèt miniskil ki koresponn ak lèt majiskil "B".

B	d	p	f	b
B	b	h	j	d
B	p	q	b	d
B	k	p	b	f

Directions: The lowercase letter "b" is in the first column. Look at the four letters in the row and circle the uppercase letter that matches the lowercase letter "b."

Direksyons: Lèt miniskil "b" nan premye kolòn nan. Gade kat lèt ki nan ranje a epi antoure lèt majiskil ki koresponn ak lèt miniskil "b".

b	B	Q	K	L
b	P	B	Q	D
b	K	D	B	M
b	L	M	B	F

Name: _____ Date: ___/___/_____ Score: _____

Appendix 2.0

Letter Recognition B/b

Uppercase and Lowercase Letter

✓ Lesson Check Point

 Directions: Read each target word. Read the words in the row and circle the word that begins with a different letter.

Direksyons: Li chak mo sib. Li mo ki nan ranje a epi antoure mo ki kòmanse ak yon lèt diferan.

Target Words				
1. body	brother	pants	boss	block
2. bow	pepper	book	boat	bliss
3. block	bread	blood	blow	door
4. blue	blink	push	blizzard	bus
5. bird	both	buns	quick	bent

 Directions: Read the words in the four boxes. Circle two words that start with the uppercase and lowercase letter "b."

Direksyons: Li mo ki nan kat kare yo. Ansèkle de mo ki kòmanse ak lèt majiskil ak lèt miniskil "b".

Big	big
Rig	dig

bag	tag
Rag	Bag

bet	Hen
ten	Bet

ban	Dan
Ban	fan

Mud	Bud
bud	mud

Boss	Toss
toss	boss

Name: _____   Date: ___/___/_____   Score: _____

Appendix 3.0

Introduction of the Letter C/c

✓ Lesson Check Point

Directions: Circle the correct letter "c" pair: uppercase and lowercase letters.
Direksyons: Antoure lèt ki kòrèk "c" pè: lèt majiskil ak lèt miniskil.

oC   Pc   Gc   Cu   cC

Directions: The uppercase letter "C" is in the first column. Look at the four letters in the row and circle the lowercase letter that matches the uppercase letter "C."
Direksyons: Lèt majiskil "C" se nan premye kolòn nan. Gade kat lèt ki nan ranje a epi antoure lèt miniskil ki koresponn ak lèt majiskil "C".

C	g	o	c	d
C	o	c	m	b
C	c	q	o	x
C	c	g	d	o

Directions: The lowercase letter "c" is in the first column. Look at the four letters in the row and circle the uppercase letter that matches the lowercase letter "c."
Direksyons: Lèt miniskil "c" nan premye kolòn nan. Gade kat lèt ki nan ranje a epi antoure lèt majiskil ki koresponn ak lèt miniskil "c".

c	Q	V	C	G
c	C	O	M	D
c	O	Q	C	N
c	C	G	Q	D

Name: _____ Date: ___/___/_____ Score: _____

Appendix 3.0

Letter Recognition C/c

Uppercase and Lowercase Letter

✓ Lesson Check Point

Directions: Read each target word. Read the words in the row and circle the word that begins with a different letter.

Direksyons: Li chak mo sib. Li mo ki nan ranje a epi antoure mo ki kòmanse ak yon lèt diferan.

Target Words				
1. club	powder	carbon	cent	change
2. child	donut	chip	circle	clip
3. confirm	cactus	money	check	click
4. compact	cargo	chance	zebra	clinic
5. chemical	chess	table	calendar	chart

Directions: Read the words in the four boxes. Circle two words that start with the uppercase and lowercase letter "c."

Direksyons: Li mo ki nan kat kare yo. Ansèkle de mo ki kòmanse ak lèt majiskil ak lèt miniskil "c".

Carbon	gallon
crop	borrow

Oil	Cash
cart	Quart

Cram	Draw
Goat	clean

Queen	cold
Chain	rain

Grasp	Pollen
college	Coast

Quick	Curl
Over	cloud

Learn to Read English With Directions In Haitian Creole

Name: _____ Date: ___/___/_____ Score: _____

Appendix 4.0

Introduction of the Letter D/d

✓ **Lesson Check Point**

 Directions: Circle the correct letter "d" pair: uppercase and lowercase letters.
Direksyons: Fè yon wonn pè lèt kòrèk "d": lèt majiskil ak lèt miniskil.

    Db   Dp   Fd   Bd   Dd

 Directions: The uppercase letter "D" is in the first column. Look at the four letters in the row and circle the lowercase letter that matches the uppercase letter "D."
Direksyons: Lèt majiskil "D" se nan premye kolòn nan. Gade kat lèt ki nan ranje a epi ansèkle lèt miniskil ki koresponn ak lèt majiskil "D".

D	t	h	k	d
D	l	b	d	t
D	f	d	h	b
D	d	k	f	t

 Directions: The lowercase letter "d" is in the first column. Look at the four letters in the row and circle the uppercase letter that matches the lowercase letter "d."
Direksyons: Lèt miniskil "d" nan premye kolòn nan. Gade kat lèt ki nan ranje a epi antoure lèt majiskil ki koresponn ak lèt miniskil "d".

d	F	B	D	H
d	B	D	E	B
d	D	F	B	M
d	G	N	H	D

Name: _____ Date: ___/___/_____ Score: _____

Appendix 4.0

Letter Recognition D/d

Uppercase and Lowercase Letter

✓ **Lesson Check Point**

Directions: Read each target word. Read the words in the row and circle the word that begins with a different letter.

Direksyons: Li chak mo sib. Li mo ki nan ranje a epi antoure mo ki kòmanse ak yon lèt diferan.

Target Words				
1. dance	dean	doe	quilt	die
2. drip	proud	doubt	droll	dot
3. disk	drift	bank	dig	drag
4. dear	does	deem	peach	dead
5. draws	quest	draft	dream	duck

Directions: Read the words in the four boxes. Circle two words that start with the uppercase and lowercase letter "d."

Direksyons: Li mo ki nan kat kare yo. Ansèkle de mo ki kòmanse ak lèt majiskil ak lèt miniskil "d".

duck	got
Dot	truck

Down	town
pen	dean

dash	Queen
pass	Draft

Glove	Dove
train	drain

Grape	pose
does	Drape

Ben	den
Dig	pig

Learn to Read English With Directions In Haitian Creole

Name: _____ Date: ___/___/_____ Score: _____

Appendix 5.0

Introduction of the Letter E/e

✓ **Lesson Check Point**

Directions: Circle the correct letter "e" pair: uppercase and lowercase letters.

Direksyons: Fè yon wonn pè lèt kòrèk "e": lèt majiskil ak lèt miniskil.

| eF | hE | cE | Oe | Ee |

Directions: The uppercase letter "E" is in the first column. Look at the four letters in the row and circle the lowercase letter that matches the uppercase letter "E."

Direksyons: Lèt majiskil "E" se nan premye kolòn nan. Gade kat lèt ki nan ranje a epi antoure lèt miniskil ki koresponn ak lèt majiskil "E".

E	c	e	s	v
E	e	x	f	h
E	z	a	d	e
E	g	w	e	x

Directions: The lowercase letter "e" is in the first column. Look at the four letters in the row and circle the uppercase letter that matches the lowercase letter "e."

Direksyons: Lèt miniskil "e" se nan premye kolòn nan. Gade kat lèt ki nan ranje a epi antoure lèt majiskil ki koresponn ak lèt miniskil "e".

e	H	F	E	X
e	E	W	Z	N
e	F	R	X	E
e	C	E	D	F

Name: _____ Date: ___/___/_____ Score: _____

Appendix 6.0

Introduction of the Letter F/f

 Lesson Check Point

 Directions: Circle the correct letter "f" pair: uppercase and lowercase letters.
Direksyons: Antoure lèt ki kòrèk "f" pè: lèt majiskil ak lèt miniskil.

    Pf   Ff   fH   Lf   Ef

 Directions: The uppercase letter "F" is in the first column. Look at the four letters in the row and circle the lowercase letter that matches the uppercase letter "F."
Direksyons: Lèt majiskil "F" se nan premye kolòn nan. Gade kat lèt ki nan ranje a epi antoure lèt miniskil ki koresponn ak lèt majiskil "F".

F	k	f	j	t
F	l	h	f	p
F	b	f	d	h
F	f	t	h	l

 Directions: The lowercase letter "f" is in the first column. Look at the four letters in the row and circle the uppercase letter that matches the lowercase letter "f."
Direksyons: Lèt miniskil "f" se nan premye kolòn nan. Gade kat lèt ki nan ranje a epi antoure lèt majiskil ki koresponn ak lèt miniskil "f".

f	E	H	F	T
f	F	K	L	E
f	T	F	Y	E
f	U	E	F	B

Name: _____ Date: ___/___/_____ Score: _____

Appendix 6.0

Letter Recognition F/f

Uppercase and Lowercase Letter

✓ **Lesson Check Point**

Directions: Read each target word. Read the words in the row and circle the word that begins with a different letter.

Direksyons: Li chak mo sib. Li mo ki nan ranje a epi antoure mo ki kòmanse ak yon lèt diferan.

Target Words				
1. fuzz	flat	frizz	Earth	fleet
2. fruit	friends	fresh	frost	house
3. flute	food	band	fix	false
4. fence	fluke	floor	flex	Yard
5. French	fume	toys	faith	flap

Directions: Read the words in the four boxes. Circle two words that start with the uppercase and lowercase letter "f."

Direksyons: Li mo ki nan kat kare yo. Ansèkle de mo ki kòmanse ak lèt majiskil ak lèt miniskil "f".

bath	Hours
Fad	fade

fan	heat
Daisy	Flint

Flip	Hold
trap	fat

flight	Drops
loves	Fool

Fling	fake
hatch	Door

trees	blood
Fear	flood

Learn to Read English With Directions In Haitian Creole

Name: _____ Date:___/___/_____ Score:_____

Appendix 7.0

Introduction of the Letter G/g

✓ **Lesson Check Point**

 Directions: Circle the correct letter "g" pair: uppercase and lowercase letters.
Direksyons: Antoure lèt ki kòrèk "g" pè: lèt majiskil ak lèt miniskil.

| Og | Gp | gQ | Gg | gU |

 Directions: The uppercase letter "G" is in the first column. Look at the four letters in the row and circle the lowercase letter that matches the uppercase letter "G."
Direksyons: Lèt majiskil "G" se nan premye kolòn nan. Gade kat lèt ki nan ranje a epi antoure lèt miniskil ki koresponn ak lèt majiskil "G".

G	p	g	j	y
G	y	j	p	g
G	g	y	q	t
G	p	y	g	j

 Directions: The lowercase letter "g" is in the first column. Look at the four letters in the row and circle the uppercase letter that matches the lowercase letter "g."
Direksyons: Lèt miniskil "g" se nan premye kolòn nan. Gade kat lèt ki nan ranje a epi antoure lèt majiskil ki koresponn ak lèt miniskil "g".

g	P	O	G	M
g	O	G	U	E
g	Q	J	O	G
g	U	C	G	O

Name: _____ Date: ___/___/_____ Score: _____

Appendix 7.0

Letter Recognition G/g

Uppercase and Lowercase Letter

✓ Lesson Check Point

Directions: Read each target word. Read the words in the row and circle the word that begins with a different letter.

Direksyons: Li chak mo sib. Li mo ki nan ranje a epi antoure mo ki kòmanse ak yon lèt diferan.

Target Words				
1. gate	grape	gaze	gift	June
2. glue	push	glance	great	gloss
3. grand	guide	grab	gross	place
4. gum	grain	gleam	joke	groom
5. golf	gone	gap	globe	down

Directions: Read the words in the four boxes. Circle two words that start with the uppercase and lowercase letter "g."

Direksyons: Li mo ki nan kat kare yo. Ansèkle de mo ki kòmanse ak lèt majiskil ak lèt miniskil "g".

grade	Girl
push	just

dance	glance
Gong	praise

Join	ball
globe	Guest

Plan	great
Queen	Glove

gown	down
juice	Greek

Go	job
group	praise

 Name: _____   Date: ___/___/_____   Score: _____

Appendix 8.0

Introduction of the Letter H/h

✓ **Lesson Check Point**

 Directions: Circle the correct letter "h" pair: uppercase and lowercase letters.
Direksyons: Antoure lèt ki kòrèk "h" pè: lèt majiskil ak lèt miniskil.

    Lh   Hf   Hh   Ph   bH

 Directions: The uppercase letter "H" is in the first column. Look at the four letters in the row and circle the lowercase letter that matches the uppercase letter "H."
Direksyons: Lèt majiskil "H" se nan premye kolòn nan. Gade kat lèt ki nan ranje a epi antoure lèt miniskil ki koresponn ak lèt majiskil "H".

H	f	h	d	t
H	h	l	t	f
H	t	k	l	h
H	d	f	h	p

 Directions: The lowercase letter "h" is in the first column. Look at the four letters in the row and circle the uppercase letter that matches the lowercase letter "h."
Direksyons: Lèt miniskil "h" se nan premye kolòn nan. Gade kat lèt ki nan ranje a epi antoure lèt majiskil ki koresponn ak lèt miniskil "h".

h	H	G	O	P
h	K	F	H	E
h	F	H	E	K
h	L	H	B	T

Name: _____ Date: ___/___/_____ Score: _____

Appendix 8.0

Letter Recognition H/h

Uppercase and Lowercase Letter

✓ Lesson Check Point

Directions: Read each target word. Read the words in the row and circle the word that begins with a different letter.

Direksyons: Li chak mo sib. Li mo ki nan ranje a epi antoure mo ki kòmanse ak yon lèt diferan.

Target Words				
1. house	touch	harp	herb	hoist
2. herb	hiss	her	hot	low
3. hope	harsh	heed	down	hide
4. hawk	kind	hark	hue	had
5. helping	haste	been	hedge	halt

Directions: Read the words in the four boxes. Circle two words that start with the uppercase and lowercase letter "h."

Direksyons: Li mo ki nan kat kare yo. Ansèkle de mo ki kòmanse ak lèt majiskil ak lèt miniskil "h".

Talk	lunch
High	house

Does	have
loud	Hard

Health	five
Trip	hill

hang	Hall
fresh	thanks

heart	Kick
look	Hawk

Hide	from
hike	drive

Name: _____ Date:___/___/_____ Score:_____

Appendix 9.0

Introduction of the Letter I/i

✓ **Lesson Check Point**

 Directions: Circle the correct letter "i" pair: uppercase and lowercase letters.
Direksyons: Antoure lèt ki kòrèk "i" pè: lèt majiskil ak lèt miniskil.

| Li | iI | It | Ji | Ij |

 Directions: The uppercase letter "I" is in the first column. Look at the four letters in the row and circle the lowercase letter that matches the uppercase letter "I."
Direksyons: Lèt majiskil "I" se nan premye kolòn nan. Gade kat lèt ki nan ranje a epi antoure lèt miniskil ki koresponn ak lèt majiskil "I".

I	y	h	t	i
I	i	j	g	t
I	j	i	y	f
I	g	y	j	i

 Directions: The lowercase letter "i" is in the first column. Look at the four letters in the row and circle the uppercase letter that matches the lowercase letter "i."
Direksyons: Lèt miniskil "i" se nan premye kolòn nan. Gade kat lèt ki nan ranje a epi antoure lèt majiskil ki koresponn ak lèt miniskil "i".

i	J	I	Y	T
i	E	D	K	I
i	B	I	N	J
i	I	T	F	K

Name: _____ Date:___/___/_____ Score:_____

Appendix 10.0

Introduction of the Letter J/j

✓ **Lesson Check Point**

 Directions: Circle the correct letter "j" pair: uppercase and lowercase letters.
Direksyons: Antoure lèt ki kòrèk "j" pè: lèt majiskil ak lèt miniskil.

| Kj | jY | Jg | Jj | Lj |

 Directions: The uppercase letter "J" is in the first column. Look at the four letters in the row and circle the lowercase letter that matches the uppercase letter "J."
Direksyons: Lèt majiskil "J" se nan premye kolòn nan. Gade kat lèt ki nan ranje a epi antoure lèt miniskil ki koresponn ak lèt majiskil "J".

J	l	j	k	b
J	j	g	y	q
J	g	i	z	j
J	q	y	j	p

 Directions: The lowercase letter "j" is in the first column. Look at the four letters in the row and circle the uppercase letter that matches the lowercase letter "j."
Direksyons: Lèt miniskil "j" se nan premye kolòn nan. Gade kat lèt ki nan ranje a epi antoure lèt majiskil ki koresponn ak lèt miniskil "j".

j	J	V	D	G
j	L	N	E	J
j	H	J	C	O
j	O	J	G	T

Name: _____   Date: ___/___/_____   Score: _____

Appendix 10.0

Letter Recognition J/j

Uppercase and Lowercase Letter

✓ Lesson Check Point

Directions: Read each target word. Read the words in the row and circle the word that begins with a different letter.

Direksyons: Li chak mo sib. Li mo ki nan ranje a epi antoure mo ki kòmanse ak yon lèt diferan.

Target Words				
1. jug	jab	jersey	jet	years
2. jade	job	guest	jack	jeep
3. jazz	jewel	jam	love	joke
4. junior	back	join	jump	jail
5. jellyfish	jolt	young	jar	joy

Directions: Read the words in the four boxes. Circle two words that start with the uppercase and lowercase letter "j."

Direksyons: Li mo ki nan kat kare yo. Ansèkle de mo ki kòmanse ak lèt majiskil ak lèt miniskil "j".

Juice	group
job	youth

grow	young
jog	Jet

Jeep	yours
foxes	jock

cares	June
jump	gloss

years	gate
Joint	junk

yoke	jean
guess	Joke

Name: _____ Date: ___/___/_____ Score: _____

Appendix 11.0

Introduction of the Letter K/k

✓ **Lesson Check Point**

Directions: Circle the correct letter "k" pair: uppercase and lowercase letters.

Direksyons: Antoure lèt ki kòrèk "k" pè: lèt majiskil ak lèt miniskil.

Lk	lK	Kk	Jk	hK

Directions: The uppercase letter "K" is in the first column. Look at the four letters in the row and circle the lowercase letter that matches the uppercase letter "K."

Direksyons: Lèt majiskil "K" se nan premye kolòn nan. Gade kat lèt ki nan ranje a epi antoure lèt miniskil ki koresponn ak lèt majiskil "K".

K	k	j	g	o
K	h	k	b	p
K	n	l	k	b
K	p	d	l	k

Directions: The lowercase letter "k" is in the first column. Look at the four letters in the row and circle the uppercase letter that matches the lowercase letter "k."

Direksyons: Lèt miniskil "k" se nan premye kolòn nan. Gade kat lèt ki nan ranje a epi antoure lèt majiskil ki koresponn ak lèt miniskil "k".

k	P	K	Y	N
k	Q	J	K	V
k	B	K	C	S
k	K	X	H	Q

Learn to Read English With Directions In Haitian Creole

Name: _____ Date: ___/___/_____ Score: _____

Appendix 11.0

Letter Recognition K/k

Uppercase and Lowercase Letter

✓ Lesson Check Point

 Directions: Read each target word. Read the words in the row and circle the word that begins with a different letter.
Direksyons: Li chak mo sib. Li mo ki nan ranje a epi antoure mo ki kòmanse ak yon lèt diferan.

Target Words				
1. knob	keep	kind	tent	knot
2. ketch	kale	krill	knit	house
3. karts	frank	key	kick	keel
4. knight	kept	tooth	knoll	keen
5. knock	frame	kelp	kedge	keg

 Directions: Read the words in the four boxes. Circle two words that start with the uppercase and lowercase letter "k."
Direksyons: Li mo ki nan kat kare yo. Ansèkle de mo ki kòmanse ak lèt majiskil ak lèt miniskil "k".

lamb	Knows
kids	Eggs

found	kind
Laugh	Knock

Enough	Friends
Kicks	knot

Knight	down
kept	Boat

keeps	Knits
Dreams	house

knob	drops
Vase	Keen

Learn to Read English With Directions In Haitian Creole

Name: _____ Date: ___/___/_____ Score: _____

Appendix 12.0

Introduction of the Letter L/l

✓ **Lesson Check Point**

 Directions: Circle the correct letter "l" pair: uppercase and lowercase letters.

Direksyons: Antoure lèt ki kòrèk "l" pè: lèt majiskil ak lèt miniskil.

Jl   Ll   Lk   lF   jL

 Directions: The uppercase letter "L" is in the first column. Look at the four letters in the row and circle the lowercase letter that matches the uppercase letter "L."

Direksyons: Lèt majiskil "L" se nan premye kolòn nan. Gade kat lèt ki nan ranje a epi antoure lèt miniskil ki koresponn ak lèt majiskil "L".

L	j	l	h	t
L	k	b	f	l
L	f	i	l	h
L	l	j	i	f

 Directions: The lowercase letter "l" is in the first column. Look at the four letters in the row and circle the uppercase letter that matches the lowercase letter "l."

Direksyons: Lèt miniskil "l" se nan premye kolòn nan. Gade kat lèt ki nan ranje a epi antoure lèt majiskil ki koresponn ak lèt miniskil "l".

l	L	H	J	K
l	T	B	L	J
l	L	J	D	N
l	J	H	L	B

Name: _____ Date: ___/___/_____ Score: _____

Appendix 12.0

Letter Recognition L/l

Uppercase and Lowercase Letter

✓ **Lesson Check Point**

Directions: Read each target word. Read the words in the row and circle the word that begins with a different letter.

Direksyons: Li chak mo sib. Li mo ki nan ranje a epi antoure mo ki kòmanse ak yon lèt diferan.

Target Words				
1. light	love	finds	luck	Latin
2. leach	live	loaf	hose	leaf
3. loam	lick	beef	laugh	league
4. leap	kitchen	lime	lamb	lend
5. lenses	learn	loud	less	dress

Directions: Read the words in the four boxes. Circle two words that start with the uppercase and lowercase letter "l."

Direksyons: Li mo ki nan kat kare yo. Ansèkle de mo ki kòmanse ak lèt majiskil ak lèt miniskil "l".

trees	dawn
Limp	lawn

Lid	Trips
land	house

Years	lease
Launch	France

Light	dance
hunch	lead

Branch	Lack
friends	leg

line	Load
Hours	Town

Learn to Read English With Directions In Haitian Creole

 Name: _____ Date:___/___/_____ Score:_____

Appendix 13.0

Introduction of the Letter M/m

✓ Lesson Check Point

 Directions: Circle the correct letter "m" pair: uppercase and lowercase letters.
Direksyons: Antoure lèt ki kòrèk "m" pè: lèt majiskil ak lèt miniskil.

Nm   Mu   Zm   Mn   Mm

 Directions: The uppercase letter "M" is in the first column. Look at the four letters in the row and circle the lowercase letter that matches the uppercase letter "M."
Direksyons: Lèt majiskil "M" se nan premye kolòn nan. Gade kat lèt ki nan ranje a epi antoure lèt miniskil ki koresponn ak lèt majiskil "M".

M	n	w	m	u
M	m	n	h	b
M	w	u	m	v
M	m	n	w	x

 Directions: The lowercase letter "m" is in the first column. Look at the four letters in the row and circle the uppercase letter that matches the lowercase letter "m."
Direksyons: Lèt miniskil "m" se nan premye kolòn nan. Gade kat lèt ki nan ranje a epi antoure lèt majiskil ki koresponn ak lèt miniskil "m".

m	M	N	Z	T
m	Y	W	M	N
m	N	Y	W	M
m	Z	N	Y	M

Name: _____ Date: ___/___/_____ Score: _____

Appendix 13.0

Letter Recognition M/m

Uppercase and Lowercase Letter

✓ **Lesson Check Point**

Directions: Read each target word. Read the words in the row and circle the word that begins with a different letter.

Direksyons: Li chak mo sib. Li mo ki nan ranje a epi antoure mo ki kòmanse ak yon lèt diferan.

Target Words				
1. milk	much	maid	mug	vain
2. mouse	mixed	norm	mall	move
3. meal	vine	male	mock	mint
4. mind	made	rain	moon	might
5. munch	mumps	mince	neck	mood

Directions: Read the words in the four boxes. Circle two words that start with the uppercase and lowercase letter "m."

Direksyons: Li mo ki nan kat kare yo. Ansèkle de mo ki kòmanse ak lèt majiskil ak lèt miniskil "m".

Name	Male
mild	wear

wax	need
Mesh	mink

very	Mill
notch	moan

munch	noun
Man	yes

mud	Mine
zoo	Next

Map	nice
whale	mole

Learn to Read English With Directions In Haitian Creole   273   Copyrighted Material

Name: _____ Date: ___/___/_____ Score: _____

Appendix 14.0

Introduction of the Letter N/n

✓ **Lesson Check Point**

Directions: Circle the correct letter "n" pair: uppercase and lowercase letters.

Direksyons: Antoure lèt ki kòrèk "n" pè: lèt majiskil ak lèt miniskil.

    mN   Mn   uN   nN   Un

Directions: The uppercase letter "N" is in the first column. Look at the four letters in the row and circle the lowercase letter that matches the uppercase letter "N."

Direksyons: Lèt majiskil "N" se nan premye kolòn nan. Gade kat lèt ki nan ranje a epi antoure lèt miniskil ki koresponn ak lèt majiskil "N".

N	u	n	y	m
N	n	h	u	z
N	y	v	n	u
N	v	u	x	n

Directions: The lowercase letter "n" is in the first column. Look at the four letters in the row and circle the uppercase letter that matches the lowercase letter "n."

Direksyons: Lèt miniskil "n" se nan premye kolòn nan. Gade kat lèt ki nan ranje a epi antoure lèt majiskil ki koresponn ak lèt miniskil "n".

n	Z	N	U	M
n	N	Y	M	W
n	U	Z	H	N
n	Y	U	N	Z

Name: _____ Date: ___/___/_____ Score: _____

Appendix 14.0

Letter Recognition N/n

Uppercase and Lowercase Letter

✓ **Lesson Check Point**

 Directions: Read each target word. Read the words in the row and circle the word that begins with a different letter.
Direksyons: Li chak mo sib. Li mo ki nan ranje a epi antoure mo ki kòmanse ak yon lèt diferan.

Target Words				
1. new	night	none	moon	neck
2. neat	round	nerve	noon	name
3. niche	near	made	norm	next
4. nook	nose	nail	neat	went
5. normal	cute	noun	nine	noise

 Directions: Read the words in the four boxes. Circle two words that start with the uppercase and lowercase letter "n."
Direksyons: Li mo ki nan kat kare yo. Ansèkle de mo ki kòmanse ak lèt majiskil ak lèt miniskil "n".

notch	moon
home	None

nip	most
you	Nose

mist	van
Night	nudge

net	Nil
word	man

verse	Nag
roll	not

nook	vote
Next	milk

Name: _____ Date:___/___/_____ Score:_____

Appendix 15.0

Introduction of the Letter O/o

✓ **Lesson Check Point**

 Directions: Circle the correct letter "o" pair: uppercase and lowercase letters.
Direksyons: Antoure lèt ki kòrèk "o" pè: lèt majiskil ak lèt miniskil.

  Qo   Oo   Co   Uo   Ou

 Directions: The uppercase letter "O" is in the first column. Look at the four letters in the row and circle the lowercase letter that matches the uppercase letter "O."
Direksyons: Lèt majiskil "O" se nan premye kolòn nan. Gade kat lèt ki nan ranje a epi antoure lèt miniskil ki koresponn ak lèt majiskil "O".

O	c	o	s	p
O	q	g	u	o
O	u	p	o	s
O	o	h	c	d

 Directions: The lowercase letter "o" is in the first column. Look at the four letters in the row and circle the uppercase letter that matches the lowercase letter "o."
Direksyons: Lèt miniskil "o" se nan premye kolòn nan. Gade kat lèt ki nan ranje a epi antoure lèt majiskil ki koresponn ak lèt miniskil "o".

o	U	J	O	P
o	O	C	U	Q
o	Q	O	Y	C
o	O	D	B	U

Name: _____ Date:___/___/_____ Score:_____

Appendix 16.0

Introduction of the Letter P/p

✓ Lesson Check Point

 Directions: Circle the correct letter "p" pair: uppercase and lowercase letters.
Direksyons: Antoure lèt ki kòrèk "p" pè: lèt majiskil ak lèt miniskil.

| Pd | Pp | Pg | Pb | Bp |

 Directions: The uppercase letter "P" is in the first column. Look at the four letters in the row and circle the lowercase letter that matches the uppercase letter "P."
Direksyons: Lèt majiskil "P" se nan premye kolòn nan. Gade kat lèt ki nan ranje a epi antoure lèt miniskil ki koresponn ak lèt majiskil "P".

P	p	b	d	q
P	g	d	p	b
P	d	g	b	p
P	p	b	g	j

 Directions: The lowercase letter "p" is in the first column. Look at the four letters in the row and circle the uppercase letter that matches the lowercase letter "p."
Direksyons: Lèt miniskil "p" se nan premye kolòn nan. Gade kat lèt ki nan ranje a epi antoure lèt majiskil ki koresponn ak lèt miniskil "p".

p	Q	B	P	D
p	H	G	T	P
p	P	Q	D	B
p	G	P	B	D

Learn to Read English With Directions In Haitian Creole

Name: _____ Date: ___/___/_____ Score: _____

Appendix 16.0

Letter Recognition P/p

Uppercase and Lowercase Letter

 Lesson Check Point

 Directions: Read each target word. Read the words in the row and circle the word that begins with a different letter.
Direksyons: Li chak mo sib. Li mo ki nan ranje a epi antoure mo ki kòmanse ak yon lèt diferan.

Target Words				
1. pace	price	quest	push	pine
2. prove	young	princess	plop	pink
3. purge	plunge	plus	pearl	guest
4. peach	good	pint	peek	pants
5. please	plane	quick	pipe	plain

 Directions: Read the words in the four boxes. Circle two words that start with the uppercase and lowercase letter "p."
Direksyons: Li mo ki nan kat kare yo. Ansèkle de mo ki kòmanse ak lèt majiskil ak lèt miniskil "p".

pen	Slate		Beep	Peep		dull	pull
Plate	den		pound	keep		full	Push

park	bark		Dry	pry		plum	lunch
Dark	Purse		Price	Try		Punch	bunch

Name: _____ Date: ___/___/_____ Score: _____

Appendix 17.0

Introduction of the Letter Q/q

✓ **Lesson Check Point**

 Directions: Circle the correct letter "q" pair: uppercase and lowercase letters.
Direksyons: Antoure lèt ki kòrèk "q" pè: lèt majiskil ak lèt miniskil.

    qQ   Qp   Oq   Gq   Qg

 Directions: The uppercase letter "Q" is in the first column. Look at the four letters in the row and circle the lowercase letter that matches the uppercase letter "Q."
Direksyons: Lèt majiskil "Q" se nan premye kolòn nan. Gade kat lèt ki nan ranje a epi antoure lèt miniskil ki koresponn ak lèt majiskil "Q".

Q	p	q	b	d
Q	j	g	q	b
Q	q	j	b	p
Q	g	b	j	q

 Directions: The lowercase letter "q" is in the first column. Look at the four letters in the row and circle the uppercase letter that matches the lowercase letter "q."
Direksyons: Lèt miniskil "q" se nan premye kolòn nan. Gade kat lèt ki nan ranje a epi antoure lèt majiskil ki koresponn ak lèt miniskil "q".

q	Q	G	O	C
q	O	S	Q	U
q	G	O	U	Q
q	C	Q	O	G

Name: _____ Date: ___/___/_____ Score: _____

Appendix 17.0

Letter Recognition Q/q

Uppercase and Lowercase Letter

✓ Lesson Check Point

 Directions: Read each target word. Read the words in the row and circle the word that begins with a different letter.

Direksyons: Li chak mo sib. Li mo ki nan ranje a epi antoure mo ki kòmanse ak yon lèt diferan.

Target Words				
1. quaint	pedal	quickly	qualm	quartz
2. quit	quotes	quail	qualify	demand
3. quiet	quaint	bunch	quake	quack
4. quite	quest	quarrel	publish	quibble
5. quarter	quake	dances	Qatar	quark

 Directions: Read the words in the four boxes. Circle two words that start with the uppercase and lowercase letter "q."

Direksyons: Li mo ki nan kat kare yo. Ansèkle de mo ki kòmanse ak lèt majiskil ak lèt miniskil "q".

quails	Quagmire
project	jumbo

Octopus	Quake
quarrel	yarn

guess	Quicken
prefix	quarter

Query	Organ
yield	queasy

quickie	pound
Quench	yogurt

judge	Orchid
quickly	Quota

Name: _____ Date: ___/___/_____ Score: _____

Appendix 18.0

Introduction of the Letter R/r

✓ **Lesson Check Point**

Directions: Circle the correct letter "r" pair: uppercase and lowercase letters.

Direksyons: Antoure lèt ki kòrèk "r" pè: lèt majiskil ak lèt miniskil.

    Rd   rV   Nr   rR   Rx

Directions: The uppercase letter "R" is in the first column. Look at the four letters in the row and circle the lowercase letter that matches the uppercase letter "R."

Direksyons: Lèt majiskil "R" se nan premye kolòn nan. Gade kat lèt ki nan ranje a epi antoure lèt miniskil ki koresponn ak lèt majiskil "R".

R	v	r	a	g
R	y	x	c	r
R	r	v	b	f
R	p	f	r	c

Directions: The lowercase letter "r" is in the first column. Look at the four letters in the row and circle the uppercase letter that matches the lowercase letter "r."

Direksyons: Lèt miniskil "r" se nan premye kolòn nan. Gade kat lèt ki nan ranje a epi antoure lèt majiskil ki koresponn ak lèt miniskil "r".

r	D	R	C	F
r	R	H	B	K
r	Q	T	R	V
r	J	K	G	R

Name: _____ Date: ___/___/_____ Score: _____

Appendix 18.0

Letter Recognition R/r

Uppercase and Lowercase Letter

✓ Lesson Check Point

Directions: Read each target word. Read the words in the row and circle the word that begins with a different letter.

Direksyons: Li chak mo sib. Li mo ki nan ranje a epi antoure mo ki kòmanse ak yon lèt diferan.

Target Words				
1. rig	rate	cares	rhythm	rock
2. rhyme	robe	reed	range	moon
3. round	rain	reach	used	raid
4. road	mold	roar	rule	ream
5. renters	rare	rail	need	risk

Directions: Read the words in the four boxes. Circle two words that start with the uppercase and lowercase letter "r."

Direksyons: Li mo ki nan kat kare yo. Ansèkle de mo ki kòmanse ak lèt majiskil ak lèt miniskil "r".

need	red		cow	rich		rib	money
Piece	Roll		part	Ramp		name	Rite

Role	noise		mouse	Realm		Reap	rip
roost	Park		rouse	peace		cats	perm

Learn to Read English With Directions In Haitian Creole   282   Copyrighted Material

Name: _____ Date: ___/___/_____ Score: _____

Appendix 19.0

Introduction of the Letter S/s

✓ **Lesson Check Point**

 Directions: Circle the correct letter "s" pair: uppercase and lowercase letters.
Direksyons: Antoure lèt ki kòrèk "s" pè: lèt majiskil ak lèt miniskil.

    Cs   Zs   sS   Os   cS

 Directions: The uppercase letter "S" is in the first column. Look at the four letters in the row and circle the lowercase letter that matches the uppercase letter "S."
Direksyons: Lèt majiskil "S" se nan premye kolòn nan. Gade kat lèt ki nan ranje a epi antoure lèt miniskil ki koresponn ak lèt majiskil "S".

S	s	c	z	u
S	z	g	s	b
S	u	s	o	z
S	c	z	g	s

 Directions: The lowercase letter "s" is in the first column. Look at the four letters in the row and circle the uppercase letter that matches the lowercase letter "s."
Direksyons: Lèt miniskil "s" se nan premye kolòn nan. Gade kat lèt ki nan ranje a epi antoure lèt majiskil ki koresponn ak lèt miniskil "s".

s	Z	S	U	C
s	U	X	S	Z
s	S	Z	C	O
s	Z	S	G	C

Name: _____ Date: ___/___/_____ Score: _____

Appendix 19.0

Letter Recognition S/s

Uppercase and Lowercase Letter

 Lesson Check Point

 Directions: Read each target word. Read the words in the row and circle the word that begins with a different letter.

Direksyons: Li chak mo sib. Li mo ki nan ranje a epi antoure mo ki kòmanse ak yon lèt diferan.

Target Words				
1. soak	shoe	scrub	zipper	says
2. sight	zero	sauce	shrimp	some
3. slow	should	slice	slide	homes
4. salt	vests	shift	scent	skip
5. snake	sheep	zoo	sand	sound

 Directions: Read the words in the four boxes. Circle two words that start with the uppercase and lowercase letter "s."

Direksyons: Li mo ki nan kat kare yo. Ansèkle de mo ki kòmanse ak lèt majiskil ak lèt miniskil "s".

zips	Skull
ponies	soon

crown	Sang
shelf	cones

green	zoo
script	Send

Shawl	zebra
combs	scoop

Sense	ships
grows	clips

sung	cliffs
Scalp	noses

Name: _____ Date:___/___/_____ Score: _____

Appendix 20.0

Introduction of the Letter T/t

✓ **Lesson Check Point**

 Directions: Circle the correct letter "t" pair: uppercase and lowercase letters.
Direksyons: Antoure lèt ki kòrèk "t" pè: lèt majiskil ak lèt miniskil.

| Tt | Lt | tF | bT | Bt |

 Directions: The uppercase letter "T" is in the first column. Look at the four letters in the row and circle the lowercase letter that matches the uppercase letter "T."
Direksyons: Lèt majiskil "T" se nan premye kolòn nan. Gade kat lèt ki nan ranje a epi antoure lèt miniskil ki koresponn ak lèt majiskil "T".

T	t	l	y	j
T	h	j	f	t
T	l	t	k	d
T	b	h	t	g

 Directions: The lowercase letter "t" is in the first column. Look at the four letters in the row and circle the uppercase letter that matches the lowercase letter "t."
Direksyons: Lèt miniskil "t" se nan premye kolòn nan. Gade kat lèt ki nan ranje a epi antoure lèt majiskil ki koresponn ak lèt miniskil "t".

t	F	T	H	J
t	T	B	F	D
t	J	F	B	T
t	H	L	T	F

Name: _____ Date: ___/___/_____ Score: _____

Appendix 20.0

Letter Recognition T/t

Uppercase and Lowercase Letter

✓ **Lesson Check Point**

 Directions: Read each target word. Read the words in the row and circle the word that begins with a different letter.

Direksyons: Li chak mo sib. Li mo ki nan ranje a epi antoure mo ki kòmanse ak yon lèt diferan.

Target Words				
1. type	tall	tomb	thigh	flag
2. tired	love	tape	tongue	twelve
3. toad	then	dance	trick	trench
4. tense	tribe	tale	twist	house
5. torn	tail	thigh	tends	boat

 Directions: Read the words in the four boxes. Circle two words that start with the uppercase and lowercase letter "t."

Direksyons: Li mo ki nan kat kare yo. Ansèkle de mo ki kòmanse ak lèt majiskil ak lèt miniskil "t".

Flame	Tough
try	desk

King	harmony
trait	Taste

label	Taught
Panel	tree

lamb	tread
food	Teach

True	kind
dream	twine

There	taint
house	Lady

Name: _____ Date:___/___/_____ Score:_____

Appendix 21.0

Introduction of the Letter U/u

✓ **Lesson Check Point**

Directions: Circle the correct letter "u" pair: uppercase and lowercase letters.

Direksyons: Antoure lèt ki kòrèk "u" pè: lèt majiskil ak lèt miniskil.

    uV   Uv   Ou   Yu   Uu

Directions: The uppercase letter "U" is in the first column. Look at the four letters in the row and circle the lowercase letter that matches the uppercase letter "U."

Direksyons: Lèt majiskil "U" se nan premye kolòn nan. Gade kat lèt ki nan ranje a epi antoure lèt miniskil ki koresponn ak lèt majiskil "U".

U	v	u	o	c
U	u	c	x	o
U	c	o	f	u
U	y	u	c	n

Directions: The lowercase letter "u" is in the first column. Look at the four letters in the row and circle the uppercase letter that matches the lowercase letter "u."

Direksyons: Lèt miniskil "u" se nan premye kolòn nan. Gade kat lèt ki nan ranje a epi antoure lèt majiskil ki koresponn ak lèt miniskil "u".

u	U	V	F	O
u	G	X	U	V
u	N	O	M	U
u	S	U	R	Z

Name: _____   Date:___/___/_____   Score:_____

Appendix 22.0

Introduction of the Letter V/v

✓ **Lesson Check Point**

 Directions: Circle the correct letter "v" pair: uppercase and lowercase letters.
Direksyons: Antoure lèt ki kòrèk "v" pè: lèt majiskil ak lèt miniskil.

| xV | Vv | vW | Mv | Uv |

 Directions: The uppercase letter "V" is in the first column. Look at the four letters in the row and circle the lowercase letter that matches the uppercase letter "V."
Direksyons: Lèt majiskil "V" se nan premye kolòn nan. Gade kat lèt ki nan ranje a epi antoure lèt miniskil ki koresponn ak lèt majiskil "V".

V	v	w	u	o
V	x	z	v	l
V	w	v	x	u
V	v	a	y	w

 Directions: The lowercase letter "v" is in the first column. Look at the four letters in the row and circle the uppercase letter that matches the lowercase letter "v."
Direksyons: Lèt miniskil "v" se nan premye kolòn nan. Gade kat lèt ki nan ranje a epi antoure lèt majiskil ki koresponn ak lèt miniskil "v".

v	W	V	U	M
v	A	Y	V	X
v	V	W	Z	A
v	X	Y	A	V

Name: _____ Date:___/___/_____ Score:_____

Appendix 22.0

Letter Recognition V/v

Uppercase and Lowercase Letter

✓ **Lesson Check Point**

 Directions: Read each target word. Read the words in the row and circle the word that begins with a different letter.

Direksyons: Li chak mo sib. Li mo ki nan ranje a epi antoure mo ki kòmanse ak yon lèt diferan.

Target Words				
1. vain	valve	vote	vent	west
2. vest	verb	vice	mouse	void
3. vogue	nuts	van	vein	vex
4. versed	voice	windy	vamp	vow
5. viewing	vague	wise	vane	verse

 Directions: Read the words in the four boxes. Circle two words that start with the uppercase and lowercase letter "v."

Direksyons: Li mo ki nan kat kare yo. Ansèkle de mo ki kòmanse ak lèt majiskil ak lèt miniskil "v".

More	Vase
Wall	valid

Vouch	click
mouse	voiced

zooms	weak
Vile	vine

Vault	wife
vet	zoo

vetch	Veil
Went	paint

noon	Volt
visa	wealth

Name: _____ Date: ___/___/_____ Score: _____

Appendix 23.0

Introduction of the Letter W/w

✓ Lesson Check Point

Directions: Circle the correct letter "w" pair: uppercase and lowercase letters.
Direksyons: Antoure lèt ki kòrèk "w" pè: lèt majiskil ak lèt miniskil.

| Wv | uW | wY | wZ | Ww |

Directions: The uppercase letter "W" is in the first column. Look at the four letters in the row and circle the lowercase letter that matches the uppercase letter "W."
Direksyons: Lèt majiskil "W" se nan premye kolòn nan. Gade kat lèt ki nan ranje a epi antoure lèt miniskil ki koresponn ak lèt majiskil "W".

W	v	y	z	w
W	x	w	v	y
W	k	v	w	x
W	w	x	y	z

Directions: The lowercase letter "w" is in the first column. Look at the four letters in the row and circle the uppercase letter that matches the lowercase letter "w."
Direksyons: Lèt miniskil "w" se nan premye kolòn nan. Gade kat lèt ki nan ranje a epi antoure lèt majiskil ki koresponn ak lèt miniskil "w".

w	W	X	Z	M
w	N	T	X	W
w	X	W	V	Y
w	Y	V	W	M

Name: _____ Date: ___/___/_____ Score: _____

Appendix 23.0

Letter Recognition W/w

Uppercase and Lowercase Letter

 Lesson Check Point

 Directions: Read each target word. Read the words in the row and circle the word that begins with a different letter.
Direksyons: Li chak mo sib. Li mo ki nan ranje a epi antoure mo ki kòmanse ak yon lèt diferan.

Target Words				
1. way	world	witch	wall	nine
2. weep	mouse	whim	worn	waltz
3. worm	win	verbal	weird	waive
4. walk	none	wake	worse	whine
5. wife	wok	whirl	volleyball	worst

 Directions: Read the words in the four boxes. Circle two words that start with the uppercase and lowercase letter "w."
Direksyons: Li mo ki nan kat kare yo. Ansèkle de mo ki kòmanse ak lèt majiskil ak lèt miniskil "w".

Whiz	Violin
Neck	won

week	Wrack
Mate	Nose

Moon	whisk
Vase	Wrath

vest	Marble
ward	Wove

Noodle	Warmth
width	Variety

well	virus
Noon	Wait

Name: _____ Date: ___/___/_____ Score: _____

Appendix 24.0

Introduction of the Letter X/x

✓ Lesson Check Point

 Directions: Circle the correct letter "x" pair: uppercase and lowercase letters.
Direksyons: Antoure lèt ki kòrèk "x" pè: lèt majiskil ak lèt miniskil.

xX   Kx   Yx   Wx   Xk

 Directions: The uppercase letter "X" is in the first column. Look at the four letters in the row and circle the lowercase letter that matches the uppercase letter "X."
Direksyons: Lèt majiskil "X" se nan premye kolòn nan. Gade kat lèt ki nan ranje a epi antoure lèt miniskil ki koresponn ak lèt majiskil "X".

X	y	z	x	v
X	x	y	v	c
X	w	x	v	y
X	z	v	m	x

 Directions: The lowercase letter "x" is in the first column. Look at the four letters in the row and circle the uppercase letter that matches the lowercase letter "x."
Direksyons: Lèt miniskil "x" se nan premye kolòn nan. Gade kat lèt ki nan ranje a epi antoure lèt majiskil ki koresponn ak lèt miniskil "x".

x	X	V	Y	Z
x	F	X	V	K
x	X	K	Z	V
x	K	V	Y	X

Name: _____ Date: ___/___/_____ Score: _____

Appendix 24.0

Letter Recognition X/x

Uppercase and Lowercase Letter

✓ Lesson Check Point

Directions: Read each target word. Read the words in the row and circle the word that does not contain a letter "x."
Direksyons: Li chak mo sib. Li mo ki nan ranje a epi fè wonn mo ki pa gen yon lèt "x".

Target Words				
1. fax	relax	sent	taxes	sixth
2. toxic	apex	oxen	cry	boxed
3. exist	milk	cortex	mix	expand
4. sixty	exact	keep	tuxedo	next
5. expel	waxy	mixed	excel	book

Directions: Read the words in the four boxes. Circle two words that start with the uppercase and lowercase letter "x."
Direksyons: Li mo ki nan kat kare yo. Ansèkle de mo ki kòmanse ak lèt majiskil ak lèt miniskil "x".

Xylem	xylan
extra	kicks

yours	xylose
cord	Xeric

horse	Xylene
xiphoid	noun

xyster	vein
Xerox	knot

Xenon	young
house	x-axis

knight	voice
Xebec	x-ray

Name: _____ Date:___/___/_____ Score:_____

Appendix 25.0

Introduction of the Letter Y/y

✓ **Lesson Check Point**

 Directions: Circle the correct letter "y" pair: uppercase and lowercase letters.
Direksyons: Antoure lèt ki kòrèk "y" pè: lèt majiskil ak lèt miniskil.

| yX | Yk | Yy | Xy | yF |

 Directions: The uppercase letter "Y" is in the first column. Look at the four letters in the row and circle the lowercase letter that matches the uppercase letter "Y."
Direksyons: Lèt majiskil "Y" se nan premye kolòn nan. Gade kat lèt ki nan ranje a epi antoure lèt miniskil ki koresponn ak lèt majiskil "Y".

Y	y	v	a	z
Y	x	j	v	y
Y	z	x	y	k
Y	j	y	g	v

 Directions: The lowercase letter "y" is in the first column. Look at the four letters in the row and circle the uppercase letter that matches the lowercase letter "y."
Direksyons: Lèt miniskil "y" se nan premye kolòn nan. Gade kat lèt ki nan ranje a epi antoure lèt majiskil ki koresponn ak lèt miniskil "y".

y	X	A	Y	F
y	Y	V	X	Z
y	K	Y	A	X
y	J	H	X	Y

Name: _____ Date: ___/___/_____ Score: _____

Appendix 25.0

Letter Recognition Y/y

Uppercase and Lowercase Letter

✓ **Lesson Check Point**

Directions: Read each target word. Read the words in the row and circle the word that begins with a different letter.

Direksyons: Li chak mo sib. Li mo ki nan ranje a epi antoure mo ki kòmanse ak yon lèt diferan.

Target Words				
1. Yale	yak	quiz	yet	yam
2. yards	year	yes	y-axis	push
3. yahoo	join	yap	yours	yarn
4. yellow	yard	yeast	groom	yield
5. yearbook	yes	jumps	yacht	Yemen

Directions: Read the words in the four boxes. Circle two words that start with the uppercase and lowercase letter "y."

Direksyons: Li mo ki nan kat kare yo. Ansèkle de mo ki kòmanse ak lèt majiskil ak lèt miniskil "y".

quiz	goal
y-axis	Yeast

yuck	jazz
ground	Yolk

queen	Yam
goat	yet

yards	just
Yours	greet

press	Yahoo
yo-yo	guest

Youth	yarn
pride	gold

Learn to Read English With Directions In Haitian Creole

Name: _____   Date: ___/___/_____   Score: _____

Appendix 26.0

Introduction of the Letter Z/z

✓ **Lesson Check Point**

 Directions: Circle the correct letter "z" pair: uppercase and lowercase letters.
Direksyons: Antoure lèt ki kòrèk "z" pè: lèt majiskil ak lèt miniskil.

| Xz | Zz | zY | Zs | Kz |

 Directions: The uppercase letter "Z" is in the first column. Look at the four letters in the row and circle the lowercase letter that matches the uppercase letter "Z."
Direksyons: Lèt majiskil "Z" se nan premye kolòn nan. Gade kat lèt ki nan ranje a epi antoure lèt miniskil ki koresponn ak lèt majiskil "Z".

Z	z	x	n	f
Z	y	v	z	x
Z	g	z	h	y
Z	v	k	x	z

 Directions: The lowercase letter "z" is in the first column. Look at the four letters in the row and circle the uppercase letter that matches the lowercase letter "z."
Direksyons: Lèt miniskil "z" se nan premye kolòn nan. Gade kat lèt ki nan ranje a epi antoure lèt majiskil ki koresponn ak lèt miniskil "z".

z	N	A	Z	J
z	M	Z	F	N
z	Z	X	N	W
z	N	Z	W	A

Name: _____   Date: ___/___/_____   Score: _____

Appendix 26.0

Letter Recognition Z/z

Uppercase and Lowercase Letter

✓ **Lesson Check Point**

Directions: Read each target word. Read the words in the row and circle the word that begins with a different letter.
Direksyons: Li chak mo sib. Li mo ki nan ranje a epi antoure mo ki kòmanse ak yon lèt diferan.

Target Words				
1. zealous	umpire	zip	zinc	zebra
2. zoologist	zinger	zoo	whale	zero
3. zillionaire	zone	vase	zoom	zonal
4. zoophobia	zenith	zipper	zap	next
5. Zimbabwe	Zurich	zodiac	Zambia	session

Directions: Read the words in the four boxes. Circle two words that start with the uppercase and lowercase letter "z."
Direksyons: Li mo ki nan kat kare yo. Ansèkle de mo ki kòmanse ak lèt majiskil ak lèt miniskil "z".

usher	Zap
zeal	swim

zonal	sweat
under	Zinc

wheel	Zoo
vote	zone

visit	stone
zero	Zebra

Zip	zealous
sprout	violet

zigzag	speak
Zenith	west

Learn to Read English With Directions In Haitian Creole

Your Next Step:
Learn To Read English Vowels With Directions In Haitian Creole